SOCIAL WORK
AND SOCIAL JUSTICE

SOCIAL WORK AND SOCIAL JUSTICE

A Structural Approach to Practice

COLLEEN LUNDY

broadview press

National Library of Canada Cataloguing in Publication

Lundy, Colleen, 1946–
    Social work and social justice : a structural approach to practice / Colleen Lundy.

Includes bibliographical references and index.
ISBN 1-55111-035-0

1. Social service. 2. Social case work. I. Title.

HV41.L86 200   361.3'2   C2003-905396-2

Broadview Press Ltd. is an independent, international publishing house, incorporated in 1985. Broadview believes in shared ownership, both with its employees and with the general public; since the year 2000 Broadview shares have traded publicly on the Toronto Venture Exchange under the symbol BDP.

We welcome comments and suggestions regarding any aspect of our publications–please feel free to contact us at the addresses below or at broadview@broadviewpress.com.

North America
PO Box 1243, Peterborough, Ontario, Canada K9J 7H5
Tel: (705) 743-8990; Fax: (705) 743-8353
email: customerservice@broadviewpress.com
3576 California Road, Orchard Park, NY, USA 14127

UK, Ireland, and continental Europe
Plymbridge Distributors Ltd.
Estover Road,
Plymouth, PL6 7PY, UK
Tel: (01752) 202301; Fax: (01752) 202333
email: orders@plymbridge.com

Australia and New Zealand
UNIREPS, University of New South Wales
Sydney, NSW, 2052
Tel: 61 2 9664 0999; Fax: 61 2 9664 5420
email: info.press@unsw.edu.au

www.broadviewpress.com

Broadview Press Ltd. gratefully acknowledges the financial support of the Government of Canada through the Book Publishing Industry Development Program for our publishing activities.

This book is printed on 100% post-consumer recycled, ancient forest-friendly paper.

PRINTED IN CANADA

This book is dedicated to my mother Hymmi Mikkola Lundy
who worked hard so that I could have the educational
opportunities she was denied.

CONTENTS

ACKNOWLEDGMENTS

T his book draws on the ideas of many scholars and practitioners, and I am indebted to their contributions. In particular, I wish to acknowledge the passion and vision for social justice which Maurice Moreau instilled in students and colleagues and infused in his development of a structural approach to social work. The idea for this book emerged from discussions with Jennifer Keck, a social work activist and professor who, like me, had been a student of Moreau's at Carleton University. The lives of Jennifer and Maurice ended far too early; they have both left behind a legacy of social justice advocacy.

I also wish to recognize the students, faculty, and other staff colleagues at Carleton University. It is a privilege to teach in a department where critical discussion, debate and camaraderie fill the classrooms and offices.

Michael Harrison of Broadview Press was unfaltering in his support and encouragement, even when deadlines were set and unmet. The professional excellence and responsiveness of both Michael and editor Betsy Struthers are much appreciated and have made the process a pleasant one. My thanks are due to the anonymous reviewers who took the time to offer suggestions and encouragement and to Roland Lecomte who graciously agreed to write the foreword.

I am particularly grateful to Ron Crawley, my companion and partner in life. Without his support, stimulating commentary, hours of editing on earlier drafts, and a ready supply of culinary delights, the completion of the book would have been much more difficult.

FOREWORD

S ocial work history is characterized by a constant preoccupation with the dual focus on individual and social change. The difficulty that has persisted since the inception of social work as a profession is that of relating these two levels of concern. Each generation identifies the dual focus on its own terms. Mary Richmond's "wholesale" and "retail" methods, Porter Lee's "cause" and "function," and Clarke Chambers's "prophets" and "priests" identify the struggle involved in relating the "private" and the "public," the "individual" and the "social," the "personal" and the "political." Some writers have proposed choosing one over the other; others encourage maintenance and extension of the duality, placing different social work practitioners in each sphere; still others place social workers outside the duality, arguing that they provide a mediating force between the social and the individual. Finally, some contributors to the debate seek to integrate the two perspectives into a single, more effective practice by suggesting that the "personal *is* political" and that individual services and social action are parts of the same act. The challenge has been to develop theoretical frameworks and practice approaches that reflect such an orientation.

Professor Colleen Lundy has provided a coherent theoretical framework and an original practice model that move from a *dualistic* view of the "personal" and the "social" to a *dialectical* one. Her historical analysis of the evolution of this perspective into a "structural" perspective is very instructive and also quite relevant for any educator or practitioner interested in bridging the gap between "micro" and "macro" interventions. She clarifies the many ambiguities that are often present in the use of the concept "structural" and offers a clearer definition of its theoretical foundations. She also demonstrates that a progressive perspective such as the structural approach is more than a theoretical, ideological, or analytical exercise.

The originality of her contribution is her conceptualization of the direct practice component in a manner amenable to practitioners working with individuals, families, small groups, and communities. She articulates the helping process within a structural perspective through a creative use of practice situations where the helping relationship is clearly defined in dialogical terms. Assessment tools and formats, such as genograms, ecological and social network maps, and the life line, are identified within a human needs and human rights perspective. The characteristics of ethical and accountable practice are particularly well-defined. Lundy provides an interesting and convincing argument for the use of a structural approach in her description of the nature of the change process which occurs at the direct practice level, i.e., connecting *the structural* and *the personal*, through empathy, critical consciousness, and empowerment.

The chapter on professional associations and union membership is particularly illuminating. Social workers experience a tension between practicing in an ethical and competent manner and implementing policies and program regulations in the context of program cutbacks and mean-spirited governments. There may be a crisis in the social services, but the author correctly suggests that it is not a crisis stemming from social work incompetence as some regulatory bodies tend to suggest. Rather, it is a crisis of underfunding and of structures that perpetuate inequalities and oppression.

The structural approach was developed in the 1970s within a socioeconomic and political climate that lent itself to change. We were witnessing the rise of the civil rights and anti-poverty movements, the women's movement, and student militancy. This was followed by a period of severe cutbacks in social welfare institutions and heavy criticism of the function and effectiveness of social work practice. The structural approach argued for a critical/generalist perspective in connecting the "personal" and the "social" which moved away from the "blaming the victim" perspectives to ones which sought to alleviate and transform the conditions in which oppressed clients found themselves. But what is its relevance today, in a context of globalization and neo-liberalism?

In the global market, the decline of social reform is increasingly leaving social needs unanswered. More than ever, social workers must understand the nature of the inequalities and oppression that stem from globalization and neo-liberal policies. Within this context, the structural approach's focus on establishing the link between "public issues" and " personal troubles," while maintaining its commitment to social change and social justice, is particularly relevant.

Professor Lundy provides a much-needed and helpful analysis of the nature of oppression, its causes and sources, its production and reproduction, its dynamics, its effects on the oppressed, including its internalization, and the social functions it carries out in the interest of the dominant groups in society. I believe that her contribution goes a long way to prepare social workers to confront the challenge of globalization and neo-liberalism and their impact on clients and social work practice.

Roland Lecomte PhD
Professor
School of Social Work
University of Ottawa

PREFACE

Above all. Always be capable of feeling deeply any injustice committed against anyone, anywhere in the world. This is the most beautiful quality of a revolutionary.

—*Che Guevara[1]*

I think social work has to find its soul and its conscience again. There needs to be a revolution in the profession.

—*Dr. David Woodsworth[2]*

The Challenge For Social Work

People working in the field of social work often face a dilemma in providing "help" to clients. On the one hand, much of the "help" that we are trained to provide targets personal and interpersonal change. At the same time, many of the issues and problems facing the people we work with are rooted in broad social, political, and economic conditions, and only a change in those conditions will "solve" them. This dilemma has sparked a series of debates within the profession about where social workers should place their efforts. Does building a profession or working for social change deserve most of our attention? Should we concentrate on individual casework or do community organization and social policy changes make more sense?

Of course, for most social workers this is very much an individual professional and career choice based on their own interests and goals. One of the main purposes of this book is to stimulate social work students and practitioners to consciously examine the relationship between the two approaches and the choices they make as professionals. While social workers are not limited to an either/or choice on this issue, this book argues that it is in their interests and those of their clients that they at least understand the relationship between individual problems and social conditions. Furthermore, a central theme is that individual recovery or change is often related to, if not determined by, change in social structures. Although an individual may approach a social worker with a seemingly individual concern such as alcohol overuse, the use of alcohol may be a way to survive an unbearable reality. For example, a fox caught in a leg-hold trap may begin to gnaw off his foot rather than die of starvation or the cold in the trap.[3] A distant observer may not see the trap beneath the snow and conclude that the fox is self-destructive and acting abnormally. Similarly, social workers need to look for the traps in the lives of people. Fully, this book advocates for an understanding of social conditions, social problems, and social change as a means of strengthening our social work practice.

Despite decades of debate within the profession, we still tend to divorce the critical analysis required for understanding broader social conditions (social welfare) from the personal and interpersonal theories and skills needed for working directly with individuals and families. For example, there may be an attempt to understand the ideas, behaviour, and feelings of individuals in the context of the socialization of their families, but there is little attempt to extend this analysis to a broader social context. Themes related to social analysis, oppression, power, and diversity are noticeably absent from these discussions. Often disparate theories and perspectives are in direct conflict with one another. The result is a tendency in direct intervention practice to individualize and pathologize problems which are often symptomatic of broader social, political, and economic conditions. However, integrating a critical analysis of broader social conditions into our day-to-day work with individuals and families, does not mean that *all* of the problems which individuals face are necessarily rooted in the larger social and political structure. Nor does it imply that individual problems can automatically be solved with changes at the societal level or that individuals do not have responsibility for their actions. Certainly it does not also mean that social work should ignore an individual's pain and suffering if it is rooted in larger social structures.

A central thesis of this book is to situate and understand the socio-economic or structural context of individual problems and how these power arrangements and societal forces create social conditions that generate stress, deprivation, and other forms of individual problems. Such an analysis can only strengthen our individual, family, and community practice. Structural analysis involves developing an awareness of the ways in which individuals and families learn to adapt and conform to their social conditions, as well as the ways they resist and challenge them. Central to this is an understanding of social and economic conditions as well as the role of ideology in shaping the way in which individual and social problems are perceived within society. It also involves a critical awareness of the role of the social work profession in the delivery of social services within a larger socio-economic and political context.

This book agues for a social change framework in social work practice. It builds on recent attempts to develop a critical analysis of class inequality, sexism, and racism along with other forms of oppression and their impact on social work practice; essentially, it offers a structural approach to social work practice. The text is designed for social work students, social work practitioners, and others interested in developing a structural analytical perspective as well as entry level generic skills for practice in a variety of social service settings.

Organization of the Chapters

The book begins by situating the social welfare state and the delivery of social services within a broader context of the enlarging global capitalist economy. Chapter 1 explores the impact of globalization and increased international trade liberalization on the social welfare of the population. In Chapter 2 a historical account of social work developments in theory and practice is summarized and provides an understanding of the roots of common practice perspectives, as well as the ongoing tension between individual helping and advocacy for social change.

Chapter 3 distinguishes theory from models and approaches while discussing the ideology guiding them and suggests an organizing framework in which to understand the ideological and philosophical differences.

The chapter also outlines the development and foundations of the Structural approach to social work. Included here is a discussion of social structures and human rights and social justice, as well as principles for practice.

Next in Chapter 4 attention is placed on structural injustice and inequality in society while examining the multiple social factors that influence the lives of individuals on a day-to-day basis. An awareness of the role of social relationships based on social class, race and ethnicity, sexual orientation, disability, and gender is viewed as central in responding to client problems and difficulties.

Chapter 5 outlines the ethics of social work practice in addition to offering some direction in responding to ethical dilemmas and difficult situations. The role and importance of recording in social work is also discussed.

In the following three chapters the focus is on practice. Chapter 6 presents assessment, analysis, and practice skills in working with individuals and their families. The anticipated outcome of social work practice, whether with individuals, families, or communities, is positive change, yet little is known regarding the nature of change and how it comes about. Chapter 7 continues with a process for achieving change and considers the influence of objective conditions on one's subjective reality while assessing the importance of critical consciousness and empowerment in the process. Chapter 8 highlights theory and practice in group work. Chapter 9 moves the discussion into social work practice with communities and suggests strategies for joining with participants to organize for change.

Increasingly, social workers encounter stress from the nature of the social and individual problems they face in practice, funding cuts to their agencies, and expanding case-loads. The final chapter, Chapter 10, is devoted to the working conditions of social workers and the role of professional associations and unions in advancing social work practice and social justice.

Like David Woodsworth, I too believe that in many ways social work has drifted from its past social justice/human rights orientation. While this orientation has not always been prevalent or dominant within the profession, it is only through reasserting the strengths and benefits of such an approach that it will be kept as a visible option for social workers. This is especially true in a time, as we now face, where social programs are being eroded and dismantled, where individuals with problems are left more and more to their own devices and support of friends and family, and ideologies that apologize for this state of affairs are becoming more and more fashionable. It is my hope that this text will engender "fire in the hearts" of social workers and offer some guidance in the task before us of responding to individual trauma and problems while supporting positive structural change and working towards a more just society.

NOTES

1 Che Guevara, *To His Children: Che's Letters of Farewell*, trans. Carmen González, ed. (Havana: Editorial José Marti/Artex, 1995) 11.
2 "An interview with Dr. David Woodsworth, Emeritus Professor of Social Work, McGill University," *Canadian Social Work* 2. 2 (Fall 2000): 149.
3 The metaphor is credited to Bruce K. Alexander, "The Empirical and Theoretical Bases for an Adaptive Model of Addiction," *The Journal of Drug Issues* 20.1 (1990): 37–65.

CHAPTER I

SOCIAL WORK, SOCIAL WELFARE, AND THE GLOBAL ECONOMY

S ocial work as a profession has historically held a central role in the development and delivery of social welfare. The need for an organized group of socially committed professionals to respond to the social and economic needs of people emerged out of the industrialization and urbanization of the late nineteenth century and the social problems they wrought. Initially the practice of social work developed within charity organizations and gradually expanded as the responsibility for social welfare shifted more and more to the state. Social work has increasingly taken on legitimacy as a profession. Social workers were front-line witnesses to the often harmful impact of economic and political policies on the lives of ordinary people. The response by the profession over the years has been both to advocate for immediate services and resources for those in need as well as to promote social change strategies aimed at eliminating and transforming structural inequalities. Political and economic changes, both in the national and international spheres, continue to have an impact on how social workers do their jobs and, in particular, on the role of social work in social welfare delivery.

The Global Capitalist Economy

These are particularly challenging times for both those who are responsible for the front-line delivery of social welfare services and for those who access those services. People are feeling the effects of more than two decades of downsizing and cuts to social programs with the consequent erosion of social benefits. Within the context of increased mobility of capital, power has shifted even further from nation-states to transnational corporations, a shift which is being solidified through international trade agreements.[1]

The process which Karl Marx and Friedrich Engels identified in 1848 as the move to "universal interdependence of nations" continues today:

> All old-established national industries have been destroyed or are daily being destroyed. They are dislodged by new industries, whose introduction becomes a life and death question for all civilised nations, by industries that no longer work up indigenous raw material, but raw material drawn from the remotest zones; industries whose products are consumed, not only at home, but in every quarter of the globe.[2]

What is different, some argue, is the accelerated speed of trade liberalization and accumulation of capital on a global scale with its attendant erosion of sovereignty and democracy within nation-states. Transnational organizations now determine the social, economic, and political policies of countries. The result is a profound increase in the polarization of wealth and disparity within and among countries as growing numbers of people within the "global village" lack the basic needs for survival, while a small number of others accumulate the riches of the world.[3] This capitalist globalization process, under the banner of the World Trade Organization (WTO) and recent trade agreements such as the proposed Free Trade Agreement of the Americas (FTAA), ensures rights for transnational corporations while eroding the power of nation-states, and their citizens, to determine their own destiny. Ironically, "democracy" is being upheld as the necessary criterion in order to gain membership and participation in these agreements.

While there has been an expanding world market throughout the history of the capitalist mode of production, the period after World War II marked a qualitative shift to a global economy and commodity production with the removal of trade barriers. During this time, global trade and investment grew dramatically, and the world domination of the US was established through new economic structures.[4] Gary Teeple notes that the origins of these new global institutions date back to 1944 when, under US auspices, the future members of the United Nations held a conference at Bretton Woods and developed institutions to regulate and liberalize world trade.

An exchange rate mechanism set the parities of national currencies against the US dollar, and two institutions, the International Monetary Fund (IMF) and the World Bank were created. The General Agreement on Tariffs and Trade (GATT) followed in 1947 and further freed commerce by providing the institutional means for the removal of all national barriers to world trade.[5] Since the creation of the GATT there have been eight rounds of multilateral trade negotiations. In 1995, at the Uruguay Round (1986–1994), the World Trade Organization (WTO), was established to administer and regulate international trade among the 141 members. The WTO is a powerful institution managed by a 500–person secretariat based in Geneva which administers legal agreements such as the GATT, the General Agreement on Trade in Services, and the agreement on Trade-Related Intellectual Property Rights. The WTO joins the IMF and World Bank as the administrative core which manages economic interests and the global financial system.[6] The functions of the WTO include "facilitating the implementation and operation of the Multilateral Trade Agreements, providing a forum for negotiations, administering the dispute settlement mechanism, providing multilateral surveillance of trade policies, and cooperating with the World Bank and the IMF to achieve greater coherence in global economic policy-making."[7]

The Role of the Military

Globalization "can neither survive nor function without the military powers as its backbone" since at times force is required to suppress resistance to World Bank/IMF policies and to ensure the expansion of imperialism.[8] Sharma and Kumar document how imperialist powers have militarily intervened in countries and discuss four categories which render countries vulnerable:

> 1) countries unable to repay debt or interest on it; 2) countries in which the people and the government resist the imposition of WB/IMF conditions; 3) countries with socialist, semi-socialist, nationalist or left populist economies; and 4) countries that resist MNCs [multinational corporations], try to develop regional alliances and struggle to present a model of development other than that of neo-liberalism.[9]

The authors also point out how imperialist countries reward countries which "voluntarily" submit to their political, economic, and military requirements and withdraw support from those who resist. For example, during the bombing of Afghanistan in 2001 after the September 11 terrorist attacks, agreement by Pakistan to accommodate the US airforce was rewarded by a lifting of trade sanctions by the US and Japan, the provision of $500 million in US aid, and an IMF loan of $1.3 billion.

Steven Staples, in a recent review of Canada's military spending, documents how "globalization, the arms industry, and military allies such as the US and NATO push for Canada to spend more on defence—much more than is required for our basic needs." Staples points out that with 2001 military spending in excess of $7 billion (US), Canada is already one of the largest military spenders in the world, ranking the sixth highest among the 19 members of NATO and the sixteenth highest in the world. In 2001, the mightiest military power, the United States, had a defence budget of $310.5 billion (US).[10] It is estimated that in the year 2002–03, military spending in the US will exceed $400 billion.[11]

The US National Association of Social Workers recognize the US dominance in the global economy and over the World Bank, IMF, and WTO. The association is firmly opposed to a unilateral, pre-emptive military attack by the US against Iraq. In a policy statement the association recognizes that "Beyond the destruction and trauma of war is the continual drain on human and material resources—the diversion of energies and goods and services to meet military needs—while the social welfare of millions of people in the US and abroad goes unmet."[12]

Imposed Structural Adjustment Programs

Many developing countries, including those in Latin America and the former Soviet Union, must adhere to imposed Structural Adjustment Programs in order to receive IMF/World Bank loans. The imposed structural adjustment measures require countries to embrace international investment and to put out the "welcome mat" of low wages, compliant unions, environmental deregulation, privatization of public services, and diminished role of the state in social protection and social programs. Under Structural Adjustment Programs countries are required to:

- abandon domestic industry in favour of transnational corporate interests

- turn their best agricultural lands over to export crops to pay off their national debt;
- curtail spending on social programs and abandon universal health care, education, and social security programs;
- deregulate their electricity, transportation, energy, and national resources sectors;
- remove regulatory impediments to foreign investment.[13]

According to Tony Clarke, the Structural Adjustment Programs, applied to both developed and developing countries and promoted by business, include "the deregulation of foreign investment and national economies; the privatization of crown corporations and public utilities and services; the negotiation and implementation of free trade regimes; the reduction of public deficits through massive social spending cuts; the erosion of national controls over monetary policy; and the reduction of public revenues through lower corporate taxes and higher interest rates."[14] Lower corporate taxes and diminished controls over corporations are accompanied by lower wages, less social spending, and lower environmental standards.

What Do International Trade Agreements Have To Do with Social Work?

This book is not about international trade agreements. However, the international trade agreements noted above will influence the delivery of services that are essential to the social welfare of Canadians, because trade agreements are no longer just about trade in goods such as automobiles, steel, or lumber; they are increasingly about trade in services. This is made clear by the General Agreement on Trades and Services, which is currently being renegotiated to liberalize trade in services including health care, dental care, child and elder care, museums, libraries, social services, education, utilities, water, publishing, tourism, and postal services, thus paving the way for corporate privatization of these services with no restrictions. The idea is to create "a level playing field" for competition among private industries, whereby governments play little or no part in supporting their workers or families. In her assessment of the General Agreement on Trades and Services, Maude Barlow notes that "not only is the ability to deliver these services in the public sector threatened, but as well governments' authority to regulate any service—public or private—is under attack."[15]

Foreign corporations established in Canada will not be obligated to hire Canadian workers or adhere to environmental, health, or social security standards. The social and health services under attack by these policies employ the majority of social workers.

Summing up the influence of these agreements and pro-globalization structures, Clarence Bolt emphasizes that the "control of Canada's destiny will not be in the hands of Canadian legislatures, but in the hands of organizations like NAFTA, the WTO, the IMF and the World Bank, that are beyond the reach of our governments—organizations that have no loyalty or accountability to Canada or its people."[16] In response, NGOs, social coalitions, and labour unions have effectively informed citizens about the impact of the trade agreements and have mobilized them to act. Opposition to these globalization structures has taken to the streets in massive demonstrations, such as the "Battle of Seattle" in 1999 where the presence of 50,000 protesters closed down the WTO meeting. Two years late, demonstrators opposing the Summit of the Americas in Quebec City and the proposed FTAA met with the biggest security operation in Canadian peace-time history. Along with a cement-based chain link fence around a large portion of the city, 6,700 police and thousands of soldiers fired plastic bullets and over 2000 canisters of tear gas at the primarily peaceful crowds. Some protesters were arrested, kept confined in vans for up to eight hours, and then placed in jails. (For coverage of the protest see www.canadians.org.)

An important point to stress is that the effects of global capitalism are not just felt in the developing world. Corporate influences outside of Canada have had a profound impact on internal decision-making. Chossudovsky points out that it was the credit rating of Canada's public debt by Moody's (a financial market) that was a factor in the 1995–96 national restructuring which resulted in massive cuts to social programs and reduction of the government workforce.[17] Also, the role of the IMF in the cuts to social welfare in Canada is now evident. As a member country, Canada's economic performance is regularly evaluated by the IMF, which then makes "suggestions" for structural readjustment. Copies of these IMF memos to former Finance Minister Paul Martin, obtained by *The CCPA Monitor*, reveal that he *voluntarily* followed IMF suggestions in budget decisions to implement $29 billion in spending cuts over three years, including "$7.4 billion slashed from health care, education and social assistance transfers to the provinces; the elimination of 45,000 public sector jobs; large reductions in UI benefits and eligibility; the privatization of the CNR, all airports, and the air traffic control system; the end of federal funding for social housing; the cancellation of the Liberals' oft-promised national child-care program."[18]

Permitting the market to be an arbiter of social priorities has a destabilizing influence on Canadian society, to say the least. *The Growing Gap*, a recent report by the Centre for Social Justice, points out that " in 1973, the richest 10 per cent of families with children under 18 made 21 times more than the poorest 10 per cent of Canadian families. In 1996, the richest 10 per cent of families made 314 times more than the poorest 10 per cent of Canadian families." [19] The wealthiest 50 per cent of the family units now control 94.4 per cent of the wealth in Canada.[20] More and more people are trying to piece together a living by combining a number of part-time jobs. While 66 per cent of workers had full-time jobs a generation ago, today only 50 per cent are employed full-time. The number of people who hold part-time jobs has doubled to 20 per cent of the working population. Full-time unionized jobs have been replaced with temporary, contract work, which now represents 15 per cent of all jobs. Facing dim job prospects, workers have been encouraged to become self-employed, and one-half of all new jobs in the 1990s were created by workers venturing out into the market as entrepreneurs. Canadians are working more and earning less under harsher conditions. When adjusted for inflation, average family market incomes are lower today than they were in 1981. Furthermore, while one's worth on the job market has been reduced, so have unemployment and welfare benefits. Eighty-seven per cent of unemployed workers were eligible for unemployment insurance benefits in 1990, while in 1997 only 42 per cent were eligible.[21] At the same time, we saw a decrease in welfare rates and a tightening of eligibility criteria, particularly in the province of Ontario.

Not surprisingly, this austere economic climate, compounded by an uncharitable political sentiment, is bound to have a profound impact on the psychological, social, and physical health of Canadians and on their opportunities for education and employment. Governments, both federal and provincial, have abdicated their responsibility for social welfare provision by reducing funding to health care, education, the environment, and social programs. There is a disturbing trend toward privatization as governments hand over public utilities, social, and health services to the lowest bidder, thereby encouraging substandard services that are more costly to those who depend on them. These trends can only increase under trade regimes that look for profits for transnational corporations.

Unemployment, Poverty, and Social Protection

Unemployment, part-time jobs, limited contracts, and casual jobs are features of global capitalism. They are also indicators that more and more people are experiencing economic hardship if not abject poverty. For the past few years, approximately 8 per cent of Canadians and 5 per cent of Americans have been counted in the unemployment statistics.[22] Unemployed and underemployed people have a greater reliance on social programs. While people find themselves without resources to sustain dignity and health, services offered by hospitals and social agencies have been cut or closed, and social assistance has been reduced to provide less to fewer people. Insurance for the unemployed, social assistance, and other welfare benefits fail to provide for even the most basic needs of housing, food, and clothing, let alone essential toiletries, school supplies, bus fares, and non-prescription drugs.

The only alternative for many people is to rely on charity. Food banks, non-existent in 1980, now provide food for many people, including families, on a regular basis. Line-ups at soup kitchens and the increasing numbers of street people and homeless have become part of our social landscape. The ever-increasing number of hungry and homeless men, women, and children is a gauge of the depth of the social crisis and the inadequacy of the "safety net" in meeting their basic needs.[23] Government and public discussions more and more are based on the ideology of "blaming the victims" for their poverty and misfortune.[24]

According to welfare recipients such as David McGee, " To be on welfare is to be told, 'Get a job.' But the jobs aren't available... We are supposed to be writing letters and resumes, but there is no money for envelopes, stamps and things. There is no money for transportation."[25] Addressing societal inequalities and social structures that contribute to such conditions are no longer part of the political agenda, if they ever were.

Measuring Poverty

While poverty is the reality for many, the debate over how best to define and measure poverty continues. In the US, the Census Bureau sets an income threshold that reflects a family's needs according to the number of its members. These thresholds do not vary geographically but are updated yearly for inflation using the Consumer Price Index. Although the Canadian government has no mandated definition of poverty, the concept of relative poverty, where a person's situation is considered relative to others in the same region of the country, is used to measure poverty. Statistics Canada's Low-Income Cut-Off (LICO), an unofficial measure of poverty, defines people as poor if they spend more than 55 per cent of their income on food, shelter, and clothing. Social policy analysts with the Fraser Institute, a conservative "think tank," disagree with the LICO, claiming that it inflates the number of poor and arguing that poverty ought to be defined in terms of basic necessities of food, shelter, and clothing. Recently, Statistics Canada introduced the market-basket measure (MBM) that determines a poverty level according to a shopping basket of basic life essentials such as food, clothing, rent, transportation and sundries.[26] Based on a preliminary version of the MBM, Ernie Lightman found that the child poverty rate in Canada of around 18 per cent when measured by LICO dropped to 12 per cent when the MBM was used.[27] The recently released version of the MBM resulted in higher poverty rates than previous Statistic Canada calculations using the LICO—13.1 per cent of Canadians compared to 10.9 per cent.[28] However, all current provincial welfare rates remain lower than the cost of life necessities listed by the MBM and for this reason the new measure will support anti-poverty activists in advocating for change. While poverty continues to be gauged by determining whether or not a person has the basic necessities of survival, it ought to describe people's incomes and standard of living in relation to the average income earners in the society in which they live; otherwise, the poor face social exclusion and are denied opportunities to actively participate in their communities.

The Poverty Numbers

Poverty statistics indicate that more and more Canadians and Americans have slipped below government poverty lines. In 2001, 11.7 per cent of the American population was considered poor, an increase from 11.3 per cent the previous year. However, the poverty rates among African Americans (22.7 per cent) and persons of Hispanic origin (21.4 per cent) are almost twice those of the general population. Child poverty remains a concern with 16.3 per cent of children considered to be poor. In the case of children under six years of age living in a female-headed family, 48.9 per cent live in poverty.[29]

Using the LICO, in 1998, 16.4 per cent of Canadians were living below the poverty line. Poverty among children in Canada was 18.8 per cent (almost one in five), an increase of 42 per cent since 1989 when the House of Commons passed a resolution to end child poverty by 2000.[30] Most vulnerable to poverty are women who are single parents (54.2 per cent), most of whom are under 25 years old (85 per cent). In recent years there has been an alarming increase in poverty among persons of visible minority origins, the "ethnicization" of poverty, and the emergence of high poverty neighbourhoods. [31]

The process of globalization and the withdrawal of state support for social security has created conditions where the fundamental human rights of citizens are being violated. Federal governments in both Canada and the US have downloaded responsibility for social welfare on the provinces and states, resulting in a lowering of benefits, tightening of eligibility criteria, and the elimination of much-needed social programs. It is quite striking how the developments in both countries have taken a similar path. In Canada, in 1996 the Canada Health and Social Transfer (CHST) replaced the Canada Assistance Plan (CAP) and introduced a single block funding that includes health, post-secondary education, and social welfare funding. With an elimination of federal standards, provinces were free to reduce social welfare benefits and impose workfare or training for work conditions for eligibility. In the US, the 1997 Personal Responsibility and Work Opportunity Reconciliation Act (PRA) converted welfare from a federal entitlement into a block grant administered by the states. The block funding is contingent on conditions such as a mandatory work requirement for welfare recipients and a five-year lifetime limit on benefits from federal funds.[32] While the majority of states have imposed the ban, others have not.

While all families are effected by economic restructuring and an erosion of social welfare programs, sole support women and their children are among the most vulnerable. Concerned with the economic impact on women of the significant cuts to social assistance and funding to women's shelters by the Ontario government in 1996, the Ontario Association of Transition Houses submitted a report to the UN Rapporteur on Violence Against Women. The report documented the conditions endured by women fleeing abuse and called the government's actions a human rights violation. In the US, so-called welfare reform has "pushed thousands of women off the rolls into low-paid jobs, but also into dangerous welfare hotels, drug-plagued streets, and unsafe relationships."[33]

The level of poverty in Canada has not gone unnoticed by the UN. While Canada has received the distinction of being one of the best countries to live in by the UN, the organization has severely criticized the Canadian government for its disregard of the increasing rate of poverty.[34] Then, in a 2000 UN Children Fund report comparing 23 industrialized countries, Canada ranked only seventeenth, with 15.5 per cent of children living below the poverty line.[35]

The impact of joblessness, low wage employment, cuts to social welfare, and poverty is hard felt by many individuals and families. Sometimes the effects can be deadly, as demonstrated in the case of Kimberly Rogers.[36] A survey of social workers in Eastern Ontario provides a glimpse into the despair and desperation they encounter in their clients. They reported that, along with relying on food banks in their struggle to survive, clients are moving to less expensive housing (or moving in with other family members), not filling much-needed medical prescriptions, cancelling phone service, and selling possessions. Parents forgo food for themselves in order to feed their children, have no money for celebrating birthdays and holidays, and often report feeling depressed and suicidal.[37] As a last resort, some families are requesting that the Children's Aid Society provide care for their children, while other clients report turning to prostitution as a source of income or a place to stay.

The lack of subsidized housing combined with increasing rents have resulted in family homelessness. Family shelters are full of destitute families who now represent the largest single group seeking shelter accommodation.[38]

Disadvantaged youth are adversely impacted by the erosion of social welfare programs and the uncertainty of the changing labour market. Jobs lost through corporate restructuring have resulted in some older workers taking jobs that were normally done by young workers. Older workers now manage newspaper routes, check out and bag groceries, and work in the fast food industry. Correspondingly, the labour participation rate of 62 per cent for people between the ages of 15 and 24 reached a 19-year low in 1995. Since two-thirds of minimum wage earners are under 24 years of age, less than one-third of those aged 18–24 are employed with sufficient income to be able to live independently of their parents.[39] A survey of 606 youth coming to one agency revealed that 28 per cent relied on a food bank or reported being hungry, 31 per cent went to a shelter or remained on the street, 46 per cent were looking for work, and 13 per cent panhandled. The daily use of alcohol (44 per cent) and/or drugs (37 per cent) have become ways of coping with severe conditions. Yet 69 per cent of these young people continued to go to school, countering the general perception perpetuated by the media and policy makers that youth are not motivated.[40]

Understanding Individual and Social Problems in a Structural Context

The previous section outlined a series of important economic and social problems that face Canadians. A structural approach to social work practice starts with an understanding of these developments. An awareness of these problems can help guide the practice of social workers and inform our understanding of social relations, as well as personal troubles and the various resistance and coping strategies of those affected. Such an analysis can help social workers illuminate the obstacles to, as well as the strategies for, achieving advocacy, providing education, and promoting social change. Too often the social, political, and economic underpinnings of people's problems are not considered. Such a lack of understanding is more likely to lead to social workers focussing on individual deficiency and promoting only social control measures such as medical treatment, monitoring, and incarceration, rather than progressive social change and social justice.

Even if the first priority of social workers is not to challenge social inequality and advocate on behalf of women, racial/ethnic minorities, or an exploited class of people, an understanding of the principal divisions within society can only assist social workers in their many areas of practice. For example, understanding the influence of large multinational corporations and their emphasis on the production of goods and services which can be sold in the marketplace for a profit, their ruthless competition with other corporations, and the need to maximize profits in the long run explains their efforts to keep workers' wages and benefits as low as possible in order to intimidate workers and increase their productivity while laying off others. An understanding of these forces helps explain the recent closure of Cape Breton coal mines in Nova Scotia. Men who had spent almost 30 years underground lost their jobs and do not qualify for a pension; the result is social strife and the intensification of various social problems for them, their families, and everyone who relies on the mining industry.[41]

Coal miners also experience the long-term impact of chronic injustice which accompanies cyclical unemployment, underemployment, and poverty, as well as racial exploitation. David Cattell-Gordon, a native of West Virginia, observed symptoms of depression, futility, anger, numbing of the spirit, and fatalism among miners and their families and identified this as part of a traumatic stress syndrome which may effect several generations.[42] As Father Bob Neville of New Waterford, Cape Breton explains, coal mining has left many men old before their time: "After twenty years in the pit, a man's body, if uninjured in an accident, is full of aches and pains and his lungs have silicosis. For many, the stress caused by the constant darkness and danger leads to life styles which are destructive to themselves and to their families."[43]

It is also important to note that not all social conflict is unhealthy. Much of it is a "natural" response to unfair policies or social inequalities. For example, when 1600 Cape Breton miners decided to launch a wildcat strike to fight the closure of the mine, it was reported that the confidence, the self-assurance, and the laughter were back, despite the fact that 200 RCMP were sent to the Prince Mine to contain the resistance of the miners. As one miner's wife said of her husband, "I don't care if he's right or wrong or wins or loses. Right now he feels like a man. And that's all that's important to me."[44] Fighting back, and even winning, does not address all of the social problems faced by Cape Breton coal-mining families, but it is an illustration of how resistance and social cohesion can play a positive role and make a difference.

There is a need to understand the role of the state within Canadian society. Whether the state at any level is perceived as a problem creator or problem solver essentially depends on who is asked and what their experience has been. The state in Canada can be viewed as including institutions such as schools and child protection and family agencies, as well as such bureaucratic structures as the Departments of Finance and National Defence. For the most part, we tend to believe that the state's role is to mediate between different groups of people for the benefit of the larger society, but many argue that the state usually functions in the interests of the rich and powerful.[45]

Our conception and understanding of the state can affect how we as social workers function within it. It can also affect our support for others who do challenge state policies and actions. For example, what do we think is the role of the state when it comes to Aboriginal peoples in Canada? How do we view the events of the summer of 1990 at the Mohawk barricades at Oka when Canadian Armed Forces were called in to assist the Sûreté du Québec (SQ) to put a stop to the uprising against expansion of a golf course into an area unsettled by land claims?[46] How do social workers view the role of the state when police are used to repress demonstrations against poverty as they did in Toronto in 2002?

While not all social workers will become involved in social protests or even openly sympathize with them, an understanding of the problems that lay behind and are the core of such struggles can enhance our practice as social workers. In *The Fiscal Crisis of the State*, James O'Connor argues that, while the state maintains the conditions in which profitable capital accumulation is possible, "the state must also create the conditions for social harmony."[47] In *Regulating the Poor*, Richard Cloward and Frances Piven provide a historical examination of social welfare practices and conclude that social welfare exists primarily to control the poor.[48] A final example of studies that can inform our practice is Gary Teeple's work in which he argues that the welfare state can be seen as, "a capitalist *society* in which the state has intervened in the form of social policies, programs, standards, and regulation in order to mitigate class conflict *and* to provide for, answer, or accommodate certain social needs for which the capitalist mode of production in itself has no solution or makes no provision"(italics in original).[49] As contradictory and inadequate as these programs are, they do redistribute income, provide social security, and represent the gains made by workers and their unions, as well as other social movements. It is for these reasons that they must be defended.[50]

Sam Gindin points out how an increase in equality and security for workers and a strengthening of social programs can actually threaten capitalism. It is for this reason that he believes that the push for neo-liberalism and the rapid globalization of the economy is intentional in order to preserve capitalism.[51]

This book focusses on the practice of social workers. Ann Withorn poignantly sums it up when she states that social workers "face the human result of all the contradictions and inefficiencies of a capitalist, racist, sexist society as well as the sheer pain and suffering that is part of life."[52] In regards to offering direct help, social workers often find themselves with two contradictory functions—the care versus control dilemma. Sue Wise views our role as carrying out the "policing of minimum standards of care for, and the protection of the rights of, the most vulnerable members of our society."[53] When we work in child protection, apprehending abused and neglected children and monitoring the progress of someone who is court-mandated to our service, we are carrying out the function of social control. At the same time we engage in the care function by offering individual and family counselling and advocating for much-needed social programs. If social work plays a contradictory role, it is because the society we live in is conflicted and uncommitted to the social well-being of its people.

In conclusion, for social workers to be consistent with their values and ethics, they must understand the inequalities in society and develop a practice approach that responds to the structural needs of individuals and families. They must be aware of their own history of organizing and advocating for social change and social justice. This history also reflects the contradictions of attraction to advocacy and social/political activism and the pressure of conformity to the goals of the state, with its associated emphasis on professionalism. The next chapter traces these tensions.

NOTES

[1] Doug Henwood, author of *Wall Street: How It Works and For Whom* (New York, NY: Verso, 1999), points out that organizations such as the World Bank hold the view that globalization as we know it is inevitable and unstoppable and notes that, even on the left, many speak of globalization instead of capitalism or imperialism to describe the process of corporate accumulation and power on an international scale. Henwood comments that "Once you understand capitalism, you see that it's always been an international and internationalizing system. Maybe we can say that the pace of that has picked up, but I don't think there is anything particularly newly international about the political economy today." In "The 'New Economy' and the Speculative Bubble: An Interview with Doug Henwood," *Monthly Review* 52.11 (April 2000): 72.

[2] Karl Marx and Friedrich Engels, *The Communist Manifesto* (1848) in *The Communist Manifesto Now: Socialist Register*, ed. Leo Panitch and Colin Leys (Halifax, NS: Fernwood Publishing, 1998) 243.

[3] Those who oppose the new globalization, such as Fidel Castro, acknowledge its reach. "Globalization is an objective reality underlining the fact that we are all passengers on the same vessel—this planet where we all live. But passengers on this vessel are traveling in very different conditions. A trifling minority is traveling in luxurious cabins furnished with the internet, cell phones and access to global communication networks... 85 per cent of the passengers on this ship are crowded together in its dirty hold, suffering hunger, disease and helplessness." Fidel Castro, "Third World Must Unite or Die: Opening of the South Summit, Havana," *Capitalism in Crisis: Globalization and World Politics Today*, ed. David Deutschman (New York, NY: Ocean Press, 2000) 279.

[4] Gary Teeple, *Globalization and the Decline of Social Reform: Into the Twenty-First Century* (Toronto, ON: Garamond, 2000). Teeple reminds us that the US was the only victor in World War II in terms of capital since other industrial powers were "economically exhausted and/or indebted to the United States" (57).

[5] Teeple 54.

[6] The fourth ministerial meeting of the WTO took place in Dohar, Qatar, on November 9–13, 2001. At the same time there were anti-WTO meetings held around the world. In Havana, the Cuban government hosted the "Enuentro Hemisferico de Lucha Contra ALCA" [Hemispheric Meeting for the Struggle Against the FTAA] (13–16 November 2001). Over 800 delegates from 34 countries met to discuss the FTAA and their resistance to it.

[7] Bernard M. Hoekman and Michel M. Kostecki, *The Political Economy of the World Trading System* (New York, NY: Oxford Press, 2001) 51. The authors are summarizing Article III of the Agreement Establishing the World Trade Organization.

8 Sohan Sharma and Surinder Kumar, "The Military Backbone of Globalisation," *Race and Class* 44.3 (January-March 2003): 23.
9 Sharma and Kumar 27.
10 Steven Staples, *Breaking Rank: A Citizen's Review of Canada's Military Spending* (Ottawa, ON: The Polaris Institute, 2002) 29.
11 Sharma and Kumar.
12 National Association of Social Workers, "Peace and Social Justice," *Social Work Speaks: National Association of Social Workers Policy Statements 2000–2003* (Washington, DC: NASW Press, 2000) 238. Also can be found at http://www.naswdc.org/.The NASW opposes unilateral, pre-emptive military action by the US against Iraq. See, for example, the October 7, 2002 letter to President George W. Bush from Terry Mizrahi, President of NASW found at the same web site.
13 Maude Barlow, *The Free Trade Areas of the Americas and the Threat to Social Programs, Environmental Sustainability and Social Justice in Canada and the Americas* (Ottawa, ON: Council of Canadians, 18 January 2001) 4.
14 Tony Clarke, "Transitional Corporation Agenda Behind the Harris Regime," *Mike Harris's Ontario: Open for Business: Closed to People*, ed. Diana Ralph, Andre Regimbald, and Neree St-Amand (Halifax, NS: Fernwood Publishing, 1990) 29. Clarke also draws our attention to how the North American Free Trade Agreement (NAFTA) and the General Agreement on Trade and Tariffs (GATT) are bills of rights for Transnational Corporations (TNCs) and how these rights supercede those for citizens of countries.
15 Maude Barlow, "The Fourth Ministerial Meeting of the World Trade Organization—An Analysis," 16 October 2001. Available at http://www.canadians.org/campaigns/campaigns-tradepub-4minmtg.html.
16 Clarence Bolt, "Our destiny to be decided more by TNCs than by MPs," *The CCPA Monitor* 6.6 (1999): 18. It is for these reasons that some 40,000 protesters, representing 800 grassroots organizations from over 75 countries gathered at the meeting of the WTO in Seattle in November 1999 to voice their opposition to growing corporate control of nation-states and the imposed economic restructuring. Similarly, in April 2001 in Quebec City, 60,000 people gathered to highlight the harmful impact the FTAA will have in terms of human rights, and on social, economic, and environmental conditions.
17 Michel Chossudovsky, *The Globalization of Poverty: Impacts of IMF and the World Bank Reforms* (London: Zed Books Ltd, 1997). This text offers a comprehensive analysis of globalization and the impact on both developed and developing countries. The author is scathing in his critique of this new international order: "The new international financial order feeds on human poverty and the destruction of the natural environment. It generates social apartheid, encourages racism and ethnic strife, undermines the rights of women and often precipitates countries into destructive confrontations between nationalities" (34).
18 Editorial, "Structurally maladjusted," *The CCPA Monitor* 9.2 (June 2002) 2.
19 Armine Yalnizyan, *The Growing Gap: A Report on Growing Inequality Between the Rich and the Poor in Canada* (Toronto, ON: Centre for Social Justice, 1998) x.
20 Steve Kerstetter, *Rags and Riches: Wealth Inequality in Canada* (Ottawa, ON: Canadian Centre for Policy Alternatives, December 2002). The report, based on data from Statistics Canada's Survey of Financial Security, can be found on the Centre's web site: www.policyalternatives.ca.
21 Yalnizyan x, xi, 57.
22 Comparing rates is difficult because of the incompatibilities in the measurement of unemployment. When adjusted to US concepts, the Canadian unemployment rate falls by 1 percentage point. See, e.g., Constance Sorrentino, "International Unemployment Rates: How Comparable are They?," *Monthly Labour Review* (June 2000): 3–20. http//www.bls.gov/opub/mir/2000.
23 Statistics compiled by the city of Ottawa in 2001 suggest that between 40 and 50 homeless people have died in shelters and on the streets in each of the previous three years. "Mission to Add Hospice for Homeless," *Ottawa Citizen*, 15 March 2001: F6
24 An excellent analysis of this practice can be found in William Ryan, *Blaming the Victim* (New

York, NY: Pantheon Books, 1971).

25 David McGee, "To Be on Welfare is to...," Eastern Branch Ontario Association of Social Workers *Bulletin* 27.3 (Fall 1998): 4.

26 "New Poverty Gauge Based on Survival," *Globe and Mail* 9 January 2003: A3.

27 Ernie Lightman, *Social Policy in Canada* (Don Mills, ON: Oxford University Press, 2003). Thanks to Ernie Lightman for clarification on the development of the MBM measure.

28 "New Yard Stick Places More People in Poverty," *Globe and Mail,* 27 May 2002: A1, A6.

29 Bernadette D. Proctor and Joseph Dalaker, *Poverty in the United States: 2001,* US Census Bureau, Current Population Reports (Washington, DC: US Government Printing Office, 2002).

30 National Council of Welfare Reports, *Poverty Profile 1998* (Ottawa, ON: National Council of Welfare), Autumn, 2000.

31 Abdolmohammad Kazemipur and Shiva Halli, *The New Poverty in Canada: Ethnic Groups and Ghetto Neighbourhoods* (Toronto, ON: Thompson Educational Publishing, 2000).

32 Under the PRA, Temporary Assistance for Needy Families (TANF) replaced Aid to Families with Dependent Children. Dorothy C. Miller, "What is Needed for True Equality: An Overview of Policy Issues for Women," *Building on Women's Strengths: A Social Work Agenda for the Twenty-First Century*, ed. K. Jean Peterson and Alice A. Lieberman (New York, NY: The Haworth Social Work Practice Press, 2001) 45–65.

33 Mimi Abramovitz, *Under Attack, Fighting Back: Women and Welfare in the United States* (New York, NY: Monthly Review Press, 2000) 25.

34 "Foodbanks Welcome UN Report," *Globe and Mail,* 31 May 1993: A3; Michael Valpy, "An Astonishing Document and How It Came About," *Globe and Mail,* 8 June 1993: A2.

35 "Canada Ranks High in Child Poverty," *Globe and Mail,* 13 June 2000: A1, A8.

36 On August 9, 2001, Kimberly Rogers—40 years old, eight months pregnant, and battling depression—died. Ms. Rogers had made the mistake of enrolling in a social service worker program and receiving student loans while remaining on social assistance (a practice which was once allowed). She was charged with welfare fraud, convicted, banned from social assistance for life, and placed under house arrest except for three hours on Wednesday mornings. A legal challenge was successful in getting temporary reinstatement of welfare benefits of $520 a month. Of her monthly income, 10 per cent was automatically withdrawn for loan restitution and $450 went for rent, leaving her with $18 a month for food and other essentials. See, e.g., Laura Etherden, "Criminalization of the Poor: Government complicity in the death of Kim Rogers," *NAPO News* 81 (December 2001): 9; "Bleak House," *Globe and Mail,* 18 August 2001. One year later, after an inquiry, the coroner's jury decided that Ms. Rogers had taken an overdose of anti-depressants and ruled that the ban was a contributing factor in her death. However, the Ontario government refused to lift the life-time ban. "Ontario to Maintain Lifetime Welfare Ban," *Globe and Mail,* 20 December 2002: A11.

37 "Observations of Social Workers In Eastern Ontario on Effects on Clients/Families of Recent Funding and Policy Changes and Strategies Clients/Families are Using to Cope," OASW Eastern Branch Survey, January-February 1996.

38 "Families Stuck in Costly 'Last Resort' Motels," *Ottawa Citizen,* 22 October 2001.

39 Anton L. Allahar and James E. Côté, *Richer and Poorer* (Toronto, ON: Lorimer, 1998) 126–29.

40 Colleen Lundy and Mark Totten, "Youth on the Fault Line," *The Social Worker* 65.3 (1997): 98–106.

41 For a year prior to the shutdown and strike the miners and their families lived in an atmosphere of uncertainty, abandonment, and powerlessness. The effect has been devastating, leading to heart attacks, family problems, and a questioning of their own worth. See, e.g., Reverend Robert Neville, "Commentary," *CBC Morning,* January 2000, reproduced with permission. Reverend Neville kindly sent me a copy of the commentary.

42 David Cattell-Gordon, "The Appalachian Inheritance: A Culturally Transmitted Traumatic Stress Syndrome?," *Journal of Progressive Human Services* 1.1 (1990): 41–57.

43 Neville. On May 16, 2001, the Prince mine workers and their families found out about the closure of the mine by hearing the news on the radio. The federal minister was not courte-

ous enough to inform them directly.

44 Neville.

45 For example, Joanne Naiman outlines how the state serves the interests of the capitalist class, composed primarily of Anglo-Saxon, wealthy, white, heterosexual, and able-bodied men and women, by the three functions of accumulation, legitimation, and coercion. Accumulation is when the state tries to create or maintain the conditions for growth of profits and capital accumulation. Legitimation is when the state tries to maintain social harmony, in large measure by legitimating the current class structure and the right of the ruling class to rule. Coercion involves the state using force to suppress the subordinate classes on behalf of the dominant class. Joanne Naiman, *How Societies Work: Class, Power and Change in a Canadian Society* (Concord, ON: Irwin Publishing, 1997) 161.

46 For an understanding of the uprising, see Kahn-Tineta Horn, "Interview: Oka and Mohawk Sovereignty," *Studies in Political Economy* 35 (Summer 1991): 29–41.

47 James O'Connor, *The Fiscal Crisis of the State* (New York, NY: St. Martin's Press, 1973) 6.

48 Frances Fox Piven and Richard A. Cloward, *Regulating the Poor: The Functions of Public Welfare*, rev. ed. (New York, NY: Vintage Books, 1993).

49 Teeple 15.

50 The fact is that the taxes paid by the working class in Canada pay for all social welfare expenditures plus military and other budgets as well. See, e.g., Ardeshir Sepehri and Robert Chernomas, "Who Paid For The Canadian Welfare State Between 1955–1988?," *Review of Radical Political Economics* 24.1 (Spring 1992): 71–88.

51 Sam Gindin, "Social Justice and Globalization: Are They Compatible?," *Monthly Review* 54.2 (June 2002): 1–11.

52 Ann Withorn, *Serving the People: Social Service and Social Change* (New York, NY: Columbia University Press, 1984) 89.

53 Sue Wise, "Becoming a Feminist Social Worker," *Feminist Praxis*, ed. Liz Stanley (London: Routledge, 1990) 236.

CHAPTER 2

HISTORICAL DEVELOPMENTS IN SOCIAL WORK

One group who have traditionally been moved to action by "pity for the poor," we call the Charitable; the other, larger or smaller in each generation, but always fired by the "hatred of injustice" we designate as the Radicals.

—*Jane Addams.*[1]

I n the early part of the last century, rapid economic growth and industrial expansion were accompanied by a rise in immigration, deplorable working conditions for labouring people, and substandard housing. There were also few resources for those who were impoverished or who faced serious social and health problems. This situation was exacerbated by major economic depressions, which resulted in massive unemployment.[2] Social work as a profession emerged in Canada and the United States as an organized response to such social and economic conditions and the resultant problems many individuals and families experienced.

Four central themes emerge as we trace the developments of the profession in Canada and the United States over the past 80 years. First, since its inception in the 1920s, the social work profession has aspired to two goals: providing services to those in need and advocating for change to social policy and social conditions. While all social workers have embraced the first goal, the profession has often been divided over whether the second has a place within social work. Those practitioners who see social change activity as part of the purpose of social work and strive to work to change social structures as well as assisting individuals and communities are part of the more radical wing. Those who focus on individual and family change, the development of treatment approaches to individual and family problems, and the enhancement and acceptance of social work as a profession argue that participation in broad social change is not the role of professional social workers. This tension between social action and individual change is evident throughout the history of social work practice. The profession consequently has been marked by periods of conservative retrenchment as well as tides of "militant professionalism" within its ranks.[3] Most would agree that radicals have been a persistent but weak force within the profession; others see the dominance of the profession by the conservative forces as complete. Indeed, Reuben Bitensky has suggested that social work's abandonment of social action and the role of the "conscience of society" for the role of "an apologist for the *status quo*" and "devoting its efforts to adjusting clients to the existing social institutions" offered the possibility of the survival of the profession and ensured a firm footing within state-sponsored social services.[4]

Secondly, in the early years of the profession, Canadian and US social work shared a common history. Social workers attended the same conferences, belonged to the same organizations, and subscribed to the same journals. But the relationship was not equal. The Council on Social Work Education (CSWE) in the US accredited Canadian schools of social work until 1970, demonstrating the degree to which social work in Canada was influenced by theoretical and practical models from our neighbour to the south. While contributions from the United Kingdom were considered, social work in Canada was most influenced by US social work developments during these years.[5]

Thirdly, theoretical developments and empirical research in other disciplines such as sociology, political science, economics, and psychology have informed social work practice in the past and continue to do so. The radical streams within these disciplines inform the social change approach of the profession, while more conservative theories and studies inform the individual-focussed approach to practice.

Finally, the ongoing search for a unifying practice framework which would bring social workers together under common principles and a generic base has persisted throughout the years. Given the degree of differing views

within the profession, it is not surprising to learn that no unifying framework has emerged.

The Early Years: Responding to Poverty and Establishing Legitimacy

Early attempts at organized response to the problems of poverty focussed
on the provision of charity and usually were based in Christian churches.
Clergy and other church leaders established charity organizations and settlement houses for the purposes of providing food, shelter, and services to the
poor. Canada's social welfare pioneers—such as J.J. Kelso, a journalist—had
laid the ground work and had mobilized community support for services
such as Children's Aid Societies, the first of which opened in Toronto in 1891.
Unlike the rest of Canada, the Maritime region (Nova Scotia, New
Brunswick, and Prince Edward Island) based their social charity response
on the English Poor Laws of 1763. The system was distinguished by poor
houses, homes for orphans, a "paupers list," and charity distributed according to who was deemed worthy by an appointed "Overseer of the Poor."

Charity Organization Societies (COS), first developed in England in
1869 and established in the US by 1877, advanced the practice of "scientific philanthropy," almsgiving, and rehabilitation of the poor. They identified those who were "deserving" of charity and provided a registry to
insure that provisions were not duplicated by participating agencies. In
1891, Mary Richmond (1861–1928), the director of the Baltimore
(Maryland) Charity Organization, advocated a "retail" approach to administering to the needy which concentrated on a case-by-case response to
individual client problems. She became a leader in establishing "friendly
visiting" as a profession and in developing casework as its primary activity. Her first book, *Friendly Visiting Among the Poor*, was a manual to guide
the practice.[6] She believed that social casework, an individualistic
approach, ameliorated the impact of industrialization through advancing personal change or adaptation.

At the same time, those who were socially minded— "some paternalis-
tic, some missionary, and some even Marxist"—established settlement
houses in communities where there was great social need and advocated for
"wholesale" social change while focussing on individual concerns.[7] Jane
Addams (1860–1935), one of the first leaders of the settlement house movement, took over the directorship of Hull House in Chicago in 1892 and gained

national stature as a social change advocate. Addams was a nationally recognized political and peace activist and a member of the Women's International League for Peace and Freedom. In 1931 she was awarded the Nobel Peace Prize for her efforts in opposing World War I and building peace.[8] Between 1907 and 1916 she published six books and more than 150 essays. Her opposition to the outbreak of war in 1914 and her support for those on the left, including Socialist presidential candidate Eugene Debs, were more than social workers at the time could accept. Therefore, her influence diminished.[9] Meanwhile, Mary Richmond, who supported the war, set out to ensure that social workers were prepared to respond to its casualties.

The two responses to poverty and social inequality and the respective approaches taken by Richmond and Addams laid the foundation on which social work as a profession would be built, and the dichotomy would endure long after they ceased to practice.[10]

Charity Organization Societies

In response to the growing numbers of poor people in North American cities that resulted from capitalist industrialization and mass immigration from Europe, organized charity was seen as "the urban community's surest safeguard against revolution." Initially, charity was distributed by volunteers who engaged in "friendly visiting," a practice which has been characterized as "an instrument of social control which assumed not only the right, but the civic duty of intervention in the lives of the poor by their economic and social betters."[11]

The charity movement social workers, guided by a desire for professional identity and recognition, turned their attention to identifying individual practice skills and techniques. Their tradition had the greatest influence on educational programs and thus on the development and direction of the newly emerging profession. Stanley Wenocur and Michael Reisch provide a thorough account of how social work followed the route taken by other established professions such as medicine in developing ties to social elites who could provide support and legitimation. It also engaged in establishing "university-based education with increasingly selective entry into the field, active professional associations to promote social work standards and to gain exclusive control over the right to practice, and development of individualistic, technological, 'scientific' methodology that would be consistent with dominant social values."[12]

Settlements

In direct contrast to the COS caseworkers who provided "friendly visiting," counselling, and material resources to those less fortunate, social workers working in the settlement house movement often lived within the community and provided assistance to the immigrant and working-class population to whom they referred as "neighbours in need."[13] Social workers practicing in the settlement tradition advanced the role of social work in the area of social justice and social activism. Emphasis was placed on group work, organizing, and community development with little interest in acquiring recognition and legitimacy for their work as a profession.

The US settlement movement led in the mobilization for social reform, and its representatives actively advocated for change in working conditions, health care, housing, child labour, child welfare, and civil rights for African Americans.[14] In 1902 Evangelia Settlement opened in Toronto—the first settlement house in Canada. Unlike their US and British counterparts, Canadian settlements tended to be church-affiliated, not secular. Allan Irving, Harriet Parsons, and Donald Bellamy suggest that this is partly due to the fact that industrialization and its accompanying social problems came later in Canada. The churches viewed charity as their responsibility, and, since they had an administrative structure that could readily respond to families and children in need, they helped develop the settlements.[15]

Early settlement work also was greatly influenced by the radical social gospel movement, considered by some to have socialist and feminist elements.[16] Social gospellers established missions, such as the Fred Victor Mission in Toronto, for transient and homeless men.[17] One member of the social gospellers was James Shaver Woodsworth, who later became a leader in the Social Welfare League and the Cooperative Commonwealth Foundation (CCF), the precursor to the modern New Democratic Party.[18] Another social gospeller, Nellie McClung, an advocate for women's rights, was elected to the federal parliament in 1921 and was one of five feminists who successfully fought in 1929 to have women in Canada regarded as persons.[19]

Settlement workers looked to sociology, economics, and political economy, as well as social gospel, for a conceptual and theoretical framework to inform their activities. They varied in their analysis of social problems and their approach to alleviating them. While some limited their response to concrete services and advocacy, others such as Jane Addams and J.S. Woodsworth strove for radical reform and political action. With some exceptions, settlement workers, like their counterparts in charity organizations, generally did not engage in class conflict and radical structural change.[20]

Establishing the Foundations of the Profession

By the end of the first third of the century the foundations of the social work profession were established. The profession constituted its title, defined its basic function and purpose, and founded professional associations and educational programs.[21] As early as 1898, the Charity Organization Societies established the first training program in social work, the New York Summer School in Philanthropic Work in New York, which increased to a full year as the New York School of Philanthropy in 1904.[22] By 1910 there were five professional training schools in the US.[23] In the same year training courses for social workers in Canada were increased to two years, and the first university program for social workers opened at the University of Toronto in 1914, followed in 1918 by a program at McGill University in Montreal. In 1919, the University of Toronto school joined 14 US schools of social work to form the Association of Training Schools for Professional Social Work (later renamed the American Association of Schools of Social Work and finally the Council on Social Work Education) and began the work of establishing educational standards and an accrediting function.[24]

The movement towards establishing social work as a profession was not without its setbacks. At the 1915 National Conference of Charities, Abraham Flexner, a recognized expert on professional schools, addressed the membership. While Flexner prefaced his comments with an admission that he lacked knowledge about social work and questioned his competence to assess whether or not social work was a profession, he nonetheless proceeded to place emphasis on the professional attribute of "intellectual activity" and, on that basis, to conclude that social work, unlike medicine and law, was not a profession since it did not possess a distinct activity, technique, or knowledge base.[25] Social workers were viewed as mediators, not professionals with expertise.

Many social work leaders considered this appraisal to be a serious setback for the fledging profession and turned their attention to the work of identifying and defining a theory and practice specific to social work. In 1917, Mary Richmond published *Social Diagnosis*, modelled after the medical profession's textbook, to guide social workers in the practice of studying, diagnosing, and treating individual problems through an interview process. Casework was identified as the technique, and social work's attention turned almost exclusively to individual counselling and away from understanding social conditions and promoting social change.

The Diagnostic and Functional Schools

The shift away from social change toward individual change or from "cause to function" was further supported by what has been coined the "psychiatric deluge," the adoption of Freudian psychoanalytic principles as the theoretical base for social work practice.[26] Richmond's casework had found a theory base in Freudian psychology, and the adoption of its central tenets greatly influenced the direction of the fledgling profession. The importance of social conditions in understanding individual behaviour was greatly diminished as attention was placed on childhood development and unresolved experiences, feelings, and thoughts, many of which were believed to be buried in the subconscious. The role of the social worker was to free the person from these damaging past experiences through intensive therapy. For example, after World War I, returning soldiers, along with their families, became a new client group in need of professional social work services, and psychoanalytic social work practice expanded.

By the mid 1920s, family agencies and child guidance clinics were established, and social workers found new settings in which to practice. During this time most graduates from the two Canadian schools of social work (University of Toronto and McGill University) were employed mainly in private family and child welfare agencies, with a few working in hospitals, settlement houses, and municipal and provincial or federal government departments. Women and men were viewed very differently by the public and the profession. The image that the public held of a social worker, according to Joy Maines, Executive Director of the Canadian Association of Social Work, "was a female dressed in mannish suits, with a straight brimmed hat, flat-heeled shoes and a very long nose for 'snooping.'" On the other hand, male social workers usually were thought to be "either reformers, retired clergymen, or wild-eyed idealists."[27]

Psychodynamic theory largely informed by Freudian theory was to dominate social work practice from the 1920s through to the 1960s. In the process, it has been argued that "the social worker departed from the stance of a doer, a provider of concrete services, to that of passive observer" and counsellor.[28] Even during the Great Depression of the 1930s, the Freudian psychological approach remained dominant.

An alternative to the diagnostic school and psychoanalytic theory was introduced by Virginia Robinson and Jessie Taft at the Pennsylvania School of Social Work in the 1930s.[29] Called functionalism, this development prompted heated debates, which continued through the 1940s and divided the social work community.

The functional school, an approach to casework based on the psychology and personality theory of Otto Rank, was considered to be a more humanistic and self-deterministic response to dealing with the problems of poverty, because it emphasized the client/worker relationship, the importance of the client's interpretation of the problem or difficulty, and the present rather than past feelings and experiences.[30] Robinson and Taft attempted to shift social work away from a dependence on psychiatry and the determinism of Freudian psychoanalytic theory.[31] They placed emphasis on the helping relationship and the participation of clients in the process. While casework and psychotherapy continued to be used, the therapeutic relationship was not shaped by the client's ego drives but by the agency's function. The purpose of a social worker's helping was influenced by the social purpose, policies, and procedures of the agency in which she was employed. For example, the purpose of family intervention by a hospital social worker would differ from that of a child protection worker. While the focus remained on individual change with little attention to the material conditions of people coming for help and a general disregard for advocacy on behalf of the client, principles of the functional approach, such as the right to self-determination and the helping relationship, can be found in social work practice approaches today.

Professional Associations.

In the immediate post World War I years, Canadian social workers were members of the American Association of Medical Social Workers (created in 1918) and the American Association of Social Workers (created in 1922); however, they saw a need for a Canadian association. Plans to establish such a Canadian association were laid during the 1924 National Conference on Social Welfare, held in Toronto. By 1926 the Canadian Association of Social Workers (CASW) was formed, and the first general meeting was held two years later.

The purpose of the CASW in its formative years was "to bring together professional social workers for such cooperative effort as may enable them more effectively to carry out their ideals of service to the community," and the membership set out "to promote professional standards, encourage proper and adequate preparation and training, cultivate an informed public opinion which will recognize the professional and technical nature of social work, issue an official organ, maintain a professional employment service, conduct research and carry on such other activities as it may deem possible."[32] The formation of the CASW was followed quickly by the establishment of three international associations that united social workers around the world—the International Permanent Secretariat of Social Workers (now the International Federation of Social Workers) founded in 1928, the International Council on Social Welfare (ICSW) also in 1928, and the International Association of Schools of Social Work (IASSW) in 1929.

Specialization and Fragmentation

As social work began to create specializations based on fields of practice—psychiatric, medical, and school social work—there was concern that the profession was becoming fragmented. To address this problem, a gathering of representatives from national organizations was held in Milford, Pennsylvania, in 1923. The objectives of the Milford Conference were to create professional unity and formulate a generic base for casework practice that was common to all, regardless of practice setting. Those attending recognized casework as the predominant, but not sole, element in social work practice and stressed the existence of common principles of "generic social case work" that could unite caseworkers into a single occupational group.[33] The final report, *Social Casework: Generic and Specific*, published in 1929, concluded that, while there were various field specializations in social work, the method of generic casework unified the profession. The report also identified the fundamental social work techniques as social case work, community organization, group work, social research, and administration, and recommended that all should be included in social work training programs. However, the profession did not have a theoretical base which would unite all the different areas of practice around generic case work.

Responses During the Depression

The 1930s, marked by massive unemployment and unprecedented poverty, produced a situation that was not responsive to the psychological intervention being used in most private agencies. The professionalization of the previous decade had resulted in a decline in social reform activities, and social workers were caught by surprise and unprepared for this upheaval.[34] Also, in the US settlement work was being undermined by the introduction of Community Chests controlled by conservative elites who supported private charity.[35] The economic crisis, so far-reaching in its devastation, presented a challenge within the profession and fostered a resurgence of the social action tradition which had been set aside. In the US, a group of social workers organized "The Rank and File Movement." They aligned themselves with labour and the poor, advocated political action, and, unlike Jane Addams and other settlement workers, moved beyond advocating better social conditions to directly exposing and challenging the capitalist system.[36]

Bertha Reynolds, a key figure in the Rank and File movement, articulated the choices ahead for the social work profession:

> Social work today is standing at the crossroads. It may go on with its face toward the past, bolstering up the decaying profit system, having to defend what is indefensible for the sake of money which pays for its services. On the other hand it may envision a future in which professional social services as well as education, medical services and the like shall be the unquestioned right of all, conferred not as a benefit but as society's only way of maintaining itself.[37]

She and other social workers of the Rank and File did not abandon working with individuals and families but infused their work with critical social analysis and activism. Through organizing efforts they successfully initiated important reform measures in areas such as social security, child, and public welfare while seeking social changes. Unlike many professionals of the time, members of the Rank and File were active in trade unions and were sensitized to, and spoke out against, racism.[38]

While there were radical movements in Canada during this time, there does not appear to have been a social work response comparable to the Rank and File. For many members of the CASW, social action "had rather a sinister connotation in the thirties." According to Joy Maines's recollection a committee was set up to consider:

...the relationship of the professional body to the large numbers of unqualified workers then unemployed. There was hot and heavy discussion during these years about whether or not CASW should throw its doors of membership wide open. The relationship of trade unions to professional associations was debated. Was there danger of a "rank and file" movement in Canada such as caused considerable flurry in the United States? CASW decided not to lower its standards![39]

In spite of the association's general lack of regard for the work of the Rank and File and its socialist orientation, articles by Bertha Reynolds appeared in Canadian social welfare journals. In 1936, in the journal of *Child and Family Welfare*, she urged social workers to join in solidarity with all workers:

The future of social casework is the future of the right of common men and women to economic justice and civil liberties, including the right to think and to participate in the making of their own life condition. If the common men and women fail to achieve those rights, no one will have them. Professional people are learning that their fate is bound up with that of all other workers. If they do not stand courageously for all human rights, they will lose their own, including the right to practice their profession as a high and honourable calling. [40]

Since the profession did not offer a radical alternative, Canadian social workers interested in working toward economic and social justice most likely joined The League for Social Reconstruction (LSR) which set out to develop a Canadian brand of socialism. The League influenced the development of social welfare policy and produced the document "Social Planning in Canada" (1935) to guide policies of the left-leaning Co-operative Commonwealth Federation, (CCF).[41] Formed in 1932, the CCF, a federation of farmer, labour, and socialist organizations, entered federal politics in the 1935 election and captured seven seats and 8.8 per cent of the vote. J.S. Woodsworth was the first party leader. The party advocated a planned economy with public ownership of natural resources, socialized health services, support for farmers, a national labour code, and disarmament and peace.[42] Harry Cassidy and Leonard Marsh, both economists and leaders in social welfare reform and social work education, were among the League's most active members.

The Depression years demonstrated the inadequacy of the existing social welfare system and the need for federally supported programs. In the US members of the Rank and File were instrumental in the passing of the 1935 Social Security Act, which gave the federal government responsibility for the aged, unemployed, persons with disability, and dependent children. Although the Rank and File was not a national organization, members were successful in providing an analysis of capitalism and drawing attention to the prevalence of poverty and inadequacy of social relief. They brought trade unionism into social work and influenced the American Association of Social Workers to take a more progressive stand on the economic and social conditions of people.

While limited in scope, these developments, and the larger social upheavals of the period, prompted social work to move beyond a psychological individual approach to social work practice. It was during this time that group work, a practice method where a social worker sees individuals in a therapeutic group, entered social work as a legitimate practice function.[43] A section on group work was included in the National Conference on Social Work in Montreal in 1935, and one year later the National Association of Group Work was formed.[44]

Social Work in an Era of Retrenchment

Social work entered a period of relative retrenchment from social change during the 1940s and 1950s when the focus was on strengthening professional associations and educational programs, as well as developing the theoretical core of social work practice. The practice approaches that emerged placed emphasis on the individual at the expense of social conditions. Herbert Bisno raised concern that the emphasis on methods and techniques placed the profession in danger of pursuing "know-how" at the expense of "know-why."[45]

During World War II, economic production increased to support the war effort, and unemployment ceased to be an urgent problem. The rise of Fascism presented a common enemy, and the struggle between the working class and the capitalists subsided. The conservatism of the 1940s and 1950s and the rise of McCarthyism with its anti-Communist and anti-socialist rhetoric took its toll on political activism. Left-wing or radical activities in all fields were curtailed, and the Rank and File social work movement disbanded.[46] According to Gerald Rothman, the movement was destroyed by the Red Scare, and the union was expelled for so-called "communist domination." Anyone associated with the union could not find an agency job, and the profession generally distanced its relationship with members of the Rank and File and failed to support them.[47]

Conservatism and McCarthyism also created difficulties for social workers who were perceived as radical or socialist. For instance, Charlotte Towle was commissioned by the Federal Bureau of Public Assistance to write a book that would provide guidelines for the supervision of public assistance workers. *Common Human Needs,* published in 1945, was quickly a success, necessitating a third printing. However, over a four-year period starting in 1949, a Commission on Government, fuelled by local business interests, questioned the efficiency of social welfare delivery and alleged that the Bureau of Public Assistance, through its publication *Common Human Needs,* was promoting the maintenance of people on welfare and thereby encouraging idleness. In 1951, the Bureau responded by destroying the plates for the book and removing all copies from circulation. Towle's offending sentence, which appeared on page 57 of the book, was: "Social security and public assistance programs are a basic essential for attainment of the socialized state envisioned in democratic ideology, as a way of life which so far has been realized only in slight measure."[48] Towle signed the copyright over to the American Association of Social Workers, and the book was reprinted in 1952 with a slight modification to the sentence which had created so much controversy. Towle continued to teach at the University of Chicago. Suspicions of her resurfaced when she signed a petition seeking clemency for Julius and Ethel Rosenberg, who had been charged with treason and were facing execution in 1953. As a result, she was denied a passport the following year.

As the Rank and File were driven underground, functional caseworkers reemerged as the "therapy people," professional counsellors practicing psychotherapy.[49] Humanistic psychology and behavioural theories joined psychoanalytic approaches in guiding social work practice. With the suppression of the radical elements within social work, traditional social workers returned to the task of building a profession and the further development of university-based social work programs. In 1947, the first Master's in Social Work program was established at the University of Toronto, and in 1951 the university opened its Doctoral program in Social Work.

In the early 1950s, social work education at the Master's level in both Canada and the US was redesigned away from a focus on specializations toward a generic curriculum that included social welfare policy, human growth and development, and the three recognized methods of the day—casework, group work, and community organizing.[50] This marked the shift away from specializations toward an emphasis on a common core and a generalist social work model that would unite all social workers. This shift was also reflected at the level of professional associations. In 1955, seven US social work associations merged to create one association, the National Association of Social Workers (NASW).

Authors such as Florence Hollis continued in the psycho-social tradition with an emphasis on diagnosis and Freudian psychology. The centrality of ego psychology and the dismissal of the social context is reflected in her views on assessment:

> Since the personality theory used in the psycho social approach is primarily Freudian, the personality system is conceptualized as a set of interacting forces designated as id, ego, and superego. The functioning of the many aspects of the ego, including how the individual's defences operate, is considered of primary importance in assessing the adequacy of the client's efforts to deal with his difficulty and the extent to which he is contributing to his own problems. Ego functioning must be understood even when the causes of the problem lie primarily in the situation rather than in the client's personality.[51]

A central task of social workers practicing from the diagnostic school was to assess the client's situation and/or problem and determine an intervention. Helen Harris Perlman, in *Social Casework: A Problem Solving Process*, developed an approach based on John Dewey's principles of problem-solving and viewed the person as active agent in the process, rather than a passive recipient of professional assessment and services. Perlman attempted to bridge the diagnostic and functional schools by promoting problem-solving as the function of social work while retaining the foundations of ego psychology. She described the problem-solving process as gathering facts (study), assessment (diagnosis), and selection of a course of action (treatment). She also recognized that the client must have the material means, such as money, recreational opportunities, or child care, in order to resolve the problem.[52]

However, the emphasis on ego functioning and the disregard for structural causes of client difficulties was out of step with the rediscovery of poverty and the movements for equality and justice of the 1960s. In the context of this social unrest and organized resistance, the practice of psychotherapy lost credibility. Increasing numbers of social workers were returning to community-based practice, and in 1962 the Council on Social Work Education finally recognized community organizing as a legitimate specialization. The buoyant economy of the time produced a proliferation of services and agencies and an immense growth in social work.

It was during this time that social workers considered a theoretical framework for practice that viewed people in the context of their environments. Sociologist C. Wright Mills made the distinction and connection between "private troubles and public issues" in his book *Power, Politics and People.*[53] During the Depression, Mills noted the difference between the personal predicament of being unemployed and the public issue of structural unemployment. William Schwartz, drawing on this connection between "private troubles and public issues," proposed that a social worker's role was "neither to 'change the people' nor to 'change the system' but to change the ways in which they deal with each other."[54] This mediating role shifted away from strictly a psychotherapy focus and again brought attention to the social context. Lawrence Shulman, building on the interactionist perspective of Schwartz, developed a holistic, empirically based theory for practice that placed emphasis on skills of helping. In the third edition of his book, Shulman added a focus on families, along with individuals and groups, and incorporated oppression theory into the framework. In 1999, he extended skills of helping to working with communities in the fourth edition of the book.[55] One of the most referenced books within social work, Shulman's framework for helping has been incorporated into a number of practice approaches.

In Search of a Generalist Practice Framework

In the last 40 years, social work in Canada has come into its own as a profession with a proliferation of university-based social work programs, social work scholarship and journals, the further development of professional associations, and legislation to regulate social work. In 1970, the Canadian Association of Schools of Social Work took over the accrediting function held by the US Council on Social Work Education (CSWE), thus signalling the independent direction of Canadian social work education.

In both the US and Canada, social workers continued to be concerned about fragmentation and the absence of a theoretical approach which would unite the profession and provide relevant practice methods. Howard Goldstein commented that the theoretical core of social work had not yet been fully developed and that the profession had "a valued and effective body of services and purpose but, like a cell without a nucleus, does not contain a substantial interior."[56] As well, there was a growing recognition that psychoanalytic approaches were limited in their application to the pressing concerns facing social workers. Therefore, there was an acute interest in identifying a conceptual framework for social work that would unify social workers and link private troubles to public issues.

While some social workers turned to functional systems theory, others looked to Marxist theory based on "socialist theory and radical analysis of society, which placed social work in a political context."[57] These two ways of viewing the client within a social context influenced social work approaches in the years to follow, each offering an organizing framework to unify and develop social work practice.[58] While both connect individual experiences to a larger social system, they differ ideologically and in their analysis of individual troubles.

Functional Systems Theory

Social workers, identifying the limitations of the individual focus of the approaches to social work, saw promise in General Systems Theory to provide the long sought-for unified framework for social work practice. Models based on this functional systems theory, such as Howard Goldstein's *Social Work Practice: A Unitary Approach* (1973) and Allen Pincus and Anne Minahan's *Social Work Practice: Model and Method* (1973), challenged the psychoanalytic approach of looking to the individual for the source of the problem; instead, they connected the person and problem with the environment.[59] They viewed society as an assembly of individuals in various sized units (called subsystems), all interacting in relative harmony within the larger system. The central assumptions were that people depend on systems and that problems are the result of a breakdown between people and the systems with which they interact, whether family, school, workplace, church, or welfare office. The primary goal of approaches drawing on functional systems theory was to achieve equilibrium within the family system, and although the social context was considered, the need for broad social change was disregarded.

While the authors differed in their application of systems theory, they were united in their attempt to offer models that would unify the profession and integrate the methods of casework, group work, and community practice with a focus on both the individual and society. Pincus and Minahan proposed four basic systems in social work practice: the change agent system (social worker(s) and agency colleagues); the client system (the client requesting help); the target system (people who "need to be changed to accomplish the goals of the change agent"); and the action system (change agents and others involved at work on the target system). They emphasized that "change agents are working to change *people,* not vague abstractions such as the 'community,' 'the organization,' or 'the system.'"[60] Pincus and Minahan, along with other functional-systems-based social workers, avoided the political dimension and believed that political activity was "more suited to social reform movements and political parties than to a profession."[61] While they recognized the need for social workers to be involved in social change, they offered a contradictory warning that "society will not support any activity which has an objective of bringing about fundamental changes in the very fabric of social institutions."[62]

Other variations on the systems theme include Carel Germain and Alex Gitterman's *The Life Model of Social Work Practice* (1980, 1996) based on ecological thinking that "focuses on the reciprocity of person-environment exchanges, in which each shapes and influences the other over time." Germain and Gitterman emphasized the social context and acknowledged that inequality and oppression is the reality for some in society: "This abuse of power creates and maintains social pollution such as poverty, institutional racism and sexism, repressive gender roles in family, work and the community life, homophobia, and physical and social barriers to community participation by those with disabilities."[63] However, they neglected to provide an analysis of the social structures that produce such inequality or to supply social work strategies for broad social change. Carol Meyer's *Clinical Social Work in an Eco-Systems Perspective* (1983) draws on systems, eco-systems, and ecology in a conceptual framework that claims to accommodate a number of approaches (eclecticism) including the life model.[64]

While the shift from the focus on individual deficiency prevalent in the psychodynamic approaches to attention to an individual's family and community was a welcome development, other social work scholars felt there was a lack of recognition of the political and economic power that produced unequal social relations; they turned to Marxist systems theory.

Marxist Systems Theory

Critics of functional systems theory articulated an alternative role for social work and offered a framework for practice. At different times this alternative approach in social work has been referred to as Marxist, radical, critical, or structural social work, but Marxism was the theory that most informed the early developments of this framework. Unlike functional systems theorists, there was no attempt to create social work models. Instead, a framework for practice with an emphasis on the analysis of society and social problems was the goal of Marxist practitioners. While proponents of functional systems theory were located primarily in the US, the leadership for radical practice also came from the United Kingdom, Australia, and Canada.

Radical social work approaches, based on a Marxist systems theory, placed individual problems within common experience and explored the degree to which they were socially constructed. This attention to how material conditions influence personal development and well-being moved social workers to develop practice strategies that would contribute to social justice as well as individual change. In 1975 two influential texts in radical social work were published—*Radical Social Work,* edited by British sociologists and activists Roy Bailey and Mike Brake, and *The Politics of Social Services* by American social worker Jeffry Galper.[65] Bailey and Brake clearly stated their vision for radical social work as "understanding the position of the oppressed in the context of the social and economic structures we live in. A socialist perspective is, for us, the most human approach for social workers. Our aim is not, for example, to eliminate casework, but to eliminate casework that supports ruling-class hegemony."[66] Similarly, Galper introduced his book: "The analysis is radical, in this sense, because it roots the problems of the social services in the most fundamental organizational principles of the society. The practice that is developed is radical, since it suggests that social services will not be of full service to clients and us all unless their task is seen as a struggle for the creation of a fundamentally changed society and—we believe—for a society organized on socialist principles."[67]

During the late 1970s, conservative political parties in power in North America and the United Kingdom eroded the welfare state through downsizing and cutbacks to services. Social workers writing in the radical tradition responded by producing some of the best analyses in social work literature on social welfare, the state, and social problems. "The Critical Texts in Social Work and the Welfare State," edited by Peter Leonard, made a particular valuable contribution in this regard. Among them were *Social Work Practice Under Capitalism: A Marxist Approach*, by Paul Corrigan and Peter Leonard (1978); *Class, Capital and Social Policy*, by Norman Ginsburg (1979); and Ian Gough's *The Political Economy of the Welfare State* (1979). During the same time, the London Edinburgh Weekend Return Group of social and community workers presented an excellent understanding of social welfare provision under capitalism in the book *In and Against the State* (1979).[68]

The faculty in the School of Social Work at Carleton University were the first in Canada to move toward a radical perspective as an orientation for social work education.[69] In 1972, the shift to more fully address social inequality was supported by the Carleton University Commission on the School of Social Work, which examined the curriculum and encouraged a broadened approach to practice. The Commission concluded that "in addition to the clinical ego-psychology approach, in which the client is seen as mainly having a problem requiring intervention and necessitating assistance towards adaptation, approaches to treatment should include a range of perspectives up to and including the 'Advocacy' and 'Participatory' approaches in which institutions and social processes are seen as having causal features requiring changes in which social workers must lead."[70]

Following this inquiry, under the leadership of Maurice Moreau, the School shifted from an ego-psychology model to what became called a structural approach, leaving behind the dualistic focus of individual change or social change and adopting a dialectic position of acknowledgement that both must be addressed and that change in one promotes change in the other. Carleton quickly became known as a "structural school," as a critical analysis and response was incorporated into all courses.[71] The project was also influenced by visiting scholars from the US and Britain such as Jeffry Galper, Vic George, Peter Leonard, and Mike Brake, who later joined the faculty on a full-time basis. (The structural approach is discussed in greater detail in Chapter 3.)

During these years, while the analysis of economic and political structures and policy was clearly developed, the direct practice component was less well conceptualized. Much of the early writings from a radical perspective, while articulating a clear class analysis and critique of capitalism, placed little emphasis on personal change, or on the differing experiences of women, persons with a disability, immigrant and visible minority persons, or those who identify as lesbian, gay, or transgendered. Towards the mid 1980s, these limitations were addressed by social workers who contributed to the development of woman-centred approaches, anti-racist social work, and social work with persons who have a disability and thereby transformed the framework for structural social work.[72]

One of the most important contributions to understanding individual behaviour within a Marxist systems framework came from Peter Leonard in his 1984 book *Personality and Ideology*. Leonard's development of personality under the conditions of capitalism provided the missing piece in much of Marxist social work. He outlined how the limitation of mainstream psychological theories, which hold a non-materialist view of society, "prevents them from understanding its necessarily exploitative character and therefore how this exploitative structure constructs the individual's inner experience of class, gender and ethnic status."[73] It is this understanding of the dialectic between consciousness and material existence that continues to be the core of radical social work practice.

Divisions in Social Work

The differences among those social workers who drew on functional systems theory and those who drew on Marxist systems theory were highlighted as social work educators returned to the task of conceptualizing a unified model for social work that would unite professional specializations and set out to clarify social work's mission, purpose, and common base. Much of the debate centred on defining the difference between practitioners who were considered generalists and those who were called specialists. These discussions took place at two working meetings on conceptual frameworks, and the contributions, which were published in the 1977 and 1981 issues of *Social Work*, reflect the differing views of generalist practice and the purpose of social work and its ideological underpinnings.

According to Anne Minahan and Allen Pincus, a generalist is defined as a person with "a broad view who can look at an entire social situation, analyze the interactions between people in all the resource systems connected to that situation, intervene in those interactions, determine which specialists are needed from a variety of disciplines, and coordinate and mobilize the knowledge and skills of many disciplines."[74] In their view, if the social worker has been prepared at a graduate level, he or she could become more of an expert generalist rather than a specialist. Specialized knowledge and skills were influenced by the practice setting, not so much by university preparation.

For others the first division of social work methods was whether or not a social worker was employed in direct service activities (counselling, advocating, providing resources and information, and making referrals) or indirect service activities (policy analysis, administration, program development and evaluation, and community planning).[75] A second level of specialization would then be determined by the specific practice setting and the client population.

Ideological difference also surfaced during these discussions. Those attending the second meeting in 1979 produced a very general "Working Statement on the Purpose of Social Work" and encouraged colleagues to make comments and critique the statement.[76] John F. Longres felt that a major limitation of the statement was its lack of attention to the ideological differences among social workers. An advocate for radical social work, he referred to the political nature of social work practice and how "theoreticians and practitioners alike are attempting to integrate radicalism into everyday, face-to-face practice with individuals, families, and communities rather than allowing it to be separated off as something that exists apart from contact with clients." Longres explained that radical practice works toward "a change *of* the system, not change *in* the system" and is guided by a socialist vision. [77] An opposing view was presented by Carol Myer, who, while recognizing the reality of increasing social inequality and the need for political action, held that it should not be part of the social work role and that such activities would be detrimental to the profession: "The idea in the last decade that social workers would change the social system through professional pursuit not only has been proven wrong (the system is worse) but has shaken public confidence in what social workers have been able to do." She concluded that "social workers can be more politically conscious and active, but politics ordinarily is not the domain of professional practice."[78] While there is relative consensus that social workers are generalists, there continues to be differences as to the practice framework that best serves social work and the needs of its clients.

The Arrival of Postmodernism

In the 1990s, some social work practitioners and academics began to consider the merits of postmodernism as a way of better informing the profession.[79] Peter Leonard, Janis Fook, and Bob Mullaly, all who have made significant contributions to radical social work, now incorporate postmodern theory to some degree.[80]

Although the complexities of, and variations in, postmodern theory cannot be elaborated here, several tenets which are integral to the theory are discussed. Postmodernism is a critique of the foundations of "modernity" and its focus on science, reason, and truth; it questions the relevance of universal claims and "grand theories," "grand narratives," or "totalizing theories" such as Marxism, socialism, and capitalism,[81] which are claimed to automatically overlook individual experience and other forms of oppression. Postmodernism, rooted in linguistic theory, holds that truth is a product of language or social discourse and is not objective or universal. Postmodern thinkers or "anti-truth tellers," as described by Joan Laird, hold that "knowledge does not develop from 'proven' or empirically-tested theory or hypothesis, it does not reflect any objective truth but is a product of social discourse; particular 'knowledges' are seen as social constructions, stories that have been shaped in contexts of power relationships in which they were crafted."[82]

Bob Mullaly suggests a continuum: at one end "postmodernism is a conservative, individualistic, and nihilistic doctrine, which holds that there is no potential for solidarity among oppressed persons or for social change efforts" and at the other end are those who, based on criticism of modernity, are attempting to revitalize critical social theory.[83] Similarly, Vodde and Gallant suggest that a narrative-deconstructivist practice drawing on postmodern theory provides a solution to the micro-macro split in social work and therefore unifies clinical and social action in pursuit of social justice.[84] They, too, distinguish between the purely linguistic orientation of postmodernist practice and one which focusses on language within a social justice framework, advocating for the latter, which they believe is represented in the narrative approaches that have been largely credited to Michael White and David Epston.[85]

Narrative therapy has gained in popularity in both Canada and the US, and White has been credited for bringing family therapy into the "postmodern world."[86] The goal of narrative approaches is to help people become authors of their own "stories," and to deconstruct and revise old problematic "stories."[87] The premise is that people are held back by an "old story" which may have helped them survive in the past but is no longer useful. In the postmodern deconstruction and revision, "no person, no theory, no point of view has privilege at the expense of anyone else's."[88] The process of deconstruction is to discover realities not initially evident—to question assumptions regarding beliefs, concepts, and practices.

The acceptance of all stories as equal creates difficulty when responding to situations rooted in injustice, such as the case of women who are beaten by their partners. If all "stories" are equal, are reactionary theories and views in regards to social class, gender, and race to be accepted as valid? Joan Laird, who incorporates social constructionism and narratives in her work with women raises caution in its application. She notes that since these theories and models have emerged during an era of political conservatism, "we could be lulled into thinking that everyone has equal power to shape his or her own story, forgetting that we must always be sensitive to the fact that our individual stories take shape in a powerful sociopolitical context."[89]

The use of creative questioning, externalization of the problem, and respect for local knowledges—all components of narrative therapy—have informed a number of practice approaches and have offered some creative ways of working with individuals and families. For example, Charles Waldegrave and his colleagues at the Family Centre in New Zealand have utilized postmodern concepts to complement modern approaches to practice. "Just Therapy," guided by the principles of spirituality, justice, and simplicity, recognizes the social and economic context of colonization and the injustices to the indigenous Maori, the impact of increasing poverty among low-income families, gender inequality, and racism in their society.[90] Waldegrave's social justice framework for practice is grounded in the culture, conditions, and experiences of the families which come to the Centre.

While postmodernism has its proponents in social work, it also has its critics. Much of the criticism is directed at the relativism and potential conservatism in its application to social work. Feminist scholars have pointed to how postmodernism ignores power and gender relations and marginalizes feminist contributions to family therapy.[91] Others hold that its tenets are extremely problematic for any emancipatory struggle. Brotman and Pollock argue that postmodernism is inherently conservative because "an undiscerning acceptance of its principles means relinquishing social work's goal of social change."[92]

The focus on differences and the many ways of knowing and even many truths creates an immense challenge to mobilize a united opposition that can advance an alternative vision for society. Postmodernists question the use of identity categories such as "working class" or "woman" because "these representations demand the suppression of the difference and instability that is inherent to each category."[93] Kenan Malik, in "Universalism and Difference: Race and the Postmodernists," critiques postmodernism for failing to understand "that while difference can arise from equality, equality can never arise from difference."[94] The emancipatory potential of postmodernism is questionable when it rejects theories of capitalism, as well as historical materialism as a method for understanding class conflict, at a time of global capitalist expansion and growing inequalities throughout the world.

Atherton and Bolland point out that postmodernism has received credit where credit was not due. They challenge the claim that postmodernism has opened up the "possibility of beginning to hear other voices—those of women, gays, blacks and other visible minorities, colonized peoples, the working class, religious groups that were forced to keep quiet so long."[95] They are correct to point out that these voices have been raised and acknowledged by feminists and other activists working towards social justice long before postmodernism. Nonetheless, postmodernists and their attention and commitment to diversity have enriched practice approaches in this regard.

Peter Leonard, a social work scholar who has written extensively on postmodernism, concludes that postmodern theory and analysis cannot "be accepted without substantial challenge and modification."[96] However, he remains convinced of its potential contributions and believes that it must be part of the work to continue the "emancipatory project in the form of feminist, socialist, anti-racist, anti-colonial, environmentalist, and other political struggles but also emphasizes a common ground underlying this diversity."[97] Leonard argues that "on its own, postmodernism is unable to provide an intellectual or practical basis for the kind of politics necessary to a new welfare project: only as linked to feminism and Marxism does it realize a capacity to move from deconstruction to reconstruction."[98]

It remains to be seen the degree to which postmodernism can contribute to the emancipatory project and offer a "solution" to social work practice and social problems in our society. In my view, broad-based social change and social justice are more likely to occur through a collective struggle based on a critique and analysis of modern society. A focus on subjectivities while retreating from the broader structures will neither serve our profession nor the people whom we serve.

As Paulo Freire has noted: "Society is transformed when we transform it. And we transform it when the organized and mobilized political forces of the popular classes and workers throw themselves into history to change the world, and not in someone's head."[99] While the quote is somewhat dated, the sentiment and the general approach remain as relevant as ever.

NOTES

[1] Jane Addams, The President's Address, "Charity and Social Justice," *Proceedings*. National Conference of Charities and Corrections (St. Louis, MO: The Archer Printing Co., 1910) 1.

[2] An excellent history of this period is provided in Michael J. Piva, *The Condition of the Working Class in Toronto—1900–1921* (Ottawa, ON: University of Ottawa Press, 1979).

[3] David Wagner, "Radical Movements in the Social Services: A Theoretical Framework," *Social Service Review* (June 1989): 264–84.

[4] Reuben Bitensky, "The Influence of Political Power in Determining the Theoretical Developments of Social Work," *Journal of Social Policy* 2, Pt.2 (April 1973): 119, emphasis in original. See also Harry Specht and Mark E. Courtney, *Unfaithful Angels: How Social Work Has Abandoned Its Mission* (New York, NY: The Free Press, 1994).

[5] Once Canadian schools had their own accrediting body and social work scholars began publishing texts on social work practice, the US influence lessened.

[6] Mary Richmond, *Friendly Visiting Among the Poor* (New York, NY: Macmillan, 1899).

[7] Gerald C. Rothman, *Philanthropists, Therapists and Activists* (Cambridge, MA: Schenkman Publishing, 1985) 26. Mary Richmond coined the terms "retail" and "wholesale" to distinguish between the efforts placed on individual change and those directed at greater societal change.

[8] Jane Addams wrote *Peace and Bread in Time of War* (New York, NY: Macmillan, 1922).

[9] Jane Addams and other settlement workers participated in the six-year process of appeal and mass demonstrations in support of Nicola Sacco and Bartolomeo Vanzetti, Italian immigrants and anarchists who were charged in 1920 with murder and executed by the State of Massachusetts on August 23, 1927 despite evidence pointing to their innocence. See, e.g., Patrick Selmi, "Social Work and the Campaign to Save Sacco and Vanzetti," *Social Service Review* 75.1 (March 2001): 115–34.

[10] See, e.g., Donna L. Franklin, "Mary Richmond and Jane Addams: From Moral Certainty to Rational Inquiry in Social Work Practice," *Social Service Review* (December, 1986): 504–25.

[11] Roy Lubove, *The Professional Altruist: The Emergence of Social work as a Career 1880–1930* (Cambridge, MA: Harvard University Press, 1965) 5, 14.

[12] Stanley Wenocur and Michael Reisch, *From Charity to Enterprise: The Development of American Social Work in a Market Economy* (Chicago, IL: University of Illinois Press, 1989) 89.

[13] Karen Lundblad, "Jane Addams and Social Reform: A Role Model for the 1990s," *Social Work* 40.5 (1995): 661–69.

[14] See, e.g., G. Rothman 28.

[15] Allan Irving, Harriet Parsons, and Donald Bellamy, *Neighbours: Three Social Settlements in Downtown Toronto* (Toronto, ON: Canadian Scholar's Press, 1995).

[16] Gale Wills, "Values of Community Practice: Legacy of the Radical Social Gospel," *Canadian Social Work Review* 9.1 (1992): 28–40.

[17] Donald Bellamy and Allan Irving, "Pioneers," *Canadian Social Welfare*, 3rd ed., ed. Joanne C. Turner and Francis J. Turner (Scarborough, ON: Allyn and Bacon, 1995) 89–117. The Fred Victor Mission's doors are still open in Toronto.

[18] Bellamy and Irving.

[19] McClung also published 16 books. Among the most widely read is *In Times Like These*, originally published in 1915, and more recently reissued by the Social History of Canada Series (Toronto, ON: University of Toronto Press, 1972).

[20] See, e.g., Wenocur and Reisch.

[21] A thorough account of US social work history can be found in Lubove.

[22] Wenocur and Reisch.

[23] Leslie Leighninger, *Creating a New Profession: The Beginnings of Social Work Education in the United States* (Alexandria, VA: Council on Social Work Education, 2000).

[24] Shankar A. Yelaga, *An Introduction to Social Work Practice in Canada* (Scarborough, ON: Prentice-Hall, 1985) 2–23; Wenocur and Reisch 130.

[25] Abraham Flexner, "Is Social Work a Profession," *Proceedings* National Conference of Charities and Corrections (Baltimore, MD: Hildmann Printing Co., 1915): 576–90.

[26] Richard Cloward and Francis Fox Piven, "The Acquiesence of Social Work," *Strategic Perspectives on Social Policy*, ed. J. Tropman, M. Duluhy, and R. Lind (New York, NY: Pergamon Press, 1981). In 1908 Freud's works were translated into English for the first time and appeared in American journals. In the following year he was invited to deliver a series of lectures at Clark University in Worschester, Massachusetts.

[27] Joy Maines, "Through the Years in CASW," NAC, FA 1713, MG 28I441: 2.

[28] Howard Goldstein, *Social Work Practice: A Unitary Approach* (Columbia, SC: University of South Carolina Press, 1979) 31. See also, Specht and Courtney.

[29] See, e.g., Clarke A. Chambers, "Women in the Creation of the Profession of Social Work," *Social Service Review* (March 1986): 1–33. Clarke describes Jessie Taft and Virginia Robinson as life-long companions who adopted two children into their "Boston marriage." He holds that settlement living supported such arrangements. A thorough understanding of the functional approach can be found in Virginia Robinson, *A Changing Psychology in Social Case Work* (Chapel Hill, NC: University of North Carolina Press, 1930); Jessie Taft, *Family Casework and Counseling, A Functional Approach* (Philadelphia, PA: University of Pennsylvania Press, 1935).

[30] Martha M. Dore, "Functional Theory: Its History and Influence on Contemporary Social Work Practice," *Social Service Review* 64.3 (1990): 358–74. Taft and Robinson were so committed to the ideas of Rank that they both entered into analysis with him.

[31] Noel Timms, "Taking Social Work Seriously: The Contribution of the Functional School," *British Journal of Social Work* 27 (1997): 723–37.

[32] A history of the Canadian Association of Social Workers from 1922 to 1977 can be found in the National Archives of Canada. See, e.g., "Through the Years" FA 1713, MG 28 I441; the quote is on page 2.

[33] Leslie Leighninger, "The Generalist-Specialist Debate in Social Work," *Social Service Review* (March 1980): 1–12; American Association of Social Workers. *Social Case Work, Generic and Specific: An Outline, A Report of the Milford Conference*, (New York, NY: American Association of Social Workers, 1929).

[34] Jacob Fisher, *The Response of Social Work to the Depression* (Cambridge, MA: Schenkman, 1980).

[35] Judith Ann Trolander, "The Response of Settlements to the Great Depression," *Social Work* (September 1973): 92–102.

[36] The Rank and File, a group of 15,000 social workers, outnumbered the American Association of Social Workers at the time. The movement existed for four years and produced the journal *Social Work Today*. See Michael Reisch and Janice Andrews, *The Road Not Taken: A History of Radical Social Work in the United States* (New York, NY: Bruner-Routledge, 2002); also Fisher.

37 Bertha C. Reynolds, *An Uncharted Journey, Fifty Years of Growth in Social Work* (New York, NY: The Citadel Press, 1963) 143.

38 See Fisher, 131. Fisher recounts an incident at the 1935 National Conference of Social Welfare held in Montreal where three black social workers were denied accommodation at the six hotels they approached. The conference committee, composed of Rank and File members, issued a general statement condemning racial discrimination and developed a policy to meet only in cities that insured complete access to facilities.

39 Maines 9, 10.

40 Bertha C. Reynolds, "Social Case Work: What is it? What is its Place in the World Today?," *Child and Family Welfare*, 11.6 (March 1936): 12.

41 For a history of the organization, see Michiel Horn, *The League for Social Reconstruction: Intellectual Origins of the Democratic Left in Canada 1930–1942* (Toronto, ON: University of Toronto Press, 1980). Approximately one-third of the membership came from education, social work, and the ministry. The League never exceeded 1000 members.

42 Alan Whitehorn, *Canadian Socialism: Essays on the CCF-NDP* (Toronto, ON: Oxford University Press, 1992).

43 A major contribution to this end was Grace Coyle's *Social Process in Organized Groups*, published in 1930 by R.R. Smith, the first comprehensive group work text. Coyle offered a theoretical framework and group work was legitimated as a practice.

44 Wenocur and Reisch.

45 Herbert Bisno, "How Social Will Social Work Be?," *Social Work* 1.2 (April 1956): 12–18.

46 Senator Joseph McCarthy of Wisconsin was one of the main proponents of the Red Scare. In 1938 the House of Representatives set up the Committee on Unamerican Activities which persecuted anyone with a left-of-centre political perspective; Leslie Leighninger and Robert Knickmeyer, "The Rank and File Movement: The Relevance of Radical Social Work Traditions to Modern Social Work Practice," *Journal of Sociology and Social Welfare* 4.2 (1976): 170.

47 G. Rothman 15. The ideas of the group were submerged and not heard again until the late 1960s.

48 Wendy B. Posner "Common Human Needs: A Story from the Prehistory of Government by Special Interests," *Social Service Review* (June 1995): 201. Posner's research explains how the criticism and negative press coverage of Towle's book was part of a campaign to discredit President Harry S. Truman's attempts to establish a national health care program. Charlotte Towle, *Common Human Needs* (London: George Allen and Unwin, 1973). The book originally published in 1945 has been translated into more than 10 languages.

49 G. Rothman.

50 These changes were based on "The Hollis and Taylor Report," Ernest V. Hollis and Alice L. Taylor, *Social Work Education in the United States* (New York, NY: Columbia University Press, 1951). Since Canadian social work programs continued to be accredited by the American Council on Social Work Education, the changes influenced us as well.

51 Florence Hollis, "The Psycho Social Approach to Casework," *Theories of Social Casework*, ed. Robert W. Roberts and Robert H. Nee (Chicago, IL: University of Chicago Press, 1970) 53. See also Florence Hollis, *Casework: A Psycho Social Therapy* (New York, NY: Random House, 1964).

52 Helen Harris Perlman, *Social Casework: A Problem Solving Process* (Chicago, IL: University of Chicago Press, 1957).

53 C. Wright Mills, *Power, Politics and People* (New York, NY: Oxford University Press, 1963).

54 William Schwartz, "Private Troubles and Public Issues," *The Social Welfare Forum* (1969): 40.

55 Lawrence Shulman, *The Skills of Helping Individuals, Families, and Groups*, 3rd ed. (Itasca, IL: F.E. Peacock Publishers, 1992); Lawrence Shulman, *The Skills of Helping Individuals, Families, Groups and Communities*, 4th ed. (Itasca, IL: F.E. Peacock Publishers, 1999).

56 Goldstein 53.

57 Wagner 271.

58 The journal *Social Work* produced two conceptual framework issues in 1977 and 1981.

59 Goldstein; Allen Pincus and Anne Minahan, *Social Work Practice: Model and Method* (Itasca, IL: F.E. Peacock Publishers, 1973).

[60] Pincus and Minahan, *Social Work Practice* 63, emphasis in original.

[61] Pincus and Minahan, *Social Work Practice* 27.

[62] Pincus and Minahan, *Social Work Practice and Method* 27.

[63] Carel B. Germain and Alex Gitterman, *The Life Model of Social Work Practice* (New York, NY: Columbia University Press, 1996) 7, 19.

[64] Carol H. Myer, "The Search for Coherence," *Clinical Social Work in an Eco-Systems Perspective*, ed. Carol H. Myer (New York, NY: Columbia University Press, 1983). For a comprehensive analysis of the eco-systems perspective, see Jerome C. Wakefield's two-part series "Does Social Work Need the Eco-Systems Perspective? Part 1: Is the Perspective Clinically Useful?" *Social Service Review* (March 1996): 1–32; and "Part 2: Does the Perspective Save Social Work From Incoherence?" *Social Service Review* (June 1996): 183–213). In the June 1996 journal see also the Debate with Authors, an exchange between Alex Gitterman and Jerome Wakefield.

[65] Roy Bailey and Mike Brake (eds.), *Radical Social Work* (New York, NY: Pantheon Books, 1975). It was first published by Edward Arnold Publishers in London. Jeffry H. Galper, *The Politics of Social Services* (Englewood Cliffs, NJ: Prentice-Hall, 1975).

[66] Bailey and Brake 9.

[67] Galper x.

[68] See, e.g., Paul Corrigan and Peter Leonard, *Social Work Practice under Capitalism: A Marxist Approach* (London: Macmillan, 1978); Norman Ginsburg, *Class, Capital and Social Policy* (London: Macmillan, 1979); Ian Gough's *The Political Economy of the Welfare State* (London: Macmillan, 1979); London Edinburgh Weekend Return Group, *In and Against the State* (London: Pluto Press, 1979).

[69] The development of this approach is outlined in Roland Lecomte, "Connecting Private Troubles and Public Issues in Social Work Education," *Social Work and Social Change in Canada*, ed. Brian Wharf (Toronto, ON: McClelland and Stewart, 1990) 31–51.

[70] Report on the Commission on the School of Social Work, Carleton University, Ottawa, June 1972: 6.

[71] Faculty members included Jim Albert, Peter Findlay, Roland Lecomte, Allan Moscovitch, and Helen Levine. Levine took a leadership role in ensuring that feminist theory informed the approach. See Helen Levine, "The Personal is Political: Feminism and the Helping Professions," *Feminism in Canada*, ed. Angela Miles and Geraldine Finn (Montreal, QC: Black Rose Books, 1982) 175–210.

[72] For a woman-centred approach, see Helen Marchant and Betsy Wearing (eds.), *Gender Reclaimed: Women in Social Work* (Sydney, NSW: Hale and Iremonger, 1986); Jalna Hanmer and Daphne Statham, *Women and Social Work: Towards a Woman-Centered Practice* (London: Macmillan, 1989). On anti-racism, see Lena Dominelli, *Anti-Racist Social Work* (London: Macmillan, 1988). And for social work for persons with a disability, see Michael Oliver, *Social Work With Disabled People* (London: Macmillan, 1983).

[73] Peter Leonard, *Personality and Ideology: Toward a Materialist Understanding of the Individual* (London: Macmillan, 1984) 26.

[74] Anne Minahan and Allan Pincus, "Conceptual Framework for Social Work Practice," *Social Work* 22.5 (1977): 352.

[75] Neil Gilbert, "The Search for Professional Identity," *Social Work* 22.5 (1977): 401–06.

[76] The Working Statement can be found in Anne Minahan, "Introduction to Special Issue," *Social Work* 26.1 (1981): 5–6.

[77] John F. Longres, "Reactions to Working Statement on Purpose," *Social Work* 85.

[78] Carol H. Myer, "Social Work Purpose: Status by Choice or Coercion?," *Social Work* 26.6 (1981): 74.

[79] Joan Laird (ed.), *Revisioning Social Work Education: A Social Constructionist Approach* (New York, NY: The Haworth Press, 1993); Adrienne S. Chambon and Allan Irving (eds.), *Essays on Postmodernism and Social Work* (Toronto, ON: Canadian Scholar's Press, 1994).

[80] Peter Leonard, "Knowledge/Power and Postmodernism: Implications for the Practice of a Critical Social Work Education," *Canadian Social Work Review* 11.1 (Winter 1994): 11–24; Peter Leonard, "Postmodernism, Socialism and Social Welfare," *Journal of Progressive Human Services* 6.2 (1995): 3–19; Peter Leonard, "Three Discourses on Practice: A Postmodern Re-appraisal,"

Journal of Sociology and Social Welfare 23.2 (June 1996): 7–26; Peter Leonard, *Postmodern Welfare: Reconstructing an Emancipatory Project* (London: Sage, 1997); Bob Pease and Jan Fook (eds.), *Transforming Social Work Practice: Postmodern Critical Perspectives* (London: Routledge, 1999); Bob Mullaly, *Challenging Oppression: A Critical Social Work Approach* (Don Mills, ON: Oxford University Press, 2002).

[81] Modernity generally refers to the historical period of the Enlightenment (seventeenth and eighteenth century Europe) and corresponds to the development of capitalism in Europe. For an overview of modernity, see, e.g., Leonard "Knowledge/Power and Postmodernism."

[82] Laird 4.

[83] Mullaly 18.

[84] Rich Vodde and J. Paul Gallant, "Bridging the Gap Between Micro and Macro Practice: Large Scale Change and a Unified Model of Narrative-Deconstructive Practice," *Journal of Social Work Education* 38.3 (2002): 439–58.

[85] Michael White and David Epston, *Narrative Means to Therapeutic Ends* (New York, NY: Norton, 1990).

[86] Alan Parry and Robert E. Doan, *Story Re-visions: Narrative Therapy in a Postmodern World* (New York, NY: The Guilford Press, 1994).

[87] Although not acknowledged, the concept of deconstructing, revisioning, and restorying is similar to script analysis in transactional analysis (TA) where a script is a life plan also discovered through narratives. See, e.g., Claude Steiner, *Scripts People Live: Transactional Analysis of Life Scripts* (New York, NY: Grove Press, 1974).

[88] Perry and Doan 22.

[89] Joan Laird, "Changing Women's Narratives: Taking Back the Discourse," Peterson and Lieberman 294.

[90] Charles Waldegrave, "Just Therapy," Social Justice and Family Therapy: A Discussion of the Work of The Family Centre, Lower Hutt, New Zealand; a special issue of *Dulwich Centre Newsletter* 1 (1990): 1–46.

[91] Rosemary Paterson and Salli Trathen, "Feminist In(ter)ventions in Family Therapy," *ANZ Journal of Family Therapy* 15.2 (1994): 91–98.

[92] Shari Brotman and Shoshana Pollock, "Loss of Context: The Problem of Merging Postmodernism with Feminist Social Work," *Canadian Social Work Review* 14.1 (Winter 1997): 9.

[93] Karen Healy, "Power and Activist Social Work," *Transforming Social Work Practice: Postmodern Critical Perspectives*, ed. Bob Pease and Jan Fook (London: Routledge, 1999): 117.

[94] Kenan Malik, "Universalism and Difference: Race and the Postmodernists," *Race and Class* 37.3 (1996): 4.

[95] Charles R. Atherton and Kathleen A. Bollard, "Postmodernism: A Dangerous Illusion for Social Work," *International Social Work*, 45.4 (2002): 430. They quote from Allan Irving, "From Image to Simulacra: The Modern/Postmodern Divide and Social Work," *Essays on Postmodernism and Social Work*, ed. A.S. Chambron and A. Irving (Toronto, ON: Canadian Scholar's Press, 1994) 28.

[96] Leonard, "Three Discourses on Practice" 19.

[97] Leonard "Knowledge/Power and Postmodernism" 18.

[98] Leonard, *Postmodern Welfare* xiv.

[99] Paulo Freire, "A Critical Understanding of Social Work," *Journal of Progressive Human Services* 1.1 (1990): 9.

CHAPTER 3

STRUCTURAL SOCIAL WORK: THEORY, IDEOLOGY, AND PRACTICE PRINCIPLES

The review of historical developments in social work practice approaches in the previous chapter outlines the differing theories and ideologies that have influenced the profession in the past and continue to do so today. Although theories and ideologies implicitly guide social workers in their day-to-day practice, they often are unaware of this fact. This is not a problem only for practitioners who operate outside of academia. An awareness of ideology and theory and its role in social work practice is frequently absent in social work courses and social work literature. Whether acknowledged or implicit, theories and models of practice have ideological assumptions underpinning them. This chapter discusses a number of theories that social workers draw on and the role these theories play in shaping and legitimating practice models or approaches. In particular, the principles and practices of a structural approach to social work are outlined.

Theory, Models, and Approaches

Theory is a systematically organized collection of concepts and relationships that explains a phenomenon. How we understand a certain situation is partly due to the theory on which we draw. While there is a tendency to interchange the terms theory, models, and approaches, there are distinct differences among them. Duncan Foley points out that theories offer explanations of a reality and include contradictory forces that call for change in the theory itself. "A model, on the other hand, is a representation of a theory in which these contradictory elements have been suppressed, often to allow a mathematical representation of the ideas. Models are representations not of reality but of theory," according to Foley.[1] This explains how social work models may share a similar theoretical foundation but differ in how the theory is represented. For example, functional systems theory informed the development of a number of generalist practice models in social work such as *Social Work Practice: Model and Method* (Allen Pincus and Anne Minahan), *Social Work Practice: A Unitary Approach* (Howard Goldstein), and *The Life Model of Social Work Practice* (Carol Germaine and Alex Gitterman). Similarly, postmodern theory is represented in narrative, solution-focussed, and brief therapy approaches.

Foley points out that those who strictly adopt a particular model of practice run the danger of not considering the limitations of the model and how it is a static and unchanging representation of a changing reality. Criticisms of a model are often received with a counter argument by the proponent. For example, in the 1970s, a number of social workers, including the author, were influenced by transactional analysis and gestalt therapy. We attended institutes and workshops, and some received certification as recognized therapists in the field. The practice was utilized in individual, family, and group work. Once invested in and committed to the model, we were reluctant to acknowledge the limitations of its prescriptive tenets and its disregard for the changing economic and material context of clients' lives. Similarly, when the Milan family therapy approach was critiqued because it demonstrated acceptance of traditional roles that advantaged men in the family, members of the Milan team discounted the concern.[2]

Much of the theory that informs, organizes, and guides the practice responses of social workers is derived from psychology, sociology, economics, political science, and social administration. Social work approaches are more expansive than many models or theories in that they draw on a number of theories that share similar theoretical and philosophical assumptions in order to understand individual and social problems. For example, the psycho-social approach spearheaded by Florence Hollis draws on psychoanalytic theory, ego psychology, and object relations, all independent but related theories.

Since theory takes into account and contains within itself the potential for change, it is never static, and it does not offer a fixed explanation for individual or social problems. As any experienced practitioner will tell you, there is a dynamic relationship between theory and practice in that, through the application of the theory, the theory itself is transformed.

This process of action and reflection, where theory informs practice and practice in turn informs theory, has been acknowledged by revolutionary theorist and practitioner Mao Tsetung.[3]

Malcolm Payne speaks to this relationship when he states that "the nature of social work and its theory are defined, not by some independent process of academic development and experimental testing but by what social workers actually do."[4] Paulo Freire's concept of "praxis," a process in which one's reflection on practice or action informs the next practice, speaks to this relationship of theory to practice.[5]

It has been said that "there is nothing as practical as a good theory."[6] Theory informs social work analysis, assessment, and intervention strategies. However, as practitioners respond to the urgent and complex situations before them, they often are not conscious of the particular theories that inform their actions and the overall theoretical framework that guides their practice. Social workers often view theory as too academic or abstract. In a study of expertise in social work, the researchers concluded that "social work theorizing may be more about underlying assumptions, the use of particular concepts and developing practice wisdom in a seemingly intuitive way than about using integrated theoretical frameworks."[7] At times it may seem like we are acting spontaneously, intuitively, yet our perceptions and our actions are never completely free of theory. The task for social workers is to strive to identify, analyze, and build on the theoretical framework which guides their practice and to insure that it corresponds to the conditions under which people live and the needs which they have.

Up until the 1960s, theory development in social work, as in other disciplines, had an ethnocentric bias and neglected to adequately consider differences based on gender, race and/or ethnicity, sexual orientation, and social class. This lack of awareness informed the responses of practitioners and failed certain groups of people. For example, Kohlberg's moral development theory was based on the study of young men, framed around their development and experience, and then applied to the development of both men and women. Since Kohlberg concluded that abstract ethical principles of justice were used by these young men to resolve moral dilemmas, women were found lacking when judged against this male standard. Carol Gilligan's research on young girls revealed that they struggled with moral dilemmas by focussing on relationships and the human consequences of their choices. Gilligan's discovery of these "different voices" built on, but also critiqued the work of Kohlberg.[8]

The women's movement, feminist research, and the development of women's studies programs were instrumental in transforming knowledge by introducing a gender analysis and advancing theory in the social sciences, including social work. Challenges and contributions from visible minority women have highlighted the limitations of what currently is conceptualized as feminism and further transformed feminist thought and feminist practice.[9]

In her study of the application and development of theory within social work, Donna Baines found that a number of feminist concepts were not helpful in her work with working-class women and women of colour in an inner city hospital. For example, the general understanding that women direct their anger inward and should be encouraged to express it outwardly had no relevance for the "streetsy" women with whom she had contact and who were far from passive and had no difficulty in expressing their anger.[10] While theories are helpful in guiding our practice, we must be ever mindful not to assume that all persons of a certain social category share the same experiences. Therefore, it is imperative that social workers develop cultural sensitivity and develop knowledge to respond to the differing realities of clients.

Taking Ideology Into Account

When we look at the array of models, theories, and approaches within social work and related disciplines, we discover that they all have ideologies or assumptions that are either stated or implied. A major factor influencing practitioners as they adopt theories and practice models/approaches is the fit between their beliefs and values (ideology) and those inherent in a particular theoretical approach. As Mary Bricker-Jenkins argues:

> Practice is more than stringing techniques and methods around a theoretical framework; it is also the reflection and promotion of values and beliefs. In other words, every practice model has an ideological core... In short, ideology is the glue that holds a practice system together and binds it to human conditions, institutions, and practices.[11]

Our assumptions and beliefs form the lens through which we look to understand and respond to social and individual situations. Social attitudes toward people based on their gender, race/ethnicity, class, sexual orientation, physical and mental ability, and the problems with which they are struggling are often influenced by ideology—ideology which is embedded in the policies and practices of social institutions. For example, the act of placing the full responsibility/blame on individuals for their circumstances is rooted in a particular ideology or set of ideas and beliefs.

We are usually influenced by the dominant ideology—the political, economic, and social beliefs that permeate all structures in our society— and in Canada today that is predominantly the neoliberal ideology. It holds, among other beliefs, the view that capitalism is a sound economic system and that the accumulation of wealth by corporations and rich individuals is well-earned and somehow "trickles down" to others in need. The prevailing message is that there are opportunities for all who are motivated to work; therefore, unemployment and poverty are generally viewed as the responsibility of individuals and their families. The notion of ideology holds political connotations.

One study of the ideological and socio-political assumptions within introductory social work textbooks found that "virtually all were found to contain assumptions about the political-economic structure of society, the nature of class and social class relationships, and the nature of social change."[12] The authors found that the texts fell into three equal clusters along a left-centre-right dimension. Those texts from a left perspective promote the view that the livelihoods of individuals are a product or responsibility of political, economic, and social institutions and conditions that must be improved. Those on the right place responsibility on families and individuals for their life situation and place little emphasis on larger social and material conditions.[13] Those in the centre acknowledge the importance of social conditions and engage in strategies of social reform but do not advocate significant changes to social, economic, and political structures.

Along the same lines, John Coates proposed that models of social work practice can be organized into three areas—those that stress personal deficiency, ecological factors, or the larger political economy. These correspond to conservative, liberal, and socialist/feminist ideological perspectives respectively.[14] Using Coates's distinction, social work approaches that assume that the primary source of personal difficulties lies within the individual, such as the psychoanalytic or behavioural models, can be considered as a personal deficiency approach. An ecological approach includes the models based on functional systems theory in which the broader system is considered, but not in a politically critical way. The political economy approach refers to anti-capitalist, anti-racist, and feminist models based on assumptions that individual troubles are connected to structural inequalities.

Organizing Frameworks

In the 1960s, John Horton proposed that theories of social problems could be separated into two groups, conflict or order, depending on whether they viewed society as being divided by conflict or functioning in a generally ordered way.[15] Conflict models offer a critique of capitalist structures and the production of inequality and exploitation. They emphasize the importance of a critical consciousness, collective action, and a radical restructuring of society, while order models argue that the system is structurally sound. An order analysis is most often expressed by those in power within capitalist societies, while a conflict analysis is advanced by social activists and political groups on the left who are often in opposition to those governing.

Building on Horton's order-conflict axis, Burrell and Morgan organized theories of social problems along two theoretical and two philosophical dimensions. In social work Whittington and Holland and Carniol found the framework useful and modified it for organizing social work theories/approaches and ideologies [16] (see Table 3.1).

Burrell and Morgan suggested that perspectives or theories be viewed as situated along a continuum. It does not matter simply whether or not a theory falls into either a conflict or order model, they argued, but the degree to which it adheres to the assumptions of either. Similar to Horton's order-conflict binary, the theoretical dimension of the framework situates a theory along a transformation-accommodation continuum according to the degree to which it supports radical change or the regulation of society and social problems. According to Whittington and Holland, theories of radical change assume that our society has an inherent tendency to instability and change and contains inherent contradictions (for example, between labour and capital); that the ideas, rules, and objectives of some groups dominate others; that radical change of prevailing rules and structures is necessary; that deprivation and alienation are widespread; and that emancipation is a prime objective. On the other end of the continuum, theories of regulation assume that "we live in a predominately stable, integrated and cohesive society; that there is a consensus

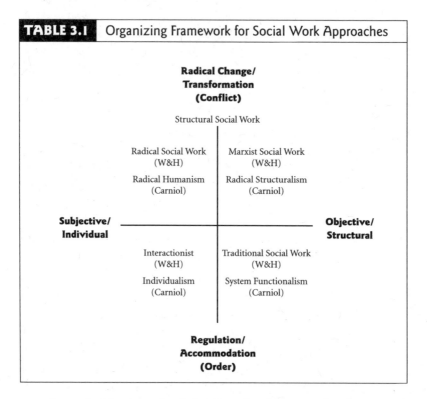

TABLE 3.1 Organizing Framework for Social Work Approaches

**Radical Change/
Transformation
(Conflict)**

Structural Social Work

| Radical Social Work (W&H) | Marxist Social Work (W&H) |
| Radical Humanism (Carniol) | Radical Structuralism (Carniol) |

**Subjective/
Individual** — — — — — — — — — — — **Objective/
Structural**

| Interactionist (W&H) | Traditional Social Work (W&H) |
| Individualism (Carniol) | System Functionalism (Carniol) |

**Regulation/
Accommodation
(Order)**

on rules and objectives; that behaviour should be regulated in accord with the prevailing social rules; that there exist social institutions to satisfy the needs of individuals and the social system (the family, education, welfare); and, finally that integration and reintegration into society are prime objectives."[17]

The philosophical dimension focusses on assumptions about how knowledge is developed and how individual and social change occurs. Theories are situated according to the degree of importance placed on subjective, individual consciousness on one end of the continuum and material conditions on the other. When the philosophical dimension is added, theories can be further distinguished by their attention to either the subjective/individual or the objective/structure. The two dimensions offer a more nuanced approach to situating theories. For example, although an order theory such as functional systems theory places emphasis on the social context when assessing social and personal problems, social structures themselves are not viewed as problematic. Solutions are found within individual or family functioning and accommodation to the structure such as readjustment and/or resocialization of the troubled individual.

The majority of the "traditional social work" approaches coincide with this perspective, according to Whittington and Holland. Similarly, social work approaches based on theories of social order can focus on a client's subjective experiences, as is the case with an "interactionist approach," such as the client-centred approach first developed by Carl Rogers.[18]

Conflict theories can differ in the emphasis placed on either agency or structure and the possibilities of social change. Radical humanist, radical feminist, and several approaches such as narrative therapy based on postmodern theory all emphasize individual subjective experiences and fall within a conflict approach. On the other hand, radical social work, socialist feminist, and Marxist-based approaches rely primarily on an objective/structural analysis and place emphasis on social, economic, and political conflict through collective action instead of attention to individual, subjective experiences.[19]

The structural approach is advocated in this book as the most promising and fruitful way of addressing social problems. It situates seemingly individual problems within social and material conditions and alienating social structures while at the same time emphasizes the importance of human agency while offering help to individuals and their families. Clearly, it is situated within the radical change/transformation approach, bridging both dimensions of the subjective and objective.

Surprisingly, there has been little attention paid to the relationship between ideology, theory building, and social work practice. However, as has been argued, certain theories share a common ideology—a set of beliefs, assumptions, and values—that offer differing views and interpretations than other theories and approaches.

Pursuing this theme, Ben Carniol presents four distinct ideological perspectives or world views of society that inform practice responses (see Table 3.1). Theories within the "regulation" quadrants are based on the ideological perspectives of individualism—"work hard and you can achieve"—and system functionalism—the belief that the system of social, economic, and political structures is sound and contributes to individual well-being. Both perspectives take a "blaming the victim" position in understanding individual and social problems since the source of the problem and the responsibility and focus for change rests with the person not with the social structures in which they live. Within the "transformatory" quadrants, Carniol situates the ideological perspectives of radical humanism, where people are viewed as inherently co-operative and which posits that a raised consciousness is instrumental in having people come together to overcome structural inequalities and create social change, and radical structuralism where emphasis is placed on a structural analysis of power and inequalities.

While a structural social work approach is considered the most useful by the author, it is important not to simply dismiss theories or approaches which may not be considered transformatory. Any concept, theory, or approach that promotes empowerment and social change is useful and can be transformed. For example, the concept of empathy as developed by Carl Rogers is useful in developing a client-centred approach and has become a central skill in all practice approaches. Empathy is the ability to understand the client's feelings and thoughts and to communicate that understanding to the client. However, because Rogers did not critique the social structures which affect people and help us understand their problems, the approach is limited. Social work theorists and practitioners such as Janis Fook and Thomas Keefe have rectified this limitation to some extent by extending the concept of empathy to include an understanding of the social context and the role it plays in consciousness-raising.[20] Consciousness-raising was also adapted by the women's movement of the 1970s as a way of teaching women to assert themselves and advocate for social change.

A structural approach to social work can be viewed as a practice that acknowledges the role of social structures in producing and maintaining inequality and personal hardship and the importance of offering concrete help to those in need or difficulty. Clearly, it draws on an array of theories and models. And yes, it is supported by and flows from a particular ideological perspective. Situated within the transformation quadrants, a structural approach, as developed here, bridges both radical structuralism and radical humanism. While not the complete answer or solution to all our practical and theoretical problems, such an approach is more relevant than ever if we are to effectively respond to the needs of individuals and their families while at the same time engaging in strategies for social change.

Structural Social Work

As we have seen, many of the issues and problems facing people in need are rooted in broad social, political, and economic conditions. At the same time, much of the "help" that we are prepared to provide is done at an individual level and assumes that problems are personal rather than a reflection of wider social structural problems. The tension between personal troubles and public issues is reflected in the social work practice goals of personal change through therapy or counselling versus social change through advocacy and activism. It is also reflected in the conflicts in the role of casework versus community organizing and the development and implementation of social policy. There have been numerous attempts to reduce the gap between "micro" (working with individuals and families) and "macro" practice (working in communities, social advocacy, and social change) and to acknowledge the importance of both functions for social work.

A structural approach to social work attempts to bridge the duality of the personal and the social, the individual and the community, and offers social workers an understanding of diverse populations in the context of social structures and social processes that generally support and reproduce social problems. In the US in the mid 1970s, Gale Goldberg and Ruth Middleman proposed a structural approach to practice in which the goal of the social worker was "to improve the quality of the relationship between people and their social environment by changing social structures that limit human functioning and exacerbate human suffering."[21] Goldberg and Middleman based their approach on two central assumptions: "Individuals' problems are not viewed as pathology, but as a manifestation of inadequate social arrangements" and "the response of the social work profession to the need for social change is the obligation of all social workers wherever they are in the bureaucracy."[22] More recently, the authors incorporated social constructionist perspectives, rooted in postmodern philosophy, and clarify that they use the term "structures" to refer to "*social* structures, such as the local school, the welfare office, or the public transit system."[23]

Maurice Moreau and his colleagues at Ottawa's Carleton University in the 1970s also set out to develop a structural approach. They turned to Marxist and feminist theories to inform their understanding of social problems and social relations in society and how social workers might respond to them.[24] This emphasis on advocacy and social change was in keeping with the profession's code of ethics, but it also addressed structural problems. Moreau identified two general social work roles: 1) to explore the socio-political and economic context of individual difficulties and to help collectivize personal troubles; 2) to enter into a helping process that facilitates critical thinking, consciousness-raising, and empowerment.[25]

Roland Lecomte recalls how the School of Social Work at Carleton University quickly became known as a "structural school" when he and others began to integrate the structural approach into all aspects of curricula.[26] Since the pioneering work of Moreau and colleagues, a structural approach to social work has been adopted by other schools in Canada and has been developed by people in the profession. Much like the radical social workers before him, Bob Mullaly, in his book *Structural Social Work: Ideology, Theory and Practice*, views structural social work as based on a socialist ideology, grounded in critical theory, and espousing a conflict view of society. For Mullaly, "The essence of socialist ideology and of radical social work perspective is that inequality (1) is a natural, inherent (i.e., structural) part of capitalism; (2) falls along lines of class, gender, race, sexual orientation, age, ability, and geographical region; (3) excludes these groups from opportunities, meaningful participation in society, and a satisfactory quality of life; and (4) is self-perpetuating."[27]

Although an understanding of the societal context is central to the approach, attention to social structures does not deny the personal element. Janis Fook, an Australian social worker, points out that "not *all* personal problems are *totally* structurally caused," but she insists that "there is *always* a structural element in any experienced problem." According to Fook, "the structural element will always interplay with personal factors such as biography, current life events, emotional and psychological characteristics, genetic inheritance, physical health, and so on to create a unique personal situation."[28]

Clearly, focussing on the social and economic context does not imply that individual change work is ignored or set aside. Nor does it suggest that individuals are not responsible for their actions. Structural social work recognizes that one's life circumstances and difficulties are connected to one's economic and social position in society and that social work intervention at both the level of the individual and social structures is needed. In essence, since powerlessness and inequality are structurally produced, they require structural solutions. However, not all social workers whose practice goals are transformatory consider what they do as structural social work. While structural social work may share similarities with strength-based, empowerment and anti-discriminatory approaches,[29] the primary differences are the former's critical analysis of the social structures in society and attention to social justice and human rights.

The Role of Social Structures

While the nature and role of social structures is central to a structural social work approach, they tend to be viewed as static structures in the social work literature. But as Wallace Clement points out, "Social structures are products of the dynamics of power and resistance; domination and struggle are the motors of history. In other words, the structure of any social formation is the complex outcome of ongoing class and social struggles." Clement therefore defines social structures "as sets of enduring relationships among and between key institutions, including the state, capital, and labour... The social structure is social in the sense it is the product of relations between people; it is a structure in the sense of a relatively stable ordering of these relationships into what are often know as institutions. Social structures are as intimate as the family, based on the ideology and practice of patriarchy, or as abstract as the mode of production (the way a society produces and reproduces its material conditions, in Canada's case through capitalism)."[30] With this in mind, a social worker who utilizes a structural approach in responding to an individual's problems and needs considers not only the material and social conditions of clients but also the social relationships and institutional formations which may be contributing to the client's problems and acting as barriers to meeting their needs.

In the case of assisting a woman who has been physically assaulted by her male partner, an understanding of her social class, race and ethnicity, age, abilities and disabilities, and regional origin, along with an understanding of how these factors and gender inequality impact on her situation, will provide a better assessment and guide the social worker's response as a professional. For example, women in partner relationships with men who are unemployed or where the family income is below $15,000, have been shown to be more likely to suffer violence from their male partners.[31] In such situations a man's patriarchal beliefs intersect with tensions and stress that exist in the lives of many couples who struggle to support a family with very little economic resources. Also, if the woman is neither employed nor economically independent, her opportunities for alternative safe and secure housing are reduced. Women who leave shelters often return to abusive partners because they cannot support themselves and their children. Aboriginal and Black women may have experienced discrimination and racism from the police and service providers, and many women have encountered the sexism that is prevalent within social structures such as the family, schools, government, criminal justice system, and church. A woman with a disability may face inaccessible shelters and increased vulnerability. As a woman, she may also have internalized stereotypes and negative messages about her own worth from her partner, other family members, and the social institutions and structures to which she is exposed or is part of. Despite this array of oppressive factors, it is important to recognize the woman's strength and how she has survived the impact of these forces. In understanding her particular situation and the social factors that either restrict or offer possibilities, we can offer her the professional support she needs.

By our actions as social workers, in conjunction with those of many other people, we maintain or change social structures within particular interactions, while we are also restrained and curtailed by them. The view that social structures and social relationships are not fixed but a result of tensions, conflict, and contradictions is part of a dialectical understanding of society.[32] For example, although the mandate of children's aid societies is the protection of children and the support of families, the inadequate state funding of the service creates a situation in which overworked social workers in such agencies are given the impossible tasks of overseeing the care of children at risk. Furthermore, state policies are partly responsible for more and more families descending into poverty conditions which place even more demand on existing state-funded programs and services. The need for decent wages and benefits as an alternative to poverty requires an appreciation of the struggle of workers for safe working conditions and a job that provides a living wage. Similarly, the welfare state and its social programs are the product of the struggle by labour unions and other social movements and community groups. Indeed, the welfare state and programs are better understood historically as a concession by the "ruling class" to the working class and its allies. This concession was also a victory for the working class, but a limited victory.

Social Justice and Human Rights

While social work has a long history of promoting the principles of social justice and human rights, often these principles are not demonstrated in practice approaches and social work responses.[33] The National Association of Social Workers endorses fundamental human rights as a foundation principle for social work theory and practice.[34] However, the relationship between social justice and social work "is decidedly uneasy, fraught with tension, contradiction and conflict at both the ideological, conceptual and theoretical levels as well as the levels of policy and practice."[35] Social workers hold a key, and at the same time contradictory, position in society as they establish principles of social justice within a political and economic context which is based on, and supports, exploitation and inequality.

Michael Reisch provides an historical account of the development of the concept of social justice in social work and summarizes the current challenge facing social workers practicing within a social justice framework.[36] Reisch points out that social justice was viewed as an alternative to charity. However, the establishment and growth of the welfare state in the 1930s, viewed by many as a means to address the structural inequalities in society, has not been a successful means for achieving social justice. With the ongoing privatization and erosion of social welfare programs, and the implementation of authoritarian welfare policies by agencies, there is the concern that instead of tackling social injustice, social work has internalized the new right-wing doctrines.[37] Since capitalism is the fundamental cause of much of the social and economic injustice the poor experience, the degree to which social justice is possible within a market economy has been questioned.[38]

Gary Craig, a professor of social justice, argues that in order to achieve social justice governments must confront the inequities of capitalism. Craig views social justice as:

> a framework of political objectives, pursued through social, economic, environmental and political policies, based on an acceptance of difference and diversity, and informed by values concerned with:
> - achieving fairness, and equality of outcomes and treatment;
> - recognising the dignity and equal worth and encouraging the self esteem of all;
> - the meeting of basic needs; maximizing the reduction of inequalities in wealth, income and life chances; and
> - the participation of all, including the most disadvantaged.[39]

Conditions of injustice and inequality violate the basic human rights of people. The United Nations' "Universal Declaration of Human Rights," was introduced in 1948 as a common standard for economic, cultural, and social rights (see Appendix A). The National Association of Social Workers endorses this human rights document. Summarizing the Declaration, all people have:

the right to a standard of living that is adequate for the health and well-being of all people and their families, without exception, and the essential resources to meet such a standard; the right to adequate food and nourishment; the right to adequate clothing; the right to adequate housing; the right to basic health care; the right to an education; the right to security in the event of unemployment, sickness, disability, widowhood, old age, or other lack of livelihood beyond one's control; the right to necessary social services; and the right not be subjected to dehumanizing punishment.[40]

Social workers witness first hand the atrocities of poverty, homelessness, social exclusion, battering, discrimination, and exploitation facing people. Thus, a commitment to social justice and human rights informs the practice of structural social work.

Principles and Practices of Structural Social Work

Structural social work is a practice framework that acknowledges the role of social structures in producing and maintaining inequality and personal hardship and uses this knowledge and understanding to assist clients. Because of this, the structural social work approach prepares social workers to be generalist practitioners and to work in individual, family, group and community practice, social policy and administration.

One of the traditional divisions in social work has been practice versus policy, as social workers identify with either being in direct service (individual, group, family or community work, providing referrals, advocating) or indirect service (social policy analysis and development, program development, and social administration). A structural approach to social work considers this division to be an artificial one. For most social workers, knowledge and expertise are not so easily polarized. While a social worker may be employed in a direct service role as a child protection worker, with specific intervention skills, she will have a conceptual understanding of children and youth in crisis as well as the policies and laws that affect her clients and limit possible interventions. Similarly, an executive director of a community health centre will draw on her policy expertise, as well as an awareness of community and direct practice concerns and strategies, in response to social welfare and social justice concerns.

Whether or not there are practice skills unique to a radical structural approach or whether helping skills can be applied within such an approach has been a topic of debate. Jeffry Galper supported the latter position. "The best practice techniques from a liberal or humanitarian perspective will provide radical practice with a methodology of intervention at the level of technique," he argued, but it is "The use to which technique is put, rather than technique itself, distinguishes radical from conventional practice." [41] Janis Fook, also reluctant to disregard traditional approaches argued that "Radical casework both *incorporates* potentially radical elements of traditional casework and *extends* these."[42] Similarly, Maurice Moreau believed that there were no interviewing skills specific to the approach and that various helping techniques could be utilized as long as they did not depoliticize the client's problem or mystify and further alienate and oppress the person.[43]

Moreau decided to study the application of the structural approach. He surveyed front-line social workers who were graduates of the Carleton School of Social Work and who were using the structural approach in their practice. He also examined taped examples from practice sessions submitted by the social workers. Based on an analysis of both the surveys and the taped practice sessions, Moreau and his research team were able to understand what structural social workers do in practice. They found that "Workers are primarily helping people develop and elaborate a new understanding of thoughts, feelings and behaviours, engaging in various facets of contracting, validating clients, helping to operationalize, coach and support new strategies with people and gathering data on and making links to material conditions."[44] Moreau concluded that overall there were five goals that guide structural social work practice, and he identified how these goals or "practices" were operationalized.[45] A discussion of the five goals and their operationalization follows.

1. Defence of the Client

Social workers help defend client entitlements and rights and encourage clients to "defend themselves against an often bewildering and unfriendly system."[46] As an ally and advocate, the social worker provides information concerning rights and entitlements and agencies' resources and structure, appeals decisions, writes letters, accompanies clients to meetings, and, at times, subverts and challenges oppressive agency policy and procedure.[47] Social workers with full knowledge of benefits will be able to access much needed benefits for clients. For example, it was recently reported that thousands of senior citizens in Canada who were living in poverty did not know that they were eligible for the Guaranteed Income Supplement to the Old Age Pension, a situation that social workers could help to rectify. Social workers have knowledge about the various benefits and programs which someone may be eligible for and can offer guidance in the application process and appeals process if necessary. Challenging policy often puts the social worker in direct conflict with the employer and the state. In such situations, the social worker engages in an ethical decision-making process to assess the risks facing the client and determines the best strategy to pursue.[48] Also it is important for the social worker to have the support of a union and/or the professional association.

2. Collectivization

This goal is about helping inform clients about how their difficulties are shared by others, potentially reducing isolation and alienation. This is done by normalizing the problem by connecting clients with a support network, thus reducing isolation. The social worker also recognizes and assists the client in questioning the limits of individual solutions when there is also a need for social change through collective action.[49] One social worker described how she practiced collectivization in her group for incest survivors by taking:

> ... the blame off them in terms of them seeing their situation as an individual problem. I like to talk about how other people may be in the same situation as them, and it is not because of their individual failing or inadequacy that they are in that situation. In my sexual abuse survivors group, I use educational materials, that is, other women's stories of being abused and how they got through it and the things they did for themselves to get stronger and to change and feel better about themselves. I distribute material talking about the prevalence of sexual abuse so these women do not think "it is a private shame, it just happens to us."[50]

Collectivization normalizes and demystifies the client's problem and provides and can contribute to empowerment.

3. Materialization

Materialist analysis, a fundamental tenet of structural social work practice, is an understanding of material conditions under which people live and the ways in which these conditions impact on their perceptions of themselves and the problems they experience. An assessment of a client's situation and particular problem is then followed by acquiring as many resources as possible—both "hard" resources such as shelter, money, food, and social services and "soft" resources such as respect, caring, and social recognition.[51] Not surprisingly, a lack of money and material resources were major concerns for many of the clients of social workers in Moreau's study. One practitioner summed up the situation:

> [Y]ou know that the real issue is that this woman doesn't need to be with a counsellor. She needs money. If she had a better roof over her head, if she had more money coming in, if she had a male partner who didn't beat her up, she wouldn't be in this office because someone told her she was crazy and needed help.[52]

The same practitioner emphasized that the structural approach to helping single mothers is not simply an intellectual or mechanical exercise.

> The orientation that I bring to my work with clients is always keeping the social analysis on the back burner so that right away when someone comes in, you're able to put them in a context, for example, single mother, there's not much money, there's no supports, she is isolated and there's a good deal of stigma in terms of being a single mother. There's a lot of being treated as a second-class citizen in terms of being a woman. [53]

Another social worker describes how a materialist understanding of violence and an applied collectivist concept can be used in helping the perpetrators of violence against women:

> It is very important to understand men's behaviour as more than simply a personal response or personal behaviour that is located in that individual relationship. The first thing we try and do throughout the programme is to continually make connections between the men's behaviour that they are exhibiting in a relationship and the

behaviour of men in the community, in this city, in this society, which in many ways mirrors what they are doing. Part of it is making those links between what you do in the privacy of your own home and helping men see that it has a big connection with the roles of women and men in the society in which we live.[54]

4. Increasing Client Power in the Worker-Client Relationship

Reducing the power differential between client and worker is integral to the helping relationship and can be advanced, according to Moreau and Frosst, by "maintaining respect for the client's dignity and autonomy, validating strengths, articulating limits to the professional role, clear contracting, reducing distance, sharing the rationale behind interventions, encouraging self-help and the use of groups, and self-disclosure."[55] This process can also include using first names; demystifying the social work role by employing simple language and avoiding jargon and diagnostic/medical terminology, ensuring that clients see what is written and hear what is being said about them; and protecting confidentiality. The utilization of a contract that clarifies purpose, goals, and tasks puts much of this in place. One social worker described empowerment of the client as:

> ... not me solving their problems. They solve them but I am a catalyst to connect the energy so they can increase their understanding. I don't take over other people's problems. I try to empower them to own the problems and to also own the solutions.[56]

5. Enhancing the Client's Power Through Personal Change

According to Moreau and Frosst, this practice aims to "maximize the client's potential to change thoughts, feelings, and behaviours that are self-destructive and/or destructive to others while acknowledging the impact of the societal context."[57] This goal is achieved by identifying and communicating strengths, assisting the client in obtaining a critical understanding of the connection of his or her personal problem within the social context, and supporting the client in personal goals. Social workers can thus enable people to gain an understanding of their situation by joining with them in exploring the range of possibilities for changing their circumstances.

It is important to note that the goals and practices discussed above are not all in play at one time or in every case. In the client sessions submitted by self-identified structural social workers, Moreau and his associates identified a total of 1,737 interventions: 50.7 per cent reflected the goal of enhancing client power through personal change; increasing client power in the worker-client relationship accounted for 22.3 per cent of interventions; and materialization accounted for 17 per cent, defence of client 6 per cent, and collectivization 4 per cent.

Summary

While the goal of all social work is change, it is the nature and method of change that distinguishes the structural approach from others. The structural approach is based on a critical analysis of the social, economic, and political context and promotes a restructuring of the social structures that exploit and dehumanize people. Within this framework social workers draw on, and at times adapt, theories and practice skills that have been developed over the years and have become the core of social work helping and relationship building. The focus, grounded in a long tradition within social work of advocating for social justice, is on empowerment and social change. While it is within a radical tradition, it is also in keeping with the profession's code of ethics which places emphasis on advocacy, equality, and social justice.

NOTES

[1] Duncan K. Foley, *Understanding Capital: Marx Economic Theory* (Cambridge, MA: Harvard University Press, 1986) 10.

[2] In a published interview with family therapist Mara Selvini Palazzoli, one of the founders of Milan systemic family therapy, the interviewer raises criticisms of her approach, particularly in regards to ignoring the wider social context and the inequality of women. In her response she does not acknowledge the importance of women's inequality for family practice models such as her own. "An Interview with Mara Selvini Palazzoli," *Networker* (September-October 1987): 26–33.

[3] Mao argues that there can be no knowledge apart from practice. "Knowledge begins with practice, and theoretical knowledge that is acquired through practice must then return to practice." The process is practice, knowledge, again practice, and again knowledge. Mao Tsetung, "On Practice," *Selected Readings From the Works of Mao Tsetung*, (Peking: Foreign Languages Press, 1971): 76.

[4] Malcolm Payne, *Modern Social Work Theory: A Critical Introduction* (Chicago, IL: Lyceum Books, 1991) 35.

[5] Paulo Friere, *Pedagogy of the Oppressed*, 30th anniversary ed. (New York, NY: Continuum, 2001).

[6] Kurt Lewin, "Problems of Research in Social Psychology (1943–1944)," *Field Theory in Social Psychology: Selected Theoretical Papers*, ed. D. Cartwright (Chicago, IL: University of Chicago Press, 1976) 155–69.

7   Jan Fook, Martin Ryan, and Linette Hawkins, "Toward a Theory of Social Work Expertise," *British Journal of Social Work* 27 (1997): 407.

8   Carol Gilligan, *In a Different Voice: Psychological Theory and Women's Development* (Cambridge, MA: Harvard University Press, 1982).

9   Aida Hurtado, *The Colour of Privilege: Three Blasphemies on Race and Feminism* (Ann Arbor, MI: University of Michigan Press, 1996).

10 Donna Baines, "Feminist Social Work in the Inner City: The Challenges of Race, Class, and Gender," *Affilia* 12.3 (1997): 297–317.

11 Mary Bricker-Jenkins, "Hidden Treasures: Unlocking Strengths in the Public Social Services," *The Strengths Perspective in Social Work Practice*, 2nd ed., ed. Dennis Saleeby (New York, NY: Longman, 1997) 138.

12 Paul H. Ephross and Michael Reisch, "The Ideology of Some Social Work Texts," *Social Service Review* (June 1982): 273.

13 Ephross and Reisch 280.

14 John Coates, "Ideology and Education for Social Work Practice," *Journal of Progressive Human Services* 3.2 (1992): 15–30.

15 John Horton, "Order and Conflict Theories of Social Problems as Competing Ideologies," *The American Journal of Sociology* LXXI.6 (May 1966): 701–13.

16 See, e.g., Gibson Burrell and Gareth Morgan, *Sociological Paradigms and Organizational Analysis* (London: Heinemann Educational Books, 1979); Ben Carniol, "Clash of Ideologies in Social Work Education," *Canadian Social Work Review* (1984): 184–99; Colin Whittington and Ray Holland, "A Framework for Theory in Social Work," *Issues in Social Work Education* 5.1 (Summer 1985).

17 Whittington and Holland 29.

18 Carl R. Rogers. "The Interpersonal Relationship," *Interpersonal Helping: Emerging Approaches for Social Work Practice*, ed. Joel Fisher (Springfield IL: Charles C. Thomas Publisher, 1973) 381–91.

19 David Howe in his book *An Introduction to Social Work Theory* (Aldershot: Wildwood House, 1987) provides descriptive names for social workers who situate themselves within each of the quadrants. According to Howe, there are the "Raisers of Consciousness" (radical and feminist approaches), the "Revolutionaries" (Marxist approaches), the "Seekers After Meaning" (client-centred approaches), and the "Fixers" (psycho-social, behavioural, and functional systems approaches).

20 Janis Fook, *Radical Casework: A Theory of Practice* (St. Leonards, NSW: Allen and Unwin, 1993); Thomas Keefe, "Empathy: The Critical Skill," *Social Work* 21.1 (1976): 10–14; Thomas Keefe, "Empathy and Critical Consciousness," *Social Casework* 61.7 (1980): 387–93.

21 Gale Goldberg, "Structural Approach to Practice: A New Model," *Social Work* (March 1974): 150. Ruth R. Middleman and Gale Goldberg, *Social Service Delivery: A Structural Approach to Social Work Practice* (New York, NY: Columbia University Press, 1974). In 1989 the authors published an updated version of the text.

22 Gale Goldberg Wood and Ruth R. Middleman, *The Structural Approach to Direct Practice in Social Work* (New York, NY: Columbia University Press, 1989) 16.

23 Ruth R. Middleman and Gale Goldberg Wood, "So Much for the Bell Curve: Constructionism, Power/Conflict, and the Structural Approach to Direct Practice in Social Work," *Revisioning Social Work Education: A Social Constructionist Approach*, ed. Joan Laird (New York, NY: The Haworth Press, 1993) 132, emphasis in original.

24 For a summary of the development of the structural approach, see Lecomte 31–51; Maurice Moreau, "A Structural Approach to Social Work Practice," *Canadian Journal of Social Work Education* 5.1 (1979): 78–94.

25 Maurice Moreau, "Empowerment Through Advocacy and Consciousness-Raising: Implications of a Structural Approach to Social Work," *Journal of Sociology and Social Welfare* 17.2 (June 1990): 53–67.

26 Lecomte.

27 Bob Mullaly, *Structural Social Work: Ideology, Theory, and Practice* (Don Mills, ON: Oxford University Press, 1997) 124.

[28] Fook, *Radical Casework* 74–75, emphasis in original. During a sabbatical in Australia Maurice Moreau met Fook.

[29] See, e.g., Dennis Saleebey (ed.), *The Strengths Perspective in Social Work Practice*, 3rd ed. (Boston, MA: Allyn and Bacon, 2002); Lorraine M. Gutierrez, Ruth J. Parsons, and Enid Opal Cox, *Empowerment in Social Work Practice: A Sourcebook* (Pacific Grove, CA: Brooks/Cole Publishing, 1998); Neil Thompson, *Anti-discriminatory Practice* (London: Macmillan, 1993).

[30] Wallace Clement, "Canada's Social Structure: Capital, Labour, and the State, 1930–1980," *Modern Canada 1930 -1980's*, ed. Michael S. Cross and Gregory S. Kealey (Toronto, ON: McClelland and Stewart, 1984) 81–82.

[31] The 1993 Canadian Violence Against Women Survey reports that men living in families where the joint income is less than $15,000 and unemployed men had rates of violence twice as high as those in upper income categories and employed men. A discussion of the findings can be found in Holly Johnson, *Dangerous Domains: Violence Against Women in Canada* (Scarborough, ON: Nelson, 1996).

[32] "The *dialectic* is both a way of thinking and an image of the world. On the one hand, it is a way of thinking that stresses the importance of processes, relations, dynamics, conflicts, and contradictions—a dynamic rather than a static way of thinking about the world. On the other hand, it is a view that the *world* is made up not of static structures but of processes, relationships, dynamics, conflicts, and contradictions." George Ritzer, *Contemporary Sociological Theory*, 2nd ed. (New York, NY: Alfred A. Knopf, Inc, 1988) 18, emphasis in original.

[33] It is encouraging to see special issues on social justice recently appear in two social work journals: *British Journal of Social Work* 32 (2002) and the *Journal of Contemporary Human Services* 83.4 (2002).

[34] National Association of Social Workers, "International Policy on Human Rights," *Social Work Speaks: NASW Policy Statements* (Washington, DC: NASW Press, 2002) 178–86. Also found at http://www.naswdc.org/.

[35] Matthew Colton, "Editorial," *British Journal of Social Work* 32 (2002): 659.

[36] Michael Reisch, "Defining Social Justice in a Socially Unjust World," *Families in Society: The Journal of Contemporary Human Services* 83.4 (2002): 343–54.

[37] Colton 659–67.

[38] Gary Craig, "Poverty, Social Work and Social Justice," *British Journal of Social Work* 32 (2002): 669–82; Gindin 1–11.

[39] Craig 671–72.

[40] National Association of Social Workers, "International Policy on Human Rights," 181.

[41] Jeffry Galper, *Social Work Practice: A Radical Perspective* (Englewood Cliffs, NJ: Prentice-Hall, 1980) 131.

[42] Fook, *Radical Casework* 43, emphasis in original.

[43] Moreau, "A Structural Approach to Social Work Practice."

[44] Maurice Moreau and Sandra Frosst, *Empowerment II: Snapshots of the Structural Approach in Action* (Ottawa, ON: Carleton University Press, 1993) 309.

[45] Maurice Moreau, *Empowerment Through a Structural Approach to Social Work: A Report From Practice* (Ottawa, ON: Carleton University, 1989); Moreau and Frosst, Sadly, Maurice died before completion of all the data analysis and the second report was authored by a project committee of colleagues and friends.

[46] Moreau and Frosst 60.

[47] See Moreau and Frosst 163.

[48] When social workers in Labrador refused to implement a policy because it was culturally inappropriate and potentially harmful to the health of the Innu, they lost their jobs. See Colleen Lundy and Larry Gauthier, "Social Work Practice and the Master-Servant Relationship," *The Social Worker* 57.4 (1989): 190–94. This case is also discussed in Chapters 5 and 10.

[49] Moreau and Frosst 181.

[50] Moreau and Frosst 69.

51 Michele Bourgeon and Nancy Guberman, "How Feminism Can Take the Crazy out of Your Head and Put it Back into Society: The Example of Social Work Practice," *Limited Edition: Voices of Women, Voices of Feminism*, ed. Geraldine Finn (Halifax, NS: Fernwood Publishing, 1993) 301–21.

52 Moreau and Frosst 75.

53 Moreau and Frosst 75.

54 Moreau and Frosst 89–90.

55 Moreau and Frosst 126.

56 Moreau and Frosst 92.

57 Moreau and Frosst 145.

CHAPTER 4

THE IMPORTANCE OF INEQUALITY AND SOCIAL LOCATION

A critical awareness of structural injustice and inequality helps us to understand the concerns of diverse populations and to challenge inequality, exploitation, and discrimination. We begin by examining the multiple social factors that influence individuals on a daily basis. This includes our relationship to those who hold economic and decision-making power, since it shapes how we see ourselves, influences our opportunities, and impacts on the ways in which we relate to others. A progressive structural approach starts with such an awareness.

For example, the "flower power" exercise, originally developed for anti-racist work, is a tool designed to help people to determine who they are in relation to those who hold power in this society (Figure 4.1). It can assist social workers in understanding social relationships in society.

The core of the flower is segmented with identity markers such as age, sex, social class, religion, language, education, and so on. Participants think of a particular period in their lives and indicate, on the inner petals, those factors that reflect their social identity at that time. This can be done individually or in pairs. On the larger petals, as a group, they list the dominant social identity. They are asked to reflect on where they are in relation to the outer petals, "the dominant group in society that controls the economic, political and social participation of other members of society."[1] This group usually consists of white, male, heterosexual, upper-class, middle-aged, and able-bodied people. The exercise recognizes the complexity of who individuals are and how they may be privileged or disadvantaged relative to others. Participants can also think about what

FIGURE 4.1 The Power Flower

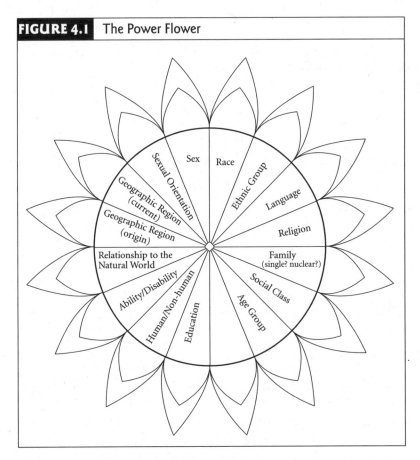

"The power flower" by Margie Bruun-Meyer/ArtWork, from *Educating for a Change* by Rick Arnold, Bev Burke, Carl James, D'Arcy Martin, and Barb Thomas (Between the Lines, 1991). Reproduced by permission.

has changed over the years, whether they had difficulty in deciding on some of the identity petals, and how their identity is a social product, influenced by interaction with others. Blank petals encourage people to add another aspect of their identity.

Social relations based on gender, sexual orientation, race/ethnicity, and social class intersect with each other to produce a complex pattern with specific effects influenced by a changing historical, political, and social context. The impact and effects of inequalities are not simply added onto one another but are multiplicative.[2] These points of intersection have been described as " a series of tangled knots" where "the tensions pulling on these knots shift and change daily"[3] as social and political conditions change. For example, a black youth living in Somalia may not experience racism based on the colour of his or her skin, but would do so on relocating to Canada. Similarly, in the US for several months after September 11, 2001 and the announcement of the "war on terrorism," racist attacks and racial profiling increased for those who were, or appeared to be, of Arab origin.

Taking Social Class Into Account

Definitions of social class generally fall into two areas: class as stratified by occupation and income and class as a product of unequal social relations within capitalist societies. It is the latter perspective that usually informs a structural approach to social work.

Wallace Clement regards social classes not as static economic categories but rather as social relationships that are in the process of constant change and that are connected to and affected by other associations.

> Not all social relations are class relations, but class affects all social relations; that is, gender, region, ethnicity, and so on are all relational concepts that are affected by class (although class does not determine these relations). This does not mean that gender, regional or ethnic groups are "classes." A key corollary in this argument is that classes never exist in isolation. Conversely, classes are always conditioned by other social relations.[4]

While social classes in traditional Marxist terms are determined by two relations—whether or not one has direct ownership of capital and whether or not one controls the labour of others—advanced capitalism has created intermediary classes. Wallace Clement and John Myles, drawing on empirical data from five advanced capitalist countries, tackle the problem of where to situate those who are in senior management and supervisory positions. They identify four classes of advanced capitalism: the capitalist-executive, old middle, new middle, and working classes. According to them, the two distinguishing factors determining class location are whether or not one controls the means of production and/or the labour of others. Drawing on their research, the class break-down in Canadian society is illustrated in Table 4.1.[5]

TABLE 4.1		
	Command Labour Power of Others	
Command Means Of Production	Yes	No
Yes	Capitalist-Executive (6.2%)	Old Middle Class (11.3%)
No	New Middle Class (24.9%)	Working Class (57.6%)

The capitalist-executive class includes those who are self-employed with at least three employees and executives who make decisions about production, budgets, and hiring. The new middle class is composed of those in managerial or administrative positions who oversee the work of others, while the old middle class are self-employed, small business owners with up to two employees. As the illustration indicates, the majority of workers have control over neither the labour power of others nor the means of production; they form the working class.

Clement and Myles offer a clear understanding of the class formation in industrial western countries and demonstrate how the development of capital impacts on social class itself. Although a new middle class has emerged in the late twentieth century, the majority of workers in Canada continue to comprise the working class.[6] Increasingly, one's social class influences educational opportunities, access to health care, level of health, general social and emotional well-being, and the ability to fully participate in society.

For most people, class position is the least understood factor in their lives and is seldom addressed when identifying social location. Generally, the tendency is simply to believe that one belongs to the "middle class" since that includes the notion of having "made it." This is reinforced by the tendency to determine class by income.[7] Those "less fortunate" are commonly referred to as "lower class," "economically disadvantaged," or "poor." The radical and Marxist traditions within social work emphasize class formation and class location as an important factor in understanding the current economic crisis and how it affects growing numbers of people.

But why do so few identify themselves as members of the working class and recognize their potential power? Joanne Naiman reminds us that this omission is intentional—a low degree of class consciousness among the working class is required for the maintenance of any class-based society.[8] We grow up learning very little about the history of working-class contributions to society and resistance against capitalist exploitation and do not find such an analysis in our school books or newspapers or on television.[9] And yet developments such as these have been a powerful force in recent and past worker uprisings. Also, history has shown that social and political change is possible when members of the working class identify their own interests, come together in solidarity, and realize the power they hold in numbers.

Race, Ethnicity, and Cultural Diversity

Canada is one of the most culturally diverse countries in the world. The Canadian Census lists more than 100 ethnic groups, and Statistics Canada projects that by 2016 the number of "visible minority" Canadians will increase to 7.1 million (from 2.7 million in 1991) representing 20 per cent of the total population.[10] An understanding of ethnicity, race, and racism is essential if social workers are to develop competence in cross-cultural practice.

Ethnicity refers to social factors that define a group according to some shared experience in regards to language, religion, and/or nationality and ancestry. One's ethnicity "interacts with economics, race, class, religion, politics, geography, the length of time since migration, a group's specific historical experience, and the degree of discrimination it has experienced."[11] At certain times race has been used to classify people hierarchically according to external physical characteristics (such as skin colour, facial features, and hair type), nationality or ethnicity, religion, or language group. The concept of race is an arbitrary social category and has no biological or scientific basis. For example, Vic Satzewich notes that during certain political and historical periods in Canada, immigrants from central, eastern, and southern Europe were seen in racial terms and as inferior to the British and northern Europeans who represented "White Canada."[12] He emphasizes that such prejudice was generally short-lived and ought not minimize the personal and institutional forms of racism experienced by people of colour today.

Race "is a structure rooted in white supremacy, economic exploitation, and social privilege."[13] It has been argued that, although prejudice has existed among peoples throughout history, racism as a systemic practice originated in the development of capitalism and the context of colonial expansion.[14] Freire argues that while "one cannot reduce the analysis of racism to social class, one cannot understand racism fully without a class analysis, for to do one at the expense of the other is to fall prey into a sectarianist position, which is as despicable as the racism that we need to reject."[15] The concept of racial inferiority has been used to justify slavery, seize the lands of Aboriginal peoples, and exploit the labour of particular ethnic and language groups. Peter Li uses the term racialization to highlight the social process by which certain groups are placed in racial categories.[16] These categories are highly problematic for persons whose heritage represents several cultures or who find themselves "between races." Identifying who one is in regards to "race" is fraught with problems since the categories are limited and predetermined.[17]

Norma Akamatsu, a third-generation Japanese American, speaks of her personal experiences as a "checkerboard of disadvantage and privilege." In recalling how she experienced poverty and anti-Japanese stigma during World War II, she remembers an incident that reflects the power and inadequacy of categories based on the concept of race:

> I tell the story of a road trip to the South in 1957, in which my then 11–year-old brother needed to make an emergency bathroom stop. My father pulled up to a roadside diner, where Johnny raced to the rest rooms in the back, only to come careening out front to the car again: "The bathrooms have signs. One says 'White.' The other says 'Colored.' Where am I suppose to go?" And without skipping a beat, my mother told him firmly: "White. White. You go to the White bathroom." [18]

While race is a mythical construct, racism and anti-Semitism are not. Racism is an institutionalized system of economic, political, and ideological relations and practices through which one group exercises power and privilege over other groups. Racist beliefs and actions are not instinctively found in people, but are created within social, cultural, and political contexts where the most vulnerable are exploited by the most powerful.

The history of Canada is marked by colonial and capitalist development based on the exploitation of people.[19] Aboriginal people share the longest history of exploitation and forced assimilation in Canada. In the 500 years of European occupation, Aboriginal peoples have had lands expropriated and their languages, customs, and culture erased.[20] Residential schools, to which Aboriginal children were sent, usually far away from their families, and in which they were not allowed to speak their mother tongues, have left a particularly harmful legacy. The impact of colonialism and institutional racism is reflected in the high rates of suicide, alcohol and other drug use, and abject poverty within Aboriginal communities.

Those who immigrate to Canada and the US encounter similar forms of oppression, exploitation, and inequality. Throughout history, different racial and ethnic groups have struggled to gain basic human rights and civil liberties such as freedom from slavery, the ability to vote in elections, and the maintenance of cultural practices.

People of Jewish origin experience anti-Semitism, hostility expressed through cultural stereotypes, vandalism of synagogues and cemeteries, and hate literature. Historically, Jews in Canada have faced entrance quotas to universities, social exclusion from institutions, and immigration barriers.[21] Irving Abella and Harold Troper, in their book *None is Too Many*, carefully document the extent of anti-Semitism in Canada after World War I and during the 1930s and 1940s when Canada would not open its doors to hundreds of thousands of Jewish people, many of whom faced the Nazi death camps.[22]

Because racism is so pervasive and insidious in our society, it is likely that, at times, people will unintentionally express attitudes and act in ways that are racially insensitive.[23] Similarly, social workers, despite the fact that they may be committed to racial justice and equality, may at times respond in ways that are racially insensitive. Therefore, part of the struggle also involves an openness to feed-back on actions or statements, a willingness to acknowledge one's own racial or ethnic insensitivity, and a commitment to personal and political change.[24]

Women's Long March to Equality

An examination of gender relations in this society highlights the pervasive power men as a group have relative to women as a group and the social, political, and economic subordination that women face. Despite the fact that women make up the majority of the population in Canada and throughout the world, they are a minority in positions of decision-making and power. After decades of struggle for equality, women still are not represented in politics in some jurisdictions. A 2002 study of 182 parliaments worldwide reports that women hold only 14.6.per cent of all parliamentary seats, essentially the same number as in 1988. Sweden placed first with 45.3 per cent of women in Parliament, while Canada ranked thirty-sixth with 20.6 per cent of the seats in the House of Commons filled by women. Britain was forty-ninth with 17.9 per cent, and the US ranked fifty-ninth with a mere 14.3 per cent of the seats in the House of Representatives filled by women.[25] The study found that women in Western democracies have lagged behind, while those in developing countries are gaining seats in parliaments.[26]

Women continue to earn less than men; are overrepresented among the poor and unemployed; are absent from positions of decision-making, whether in government, business, or organizations; and endure severe forms of violence in their communities, workplaces, and homes. The nature of women's inequality can be understood by examining women's role in the labour force and in the home—women's underpaid and unpaid work.

Women's Work

In the past 50 years, female participation in the labour force in Canada has increased from 24 per cent in 1951 to 57 per cent in 1996; however, their occupations have not varied significantly. [27] Despite some progress in entering traditionally male professions, women continue to be concentrated in occupations that are low in pay and prestige: clerical (25.0 per cent), service (17.5 per cent), sales (10.2 per cent), and nursing (9.1 per cent). The increased rate of women in the workforce parallels the rise of the service sector in Canada. While 67 per cent of those employed in the service sector were women in the early 1950s, by the 1990s this figure increased to 80 per cent.[28] Many women work at part-time, low-paid jobs (McJobs, as they are sometimes called) with little or no possibility of advancement, few employment-related benefits, and little control over their labour. Such work does not offer them independence nor is it a solution to poverty. In fact, in recent years more and more women are working two or three jobs in order to make ends meet.[29] Women working full-time continue to earn 73 per cent of what men earn even in female-dominated occupations. In 1994, 26.1 per cent of women were working part-time compared to 10 per cent of men. Unemployment rates (1991) are higher for women overall, and this is particularly so for immigrant women who arrived after 1986 (18.4 per cent), visible minority women (13.4 per cent), Aboriginal women (17.7 per cent), and women with disabilities living in households (16 per cent).

As federal and provincial governments cut back on social programs, more and more women and children live in poverty. Monica Townson recently reported that women's poverty at 19 per cent has reached the highest rate in the last two decades. Equally disturbing is the fact that 56 per cent of sole support mothers are poor, little changed from the 52 per cent reported in the 1967 Royal Commission on the Status of Women. Since pensions, such as the Canada Pension Plan, are based on one's life-time earnings, poverty accompanies women into retirement. Elderly women who do not have work-related pensions are also likely to find themselves impoverished. In fact, half of the women in Canada over 65 are poor.[30] In the case of Aboriginal women, 43 per cent in 1996 had incomes below the poverty line, compared to 20 per cent of non-Aboriginal women and 35 per cent of Aboriginal men.[31]

Even though women's participation in the workforce has increased, they continue to do two-thirds of the unpaid work in the household—child care, housekeeping, food purchasing and preparation, care for the ill and elderly family members, and maintenance and repair. In families with children women spend more than twice as much time on domestic

FIGURE 4.2

From: *Not for Nothing* (St. John's, NF: Women's Unemployment Study Group, 1983) 54.

work as men. Among couples without children, women do 60 per cent more of the domestic labour than men.[32] There are few resources to support the family, and the economy depends on women to take on the tasks necessary to ensure the emotional and physical well-being of family members. Women are expected to support and care for family members, providing the services that were previously offered by the state. Therefore, the lack of affordable and quality care for vulnerable family members, and the funding cuts to hospitals and specialized programs for children, persons with disabilities, and the elderly have a greater impact on women. Women's work within the family is essential in order for the current economic and political system to carry on. Yet, this unpaid "domestic" work is ignored, unpaid, and undervalued. [33]

Unlearning Sexism

Patriarchy, both a system of social structures and an ideology, in the household and in the public realm, supports the exploitation and oppression of women by men. Women face sexism and stereotyping in their private and public lives. The patriarchal nature of the traditional family is characterized by compulsory heterosexuality, violence against women, and the exploitation of women's labour. Women continue to be portrayed as less capable and intelligent than men, promiscuous, and over-emotional. Since patriarchy, as an ideology, is entrenched in laws, policies, and practices, it becomes internalized by both males and females at a young age. It is not uncommon to find sexist stereotyping and attitudes toward women among professionals, including social workers.

Paulo Freire acknowledged the power of ideology in shaping attitudes and views and spoke of his own struggle to unlearn sexism. Although he was fully committed to women's equality with men, he described his struggle as a Latin American male influenced by a sexist culture and recognized how he could be progressive in discourse while his actions could be reactionary. Freire realized that his struggle to be non-sexist and to lessen the distance between what he said and what he did required "a progressive obsession." [34] It is not surprising that men, although committed to gender equality, may at times act in ways that reflect sexist beliefs.

Generally, masculinity—what it means to be a man in our society—is tied to power and aggression and is reproduced and reinforced by men in their day-to-day practices. There is no question that men as a group share greater privileges than women as a group. Although all men benefit from women's oppression, they do so to varying degrees. Also, the problem does not lie solely with men overall—that is too simplistic a position. Working-class men, for instance, are frequently engaged in exhausting and danger-ous work and are exploited by their employers. Some men (as do women) face increased insecurity in the workforce as they age, if they are unskilled, have a disability, or are a person of colour. Thus, the majority of men may feel that they have little power in their daily lives, and yet they encounter the societal expectation that to be a man is to be powerful, economically and socially. So, along with acknowledging men's structural power and privilege, it is imperative at the same time to understand how male priv-ilege and institutional power is reduced for working-class men, men of colour, men who have a disability, and gay men.

Women's Rights are Human Rights

Although women's rights were enshrined in the *Universal Declaration of Human Rights* in 1948, many countries often lack the political and cultural will to protect and promote these rights. Women activists argue that the systematic subordination of women is a violation of human rights and hold that the "lack of understanding of women's rights as human rights is reflected in the fact that few governments are committed, in domestic or foreign policy, to women's equality as a basic human right."[35] In 1993, women's rights were highlighted at The World Conference on Human Rights in Vienna, and violence against women was recognized as a human rights issue for the first time.[36]

A renewed global struggle for women's rights is taking place. In 2000, women marched in the World March of Women in 159 countries. They then moved the campaign to the UN Building in New York and organ-ized a Global Rally where women's delegates met with UN Secretary General Kofi Annan and leaders of the World Bank and the International Monetary Fund. The March demonstrates women's potential and has given further impetus to the women's movement.

Sexual Diversity

The lesbian and gay liberation movement, now over 30 years old, has been successful in educating the public and advocating for changes to laws and policies in areas of sexual orientation and concepts of gender identity and gender relations.[37] Despite this progress, heterosexism and homophobia are pervasive in our society and continue to deny gay, lesbian, bisexual, and transgendered persons full participation in society. In order to achieve fundamental social change, Tom Warner, a leading gay activist in Canada, recognizes the importance to gays and lesbians of gaining a positive consciousness of themselves and of actively opposing "the repression of sexuality and combating sexual stereotyping, sexism, heterosexual supremacy, violence, hatred, bigotry, and hypocrisy."[38]

Heteroesexism is an ideology that considers heterosexuality as "natural" and any other form of sexuality and intimate relationship unnatural, while homophobia is the irrational fear, hatred, and intolerance of gay men and lesbian women based on myths and stereotypes. Heterosexism has the social and institutional power that supports homophobia while enforcing heterosexual superiority.[39] Suzanne Pharr argues that homophobia, heterosexism, and sexism work effectively together to promote and reinforce compulsory heterosexuality, patriarchal power, and the nuclear family.[40] Heterosexuality as a norm is entrenched in laws, social and cultural practices, and educational institutions.

The cost to gay and lesbian persons has been invisibility, an internalization of harmful beliefs, and threats to their personal safety. Homophobia supports vicious attacks against those who are viewed as gay. Along with derogatory names such as "fag" or "dyke," men and women also face violence and literally fear for their lives.

Cases such as the 1998 brutal killing of 21–year-old Matthew Shepard, a gay man living in Wyoming, who was kidnapped, severely beaten, tied to a fence, and left to die in the cold is a message to all gay men, or men who may be seen to be gay, of the potential threat against them. Matthew Shepard's brutal murder prompted the *Journal of Gay and Lesbian Social Services* to publish a special issue "From Hate Crimes to Human Rights: A Tribute to Matthew Shepard." The guest editors, Mary E. Swigonski, Robin S. Mama, and Kelly Ward, address how homophobic hatred and hate crimes are a violation of the human rights experienced by "the community of lesbian, gay, bisexual, transgendered, and two-spirited (LGBT[2]) persons."[41] Despite the evolution of human rights since the 1948 *United Nations Declaration of Human Rights*, gay and lesbian rights do not appear in the common standards of achievement set for all countries.[42]

Social workers, like other helping professionals, have been slow to fully recognize alternative sexual orientations and to provide gay- and lesbian-positive services. For example, the social work literature does not reflect the gay and lesbian experience or struggle. In a recent examination of 12 social work journals, gay and lesbian content, not relating to HIV/AIDS, was found in only 1 per cent of the articles.[43] This in part reflects the degree of heterosexism and homophobia in society in general and within universities in particular. Jane Aronson, a social work professor, notes how lesbian faculty and students are invisible in the university and how living fragmented lives is a stressful, "self alienating and draining process."[44]

One step in developing a gay- and lesbian-positive social work practice is to develop sensitivity regarding sexual orientation and an awareness of how easily homophobia is internalized. Since heterosexism is so prevalent and present in all social structures, including universities and social welfare agencies, it is important that social workers become aware of their own homophobia and heterosexism. Robin D'Angelo developed several questions which are useful in facilitating a process of critical thinking and advancing critical consciousness in this area.[45] The process begins by examining how one was taught to view gay and lesbian persons and heterosexual persons and how one sees societal responses to them either as a group or individually. The exercise demonstrates how society teaches lesbian and gay persons to hate themselves.

Suzanne Pharr suggests an exercise that facilitates gaining awareness of the structural and personal difficulties that arise when one counters the heterosexual norm. The task is to write a letter to someone who you care about and/or who has power over you, telling them you are a lesbian woman or a gay man. An exploration of the fears that might surface will assist in increasing your critical thinking, awareness, and sensitivity to the reality faced by gay and lesbian persons.[46]

Persons with Disabilities

Persons with disabilities often encounter social workers who are ill-informed regarding physical and mental disability and/or who have patronizing attitudes towards persons with disabilities. This situation is compounded by inadequate and inaccessible social services. Of the 16 per cent of people in Canada who are considered to have a disability, 56 per cent are of working age, 43 per cent are employed, and 35 per cent are over 65 years of age.[47] Those who are restricted from fully participating in society may have sensory or visual and hearing impairments; a hidden disability such as a psychiatric condition, allergies, Multiple Sclerosis, arthritis, or learning disabilities; or may belong to the smallest but most visible group, the mobility impaired or physically disabled.[48] Disabilities may be present at birth or be acquired by injuries or illness. For social worker Michael Oliver, the definition of disability contains three elements: the presence of an impairment, the experience of externally imposed restrictions, and self-identification as a disabled person.[49]

Activists within the disability rights movement have argued that while functioning may be impaired, it is the environmental barriers and social attitudes that are disabling. It is not only the physical disability that impacts on one's quality of life but also the social and economic conditions people with a disability face. Accessible buildings, transportation and services, technical aids and personal assistance are essential in order for many persons with disabilities to fully participate in society. Unfortunately, the focus of "helping" often occurs out of a sense of charity rather than social equality, with little attention placed on material and social conditions such as discriminatory structures, laws, policy, and attitudes.

Social worker Michael Oliver, one of the leading authors on the social model of disability, contrasts it with the predominate individual model which is prevalent in society (Table 4.2).

Oliver's social model of disability places the focus on societal structures and on the material and social conditions that deny people the right to full participation in society, rather than on individual impairment, personal problems, medicalization, and individual treatment. He emphasizes the social construction and politics of disablement and the rights of those who have a disability. Social workers often assist persons with a disabling illness or injury to overcome their denial and anger to adjust to impaired functioning and arrive at a level of acceptance. "Acceptance depends, in part, on one's ability to perceive oneself as competent and whole, despite dramatic changes in the body image."[50] An accessible environment, adequate social programs, and economic security support persons with disabilities to lead active and fulfilling lives.

In regards to mental health, Iain Ferguson outlines how the members of the working class are more likely to experience mental illness and, when they do, to encounter more serious outcomes. He voices scepticism that a postmodern approach would be capable of effectively challenging this material inequality and advocates instead a class-based, political response.[51]

TABLE 4.2	Disability Models[52]
The individual model	The social model
personal tragedy theory	social oppression theory
personal problem	social problem
individual treatment	social action
medicalization	self-help
professional dominance	individual and collective responsibility
expertise	experience
adjustment	affirmation
individual identity	collective identity
prejudice	discrimination
attitudes	behaviour
care	rights
control	choice
policy	politics
individual adaptation	social change

©Michael Oliver, from *Understanding Disability*. Reprinted with permission of Palgrave-Macmillan.

While Oliver believes that only members of the disability community can define and challenge oppression based on disability, Ferguson suggests that alliances based on class can best mount a challenge to the material inequalities and stigma which people with disabilities encounter.

The Impact of Inequality and Discrimination

The situation for all disadvantaged and oppressed groups has deteriorated with the neoliberal agenda. Along with hardship due to the erosion of social programs, the current economic situation fosters discrimination such as racism, homophobia, sexism, and poor-bashing. Targetted groups also face discrimination when looking for work or housing and experience humiliation, harassment, high levels of unemployment, and brutality by the police. A recent report commissioned by the City of Toronto indicates that Black immigrants face rates of poverty as high as 40 per cent compared to 10 per cent for white immigrants.[53]

The personal costs are immense. The systematic racism and assimilation process that has devastated the lives of Aboriginal peoples is well-documented in the 1997 *Final Report* on the Royal Commission on Aboriginal Peoples.[54] In Cornel West's view, the pervasive racism in the history of Black Americans has created an intense sense of worthlessness and hopelessness, what he has termed nihilism or "the lived *experience of coping with a life of horrifying meaninglessness, and hopelessness, and (most important) lovelessness*" that results in "a numbing detachment from others and a self-destructive disposition toward the world."[55]

Since the attitudes and beliefs that are dominant in society reflect the experiences of those who are privileged and in positions of decision-making, members of equity-seeking groups often experience life as living in two worlds. In 1903, W.E.B. DuBois, a Black scholar, referred to this as double consciousness, a sense of always looking through the eyes of others to measure oneself. The result, for DuBois, was a feeling of "two souls, two thoughts, two unreconciled strivings."[56] The experience of living and walking in "two worlds" can be compounded for those who identify themselves as a member of more than one disenfranchised group; for instance as gay Aboriginal men identify themselves as "two-spirited." They often face homophobia in their Aboriginal communities and racism in the gay community.

Those who live in the margins and who encounter racism, sexism, homophobia, and stereotypes of mental and physical disability on a daily basis can begin to internalize these messages. If they internalize society's view of them as "other" or "less than," it can be easy to begin to believe that there is something wrong with them, resulting in feelings of inadequacy and/or self-blame. This price of acceptance into the centre is often a denial of who one is. Terry Tafoya likens the denial of part of ourselves as amputation. People are told "to amputate a part of themselves to be able to fit something that's rigid and not built for them in the first place. Amputate your sexuality, amputate your gender, amputate your language, your spirituality" are some of the messages. [57] Tafoya believes that people may overuse drugs and alcohol to numb the pain of amputation and that the healing process involves reclaiming wholeness.

Addressing Injustice

While there have been important achievements, injustice and inequality continue in personal practices, policies, and law. According to the Code of Ethics of the Canadian Association of Social Workers (see Appendix B), social workers have an ethical responsibility to "identify, document and advocate for the elimination of discrimination" (Section 10.1), to "advocate for the equal distribution of resources to all persons" (10.2), and to promote social justice (10.6). Clearly, these changes cannot come about without a radical restructuring of society and elimination of class exploitation.

Anne Bishop makes the point that social class is different from other forms of oppression such as racism and sexism because, while other forms of oppression help keep the hierarchy in place, class *is* that hierarchy.[58] For Bishop, class struggle becomes part of the struggle against racism, sexism, and discrimination based on disability or sexual orientation because social class cuts across all other forms of oppression. For example, financial security mediates the degree of hardship faced by persons with disabilities because it provides increased access to resources, privileges, and opportunities.

However, members of equity-seeking groups do not often include a class analysis in their struggle for change. Addressing the issue of racial identity politics, Manning Marable comments on the absence of a class awareness among members in racial minority groups as well as recognition of interests in common.[59] The absence of a class analysis was one of the obstacles in the work of the Ontario Anti-Racism Secretariat from 1992 to 1996. A critical account of the Secretariat reports that, although it was set up under the social democratic government of the New Democratic Party, most of those working within it had ties to the centrist or right-wing parties and that "virtually every senior bureaucrat dedicated to anti-racism harboured a deep distrust of class politics and any analysis of institutions as capitalist institutions."[60]

Acknowledging the role of social class does not imply that there is a "hierarchy of oppressions" or that other factors are not equally important. While Allahar and Côté, in their book *Richer and Poorer*, acknowledge the role and centrality of social class in ending all forms of inequality and exploitation, they caution that this view does not imply that race, gender, and age are less real or less important than class.[61] Because of the intersections and interlocking nature of inequality, challenging one form of oppression requires working to end all forms. The struggle to eliminate injustice and all forms of inequality is part of the struggle to transform the existing social and economic institutions of society. Whatever our starting point of critique and analysis of existing injustices, be it race, gender, disability, or sexual orientation, social class remains an important factor.

NOTES

1 Carl E. James, *Perspectives on Racism and the Human Services Sector: A Case for Change* (Toronto: University of Toronto Press, 1996) 19.

2 Patricia Hill-Collins, *Black Feminist Thought: Knowledge, Consciousness, and the Politics of Empowerment* (London: Unwin Hyman, 1990).

3 Minelle K. Mahtani, "Polarity Versus Plurality," *Canadian Women's Studies* 14.2 (1994): 16.

4 Wallace Clement, *The Challenge of Class Analysis* (Ottawa, ON: Carleton University Press, 1988) 26.

5 Wallace Clement and John Myles, *Relations of Ruling: Class and Gender in Postindustrial Societies* (Montreal, QC: McGill-Queen's University Press, 1994). Table 4.1 is a combination of two tables found on pages 16 and 19.

6 I use the term "working class" to refer to waged workers and "middle class" to mean salaried managers and professionals.

7 For example, a process currently identifies all families with incomes of between $35,000 and $69,000 as middle class. "Canadian family income slips over past decade," *Globe and Mail*, 27 January 2000: A6.

8 Naiman, *How Societies Work: Class, Power and Change in a Canadian Context*.

9 It was not until I was in my late twenties that I developed a consciousness of and pride in my working-class background. I began to fully realize the exploitative nature of a grandfather's death in a mine accident at age 34 and the struggle of miners, including my father, for a living wage and safe working conditions. I grew up in mining communities and knew the frequency of "accidents" and the vulnerability of the miners and their families to the "boom and bust" nature of the mining industry.

10 Wsevolod W. Isajiw, *Understanding Diversity: Ethnicity and Race in the Canadian Context* (Toronto, ON: Thompson Educational Publishing, 1999) 90.

11 Monica McGoldrick and Joe Giordano, "Overview: Ethnicity and Family Therapy," *Ethnicity and Family Therapy*, 2nd. Ed. Monica McGoldrick, Joe Giordano, and John K. Pearce (New York, NY: The Guilford Press, 1996) 2.

12 Vic Satzewich, "Race, Racism and Racialization: Contested Concepts," *Racism and Social Inequality in Canada*, ed. Vic Satzewich (Toronto, ON: Thompson Educational Publishing, 1998) 25–45.

13 Manning Marable, "History and Black Consciousness: The Political Culture of Black America," *Monthly Review* (July-August 1995): 72.

14 James Boggs, *Racism and the Class Struggle: Further Pages From a Black Worker's Notebook* (New York, NY: Monthly Review Press 1970) 136. Boggs reminds us that, although racial prejudice has a long history, the current systemic oppression of one race by another followed the emergence of capitalism 400 years ago; Louise Derman-Sparks and Carol Brunson Phillips, *Teaching/Learning Anti-Racism: A Developmental Approach* (New York, NY: Teachers College Press, 1997) 13.

15 Paulo Freire and Donaldo Macedo, *Ideology Matters* (Boulder, CO: Rowman and Littlefield), forthcoming. Mentioned in Freire, *Pedagogy of the Oppressed* 15.

16 Peter Li, *Race and Ethnic Relations in Canada* (Toronto, ON: Oxford Press, 1990).

17 Didi Khayatt, "The Boundaries of Identity at the Intersection of Race, Class and Gender," *Canadian Women's Studies* 14.2 (1994): 7.

18 Norma Akamatsu, "The Talking Oppression Blues," *Revisioning Family Therapy: Race, Culture, and Gender in Clinical Practice*, ed. Monica McGoldrick (New York, NY: The Guilford Press, 1998) 139.

19 The importance of acquiring a historical perspective is emphasized by Constance Backhouse in her recent book, *Colour-Coded: A Legal History of Racism in Canada 1900–1950* (Toronto, ON: University of Toronto Press, 1999). She comments that:

> Canadian history is rooted in racial distinctions, assumptions, laws, and activities, however fictional the concept of "race" may be. To fail to scrutinize the records of our past to identify deeply implanted tenets of racist ideology and practice is to acquiesce in the popular misconception that depicts our country as largely innocent of systemic racial exploitation. Nothing could be more patently erroneous. (7)

[20] In the case of the Beothuk people of Newfoundland, an entire nation was eradicated.

[21] Nora Gold, "Putting Anti-Semitism on the Anti-Racism Agenda in North American Schools of Social Work," *Journal of Social Work Education* 32.1 (Winter 1996): 77–89.

[22] Irving Abella and Harold Troper, *None is Too Many: Canada and the Jews of Europe 1933–1948* (Toronto, ON: Lester and Orpen Dennys, 1983). One of the most astonishing accounts is the "Voyage of the Damned." The *St. Louis*, a luxury liner, left Hamburg with 907 German Jewish passengers on May 15, 1939, in a desperate attempt to escape the Nazis. When refused entry to Cuba (despite having obtained entrance visas prior to leaving), the ship made unsuccessful attempts to enter Argentina, Uruguay, Paraguay, Panama, and the US. Canada, their last hope, also denied them entry, and "the Jews of the *St. Louis* headed back to Europe, where many would die in the gas chambers and crematoria of the Third Reich" (64).

[23] Kenneth V. Hardy and Tracy A. Laszloffy, "The Dynamics of a Pro-Racist Ideology: Implications for Family Therapists," McGoldrick 118–28.

[24] In 1983 I was involved in a coalition for racial equality in the US South and helped organize community responses to local incidences of racial discrimination and exploitation. After several months, a tension was evident in the meetings, and finally several Black members came forward with their concerns. Despite the fact that three-quarters of the coalition members were from the Black community, our regular meeting place was always in a part of the city recognized as "white." Further, all spokespeople to the media had been "white," as was the chair of the meetings. There was a period of silence, and then one by one we responded, acknowledging our blindness and beginning to change the practices of the coalition. Our work together was strengthened, and we continued to pursue social action strategies. We also organized a bus to the Twentieth Anniversary March on Washington for Jobs, Peace, and Freedom held on August 27, 1983.

[25] The data is compiled by the Inter Parliamentary Union on the basis of information provided by National Parliaments. "Women in National Parliaments" (1 March 2002),

[26] "Female, seeking public office? Better try Sweden," *Globe and Mail* (7 March 2003): A7.

[27] Gillian Creese and Brenda Beagan, "Gender at Work: Seeking Solutions for Women's Equality," *Social Inequality in Canada: Patterns, Problems and Policies*, ed. James Curtis, Edward Grabb, and Neil Guppy (Scarborough, ON: Prentice-Hall, 1999). 199–211.

[28] Allahar and Côté 106.

[29] In the last 10 years, the number of women working more than one job has grown by 45 per cent, compared to the 4 per cent rise in the number of men holding multiple jobs. See Statistics Canada, *Labour Force Survey*, 1999.

[30] Monica Townsend, *A Report Card on Women and Poverty* (Ottawa, ON: Canadian Centre for Policy Alternatives, April 2000).

[31] Statistics Canada Target Group Project, *Women in Canada 2000: A Gender-Based Statistical Report* (Ottawa, ON: Statistics Canada, 2000).

[32] See also Kevin McQuillan and Marilyn Belle, "Who Does What? Gender and the Division of Labour in Canadian Households," Curtis et al. 186–98.

[33] Johanna Brenner, *Women and the Politics of Class* (New York, NY: Monthly Review Press, 2000).

[34] Freire, "A Critical Understanding of Social Work."

[35] Charlotte Bunch, "Transforming Human Rights From a Feminist Perspective," *Women's Rights: Human Rights*, ed. Julie Peters and Andrea Wolpe (New York, NY: Routledge, 1995) 12.

[36] See, e.g., World Conference on Human Rights, Vienna, 1993: *Vienna Declaration and Program Action*; Fourth World Conference on Women, Beijing (1995); *Beijing Declaration and Platform* and its follow-up, *Beijing Plus 5* (2000). Documents can be found at http://www.who.int/hhr/readings/conference/en/.

[37] In June 1969, police raided a known gay bar in the Stonewall Inn, 53 Christopher Street, New York City. The riots that ensued sparked the start of the gay liberation movement. While the early movement primarily comprised gay men, lesbian women, and bisexual persons, transgendered and transsexual persons have been recognized more recently. Transgendered persons are distinct from those who are gay or lesbian. While being gay or lesbian refers to one's sexual

orientation and an emotional and sexual attraction for someone of the same sex, a trans-gendered person is defined by their gender identity, the belief about who they are as a person. The gender identity of transsexuals does not match their anatomical sex at birth, and they often undergo sexual-reassignment surgery when adults. See, e.g., Mary Coombs, "Transgenderism and Sexual Orientation: More Than a Marriage of Convenience?" *Queer Families: Queer Politics*, ed. Mary Bernstein and Renate Reimann (New York, NY: Columbia University Press, 2001) 397–419.

[38] Tom Warner, *Never Going Back: A History of Queer Activism in Canada* (Toronto, ON: University of Toronto Press, 2002) 8.

[39] Robin DiAngelo, "Heterosexism: Addressing Internalized Dominance," *Journal of Progressive Human Services* 8.1 (1997): 5–21.

[40] Suzanne Pharr, *Homophobia: A Weapon of Sexism* (Little Rock, AR: Chardon Press, 1988).

[41] Mary E. Swigonski, Robin S. Mama, and Kelly Ward, "Introduction," *Journal of Gay and Lesbian Social Services* 13.1/2 (2001): 1–6.

[42] Janice Wood Wetzel, "Human Rights in the 20th Century: Weren't Gays and Lesbians Human?," *Journal of Gay and Lesbian Social Services* 13.1/2 (2002): 15–45.

[43] Rebecca Van Voorhis and Marion Wagner, "Coverage of Gay and Lesbian Subject Matter in Social Work Journals," *Journal of Social Work Education* 37.1 (Winter 2001): 147–59.

[44] Jane Aronson, "Lesbians in Social Work Education: Processes and Puzzles in Claiming Visibility," *Journal of Progressive Human Services* 6.1 (1995): 14.

[45] DiAngelo 5–21.

[46] Pharr 42.

[47] *In Unison 2000: Persons with Disabilities in Canada*, Http://www.socialunion2000.

[48] See Joan Meister, "Keynote Address: The More We Get Together," *The More We Get Together*, ed. Houston Stewart, Beth Percival, and Elizabeth R. Epperley (Charlottetown, PEI: CRIAW and Gynergy Books, 1992) 11–18.

[49] Michael Oliver, *Understanding Disability: From Theory to Practice* (New York, NY: St. Martin's Press, 1996).

[50] Marlene Cooper, "Life-Threatening Disability in Adolescence: Adjusting to a Limited Future," *Clinical Social Work Journal* 22.4 (1994): 435.

[51] Iain Ferguson, "Identity Politics or Class Struggle? The Case of the Mental Health Users' Movement," *Class Struggle and Social Welfare*, ed. Michael Lavalette and Gerry Mooney (London: Routledge, 2000) 228–49.

[52] Oliver, *Understanding Disability* 34.

[53] *The Toronto Star* (25 July 2000): A20.

[54] Royal Commission on Aboriginal Peoples, *Final Report* can be found at http://www.indige-nous.bc.ca/rcap.htm.

[55] Cornel West, *Race Matters* (New York, NY: Vintage Books, 1994) 22–23; emphasis in original.

[56] W.E.B. DuBois, *The Soul of Black Folks* (New York, NY: Bantam Books, 1989) 3. The book was originally published in 1903.

[57] Terry Tafoya, "Finding Harmony: Balancing Traditional Values with Western Science in Therapy," *Canadian Journal of Native Education* 21 (1995): 27.

[58] Anne Bishop, *Becoming an Ally: Breaking the Cycle of Oppression* (Halifax, NS: Fernwood Publishing, 1994).

[59] Manning Marable, "Beyond Racial Identity Politics: Towards a Liberation Theory For Multicultural Democracy," *Race and Class: A Journal for Black and Third World Liberation* 35.1 (July-September 1993): 113–30.

[60] Stefano Harney, "Anti-racism, Ontario Style," *Race and Class* 37.3 (1996): 37.

[61] Allahar and Côté.

CHAPTER 5

ETHICAL PRACTICE

Situation #1

A 16-year-old girl was released from hospital after a suicide attempt. She agreed to weekly sessions with a social worker and was aware of her right to confidentiality as well as its limits regarding suicidal and homicidal thoughts. After about two months of counselling, she announced that three days earlier she had taken a kitchen knife and cut herself twice on the arm. Although the cuts were severe enough to bleed, she did not require medical attention. In fact no one else was aware of the injury. She adamantly denied wanting to end her life, saying she cut herself because she was angry and did not know what else to do. During the session she denied any suicidal ideation but could not guarantee that she would not cut herself again. She refused to tell her parents about the self-harm and warned the social worker "you can't tell them either."[1]

Situation #2

Joe is a social worker in an anonymous HIV-testing clinic. Susan, a 24-year-old married woman, tested HIV positive. Joe encouraged Susan to inform her husband Frank of her positive status and to abstain from unsafe sex practices until she had discussed her health with him. Two weeks later, Susan returned to see Joe. She was distraught and confused. She told Joe that she had been having unprotected intercourse with her husband so that he would not suspect anything was wrong. She still had not found the courage to tell Frank about her status for fear of losing him. Joe is unclear how to proceed in his role. He could take more time to work with Susan and encourage her to disclose her HIV status to her husband, but he is also concerned about warning Frank so that he can protect himself.[2]

Situation #3

The District Manger of Social Services in a remote Aboriginal community receives a government directive instructing him to implement a policy and deduct 20 per cent for "board and lodging" from social assistance recipients if they have someone living with them who has earnings, pensions, or other allowances. Members in the community are suffering from poverty and a chronic shortage of housing, and at this time there is also an outbreak of tuberculosis. The culture values sharing, and families who have some room welcome those who are in need of housing. No "rent" is charged; instead, "lodgers" help with chores and contribute towards their food. The concept of "boarder" is unknown in the communal culture of the people. The manager believes that implementing the policy would create even further hardship for the community, as well as being culturally irrelevant.[3]

Social workers regularly encounter ethical dilemmas in the context of their daily practice. They are expected to assess competing ethical principles and arrive at a decision. The decision-making process is guided by the profession's code of ethics, as well as laws, social policy legislation, and the policies of the agency. This chapter outlines the central ethical responsibilities facing social workers and gives some direction about responding to difficult situations.

Social Work Codes of Ethics

Both the Canadian Association of Social Workers (CASW), and the US National Association of Social Workers (NASW) have codes of ethics that identify the core values, ethical principles, and standards which are to guide the practice of its members (Appendices B and C). It is important that codes of ethics be regularly debated, assessed, and revised in order to respond to emerging ethical concerns and to better reflect the practice of social work.[4]

While the codes of ethics of the two professional associations have common ethical standards for social work practice, they differ in the degree of development and detail and in how they are organized. The NASW code is organized into six ethical standards: social workers' ethical responsibilities to clients, to colleagues, in practice settings, as professionals, to the profession, and to broader society. The CASW code is organized into seven statements of ethical duties and obligations, which, if breached, may result in disciplinary action: best interests of the client as the primary professional obligation; integrity, and objectivity; competence in the provision of social work services; a limit on the professional relationship; confidential information; outside interests; and a limit on private practice. Also included are three statements characterized as ethical responsibilities, which are desirable goals to be achieved but, unlike ethical duties and obligations, are not likely to form the basis of disciplinary action if breached. They are ethical responsibilities to the workplace, to the profession, and for social change.

When conflicts of interest and ethical dilemmas arise, the social worker is expected to act in a manner consistent with ethical principles and standards of the code of ethics. However, codes of ethics have been criticized for their level of abstraction, which diminishes their usefulness in guiding ethical concerns.[5] Also, in both codes of ethics, categories tend to overlap and do not easily match the ethical dilemmas many social workers encounter. It has been suggested that a more useful alternative would be to organize standards around the major conflicts they face.[6] These factors limit the accessibility and usefulness of the codes of ethics in the decision-making process.

Social work is committed to social justice and social change with and on behalf of clients. A social work client may be an individual, family, group of persons, organization, or community on whose behalf a social worker agrees to provide a service. At times the service may be mandated by a court judge who orders the social worker to provide an assessment. The practice of social work includes direct practice; community organizing; the development, promotion, and delivery of human service programs; the development and promotion of social policies; political and social action; research; and evaluation.[7] The CASW Code of Ethics stipulates that a person or group ceases to be a client two years after termination of social work service.

Social workers are obligated to practice within the code of ethics endorsed by their professional association or regulatory body. However, it is useful for practitioners to be aware of various formulations of ethical practice. It is for this reason that reference will be made to both the CASW and NASW codes of ethics.

Malpractice

Social workers can be subject to discipline if their behaviour or actions do not meet the standards of care, that is, the ethical duties and obligations, listed in the Code of Ethics. Malpractice is considered to be a form of negligence that not only violates the standards of practice but also results in some form of injury to a client. Negligence can include behaviours that result in "assault, deceit, fraudulent misrepresentations, defamation of character, breach of contract, violation of human rights, malicious prosecution, false imprisonment or criminal conviction."[8]

Frederic Reamer, one of the leading social work scholars writing in the area of ethics, holds that four conditions must be satisfied to support a claim of malpractice: (1) evidence that the social worker owed a duty to the client (e.g., the duty not to engage in a sexual relationship with the client); (2) the social worker was derelict in that duty; (3) the client suffered some sort of harm or injury; and (4) the harm or injury was the direct result of the social worker's breach of duty.[9]

Although there is little written regarding the malpractice cases involving social work, within the current climate of litigation there has been a growing interest in ethical standards and responsibilities among social workers.

The Process of Ethical Decision-Making

Since ethical dilemmas are often complex, the social work code of ethics is viewed as a necessary but insufficient tool for ethical decision-making.[10] These situations require a careful process of analysis which combines ethical, legal, and clinical concerns and which considers the social and cultural context. In the event of a conflict or dilemma, the following steps are recommended for arriving at an ethical and accountable resolution:[11]

1. Recognize the ethical issue and/or dilemma.
2. Identify and rank the conflicting social work values and standards.
3. Identify individuals, groups, and organizations likely to be impacted by the ethical decision.
4. Consider specific information regarding the issue and ethical theories. This may involve an examination of the case file and worker's case notes and/or interviews with relevant parties.
5. Examine differing courses of action and the participants involved in each and weigh the risks and benefits for each.
6. Consult with colleagues and other appropriate staff.
5. Consider other factors such as laws, social policies, and agency policies.
6. Decide on an action plan.
7. Implement, monitor, and evaluate the outcome.

While social work codes of ethics offer the minimum standards of practice expected of a social worker, agency policy may state additional expectations which may conflict with these codes. For example, an agency may have a policy opposing dual relationships (worker and client) of any form, whereas social work codes of ethics are concerned about whether or not the relationship is potentially exploitative and harmful to the client. In most cases, the guidelines in both the agency and the code of ethics are more general than specific and must take into account the context of the situation.

In a study of one agency, Amy Rossiter and her colleagues found that social workers hesitated to disclose uncertainty regarding situations of an ethical nature in their workplace because they feared that their actions would be viewed negatively by a supervisor and their professional judgment placed under question. They also commented on the lack of supervision or opportunities to process complex situations.[12] Social workers in non-unionized agencies are particularly vulnerable to unfair responses by management. Agencies have the obligation to provide social workers with the opportunity to openly discuss occurrences that raise ethical concerns. This includes adequate and regular supervision and an open, non-judgmental process for ethical decision-making. The establishment of an ethics committee to serve as a consultative body when ethical concerns arise would normalize and facilitate the examination of situations of ethical uncertainty in social work practice.

Informed Consent[13]

A valid, informed, and voluntary consent by a client is essential prior to initiating any social work intervention. Social workers are generally governed by the common law principles of consent unless they are employed in an area under statutory regulation. The consent must include information about the service being rendered as well as limits to confidentiality and disclosure. Under common law, consent is only valid if the person is legally competent and is able to understand the information and the nature of the intervention to be provided. For this reason a person signing a consent should not be intoxicated, drugged, or in severe pain. In situations where the social worker and client do not speak a common language, an interpreter should be used in order to ensure comprehension.

While in most cases the consent will be obtained in writing, implied consent or oral consent is sufficient in social work contact of an informal nature such as meeting with youth who come to a drop-in centre. Whether or not the consent is written, it is important that the social worker discuss the limits to confidentiality and the fact that consent may be withdrawn by the client at any time. In emergency situations professionals are authorized to provide services without a consent.

While there is no requirement of age to determine competency under common law, there are age-of-consent provisions set by legislation. For example, in Ontario, social workers who are employed in agencies funded by the Ministry of Community and Social Services are governed by the *Child and Family Services Act*, which holds that a child who is 16 years or older may consent to any service, and children 12 or over may provide their own consent to a counselling service without parental approval or even knowledge. If the child is over 12 but under the age of 16, the social worker is obligated to *suggest* the involvement of the parents. In regards to residential care programs, the consent of the parent or guardian is required for a child who is under the age of 16. This consent may be provided by the Children's Aid Society (CAS) if the child is in custody. For social workers employed in the educational system, the *Education Act* stipulates that the consent of parents is necessary for personality or intelligence testing on students who are below the age of 18. In the event of divorce, the parent who has custody is the one who has the right to make decisions on behalf of the child, while the parent who has access is only authorized to be informed about the situation.

In the case of young children or adults who are not capable of making a decision regarding their own personal care, the social worker relies on an appropriate third party who will act in the best interests of the client. In Canada, the *Substitute Decisions Act* authorizes a substitute decision-maker to provide consent: "A person is incapable of personal care if the person is not able to understand information that is relevant to making a decision concerning his or her own health care, nutrition, shelter, clothing, hygiene or safety, or is not able to appreciate the reasonable foreseeable consequences of a decision or lack of decision."[14]

Confidentiality

Social workers and other helping professionals are obligated to not willingly disclose information obtained from a client in confidence. When a person ceases to become a client, the social worker is still professionally obliged to maintain the same confidentiality.

Usually disclosure can only take place with the client's permission or if the law requires it. Also, it is not considered a breach of confidentiality if a social worker discloses information to others when she believes that a client is a danger to him or herself or to someone else. For instance, it is not only mandatory but required by law to report child abuse.

A discussion about confidentiality and its limits should take place early in the social work relationship, since the social worker is not able to guarantee that everything the client says will be held in confidence. The social worker can say something like:

> Normally, what you say or do is held in confidence. This means that I will not discuss your situation with anyone except workers in this agency unless I have your permission to do so. However, there are some exceptions. If you mention, or I suspect, that you or a family member have abused or neglected a child, I must report this to the Children's Aid Society. If possible, I would assist you in making the report yourself. If you say or do something that raises concern for your safety or the safety of another person, I have the responsibility of notifying the person at risk or other appropriate individuals or agencies. Also, in the case of a subpoena, your file becomes the property of the court.

Additional limits to confidentiality might include the file being used in agency research activities or file audits. In both these cases, files should not be removed from the site, and a method to protect client confidentiality, such as the use of pseudonyms or initials, ought to be in place.

It is useful for the social worker to anticipate which agencies or professionals may be important in the context of the service to the client and to obtain a release of information from the client. For example, if a social worker is providing drug treatment services to a woman and is also aware that the CAS is involved with the family, a sharing of information would be beneficial in coordinating resources and determining progress. The participation agreement or consent in some programs such as those for abusive men may contain additional limitations to confidentiality. For example, men mandated by the court are notified that their probation officers will be contacted regarding their attendance, participation, and progress. Similarly, in some programs, partners of the men have access to information about their attendance, general participation, and/or dismissal from the program, as well as the right to be notified if there is a concern for their safety.[15]

It is important to be vigilant regarding confidentiality. This involves not mentioning names or discussing someone's situation in public places. While it can be tempting to discuss a client's situation with a colleague in the cafeteria or on a bus ride home, it is a breach of confidentiality. Even though the social worker may not mention a client's full name, the circumstances and details may be overheard by others and linked to the client.

Technological innovations, such as computers, electronic mail, and answering and facsimile machines in the workplace, create additional possibilities for breaching confidentiality. A client may consent to disclosure of information to another agency, but faxing documents is a breach of confidentiality since a fax is visible to other workers, visitors, and clerical and maintenance staff while it is sitting in the machine waiting to be picked up. Faxes may be lost, and emails circulated beyond the person to whom they are addressed. Care is also required when leaving telephone messages on an answering machine in order to ensure that the message left will be heard only by the intended recipient. Moreover, the social worker should retrieve telephone and electronic messages in private. Computer screens ought to be hidden from public view in the reception area or the social work office, and access to electronic files should be restricted and secured with a password.

It is a good policy not to bring files home. Once they are removed from the agency, there is the possibility of misplacement or loss. Leaving files on buses, in taxis, or on the dining room table in view of others is a breach of confidentiality. Also, files should not be left on top of a desk as other clients may glance at the name or other staff may read through them.

At times social workers from different agencies may share the same client and may telephone each other to ask for information. Without the client's permission, each social worker is ethically bound not even to acknowledge that the person is a client, let alone disclose details about the case. Maintaining confidentiality becomes a particular challenge in settings such as the school where social workers are often approached by parents, teachers, and other school personnel for information regarding the student. There are some who strongly argue that all information should be kept in confidence (except, of course, when there is a threat of harm to the client or others) unless permission is obtained from the student.[16] This position is viewed as "too absolute" by others. Sidney Kardon, a school social worker, questions leaving parents and teachers "out of the loop" and asks "do we withhold information from a warm, affectionate teacher that a sexually abused child may become uncomfortable when touched?... Or perhaps one of my students tells me he is using drugs regularly. Do I withhold this information from his parents?"[17]

Let us consider Situation #1: a 16-year-old girl, with a history of a recent suicide attempt, discloses that she has been cutting her arm and does not want her parents notified. Here, the adolescent's right to confidentiality conflicts with the parents' right to information regarding their child. Applewhite and Joseph begin the assessment by drawing on what is known about acts of self-harm and argue that the act in this situation is one of self-harm and not suicidal behaviour. They also emphasize the importance of confidentiality for trust and the development of a relationship with adolescents. They conclude:

> From a practice perspective, keeping the adolescent's confidentiality helps to maintain the therapeutic relationship, fostering an environment in which work can continue to eliminate self-harming behavior. However, there is a chance that this behavior will continue. But since the client is an adolescent and not clearly incompetent, she should be able to choose her own behavior.[18]

Duty To Warn

Social workers have a duty to warn to protect others from potential harm. Based on the premise that public safety overrides the right to individual privacy, the landmark case *Tarasoff v. Board of Regents of the University of California* (1976) set the precedent of duty-to-warn over confidentiality. In this case Prosenjit Poddar informed his therapist, psychologist Dr. Moore, that he was planning to kill an unnamed woman (who was easily identified as Tatiana Tarasoff) when she returned from her vacation. Dr. Moore notified the campus police first by telephone and then in a follow-up letter. Although the police took Poddar into custody, they released him because he appeared rational and promised not to harm the woman. No one notified Tarasoff or her family. Two months later Poddar killed her. Tarasoff's parents sued the Board of Regents, the campus police, Dr. Moore, and his supervisor and won the case based on the court's decision that failure to warn the victim was irresponsible.[19]

A similar situation occurred in Connecticut. A third-year psychiatric resident disclosed to his psychiatrist, who was also a faculty member, that he was a pedophile. Four months after the disclosure, the resident sexually assaulted a 10-year-old boy. The question to be decided is whether or not the resident posed a threat to others that warranted disclosure by his psychiatrist.[20]

Consider Situation #2 in which the social worker faces two ethical principles that are in conflict. The balance between confidentiality and the privacy rights of an HIV-positive client against the duty to warn a partner of imminent harm is debated among social workers and other professionals. Social workers who support maintaining the right of the client to confidentiality may base their decision on the belief that ongoing education can take place in the context of a helping relationship and that clients may be encouraged to voluntarily inform their partners. Further, a breach of confidentiality about clients with HIV may jeopardize their employment and possibilities of securing insurance and housing.[21] On the other hand, a decision to warn the partner may be based on public health policy and the need to protect others from possible infection. A social worker may consider partner notification once he or she has exhausted all options to convince the client to disclose, when unprotected behaviour occurs on a regular basis, and when the threat of transmission of HIV is imminent and the victim is identifiable.[22] After weighing the risks and consequences of such situations, Reamer and Gelman argue that the duty to protect a life takes precedence over the right to confidentiality and privacy.[23]

Duty to Report

There are also situations in which social workers, fearing for the safety of their clients, have a duty to report to another agency. In the case of children under 16, both members of the public and professionals, who have reasonable belief that the child is or may be in need of protection, have an obligation to make a report to the CAS.[24] A social worker must call the CAS directly; it is not sufficient to merely inform a supervisor in the agency. A professional who neglects to report is guilty of an offence, punishable by a fine.

Boundary Issues and Dual Relationships

Dual relationships occur when social workers enter into more than one form of relationship with clients. For example, a social worker who has a therapeutic relationship with a client may also become a friend, teammate, intimate partner, or business associate. While social workers often share friendly moments with clients, the development of a friendship raises concerns regarding potential harm to the client.

Both the CASW and NASW Codes of Ethics address the issue of client contact outside the professional relationship. While they state that it is an ethical violation to have a sexual relationship and/or exploit a client in any way, they do not explicitly indicate that all dual relationships ought to be avoided or are necessarily harmful. The CASW Code of Ethics stipulates that a social worker is not to exploit the relationship with a client for personal benefit, gain, or gratification. Examples of exploitation include initiating a sexual relationship with a client or with a student assigned to the social worker, or entering into a business relationship by borrowing from or loaning money to a client.[25] The NASW Code of Ethics defines dual relationships and recognizes that in some case they are unavoidable:

> Social workers should not engage in dual or multiple relationships with clients or former clients in which there is risk of exploitation or potential harm to the client. In instances when dual or multiple relationships are unavoidable, social workers should take steps to protect clients and are responsible for setting clear, appropriate, and culturally sensitive boundaries. (Dual or multiple relationships occur when social workers relate to clients in more than one relationship, whether professional, social, or business. Dual or multiple relationships can occur simultaneously or consecutively.)[26]

These "tangled relationships," as Frederic Reamer has called them, have the potential to harm others and pose risks to social workers themselves.[27] They are more likely to occur in small geographic communities, or when a social worker belongs to an identity-based community such as the disability or the gay/lesbian community.

Increasingly, professionals are pointing out that non-sexual dual relationships are not necessarily unethical or will lead to exploitation or harm to the client, and they distinguish between "boundary violations" and "boundary crossings." Psychologist Ofer Zur identifies boundary violations as occurring when a therapist's relationship with the client is exploitative and harmful, such as typically occurs in sexual relationships, while boundary crossings include activities with the client such as going for a hike, exchanging inexpensive gifts or non-sexual embraces, sending cards, watching a client perform in a show, and accepting an invitation to attend a client's wedding or graduation. The key is that these decisions are made with the client's well-being in mind. Zur points out that not all such boundary crossings constitute dual relationships and may be an extension of the therapeutic relationship. He also argues that the prohibition of dual relationships may infringe on people's rights of freedom of association.[28]

Similarly, Karl Tomm, a family therapist, stresses that, while dual relationships can introduce complexity, they are not inherently harmful. On the contrary, he argues, "the additional human connectedness through a dual relationship is far more likely to be affirming, reassuring, and enhancing, than exploitative. To discourage all dual relationships in the field is to promote an artificial professional cleavage in the natural *pattern that connects* us as human beings."[29] Feminist therapist Miriam Greenspan holds that the emphasis on maintaining boundaries in therapeutic relationships is based on a male distance model where "distance is enshrined" and "connection is seen as inherently tainted and untrustworthy."[30]

Reamer cautions about the possibility of social workers meeting their own emotional needs in dual relationships and gives the following example:

> A social worker in a public child welfare agency was responsible for licensing foster homes. The social worker, who was recently divorced, became friendly with a couple who had applied to be foster parents. The social worker also became involved in the foster parents' church. The social worker, who approved the couple's application and was

responsible for monitoring foster home placements in their home, moved with her son into a trailer on the foster parents' large farm.[31]

In this case, the dual relationship of friend and social worker is likely to interfere with the supervision of the foster home placement and may place the child at risk. Not all situations are so clearly identified as problematic.

When a dual relationship is being contemplated, the social worker should examine the situation from the perspective of the client and assess potential harm. Gottlieb has developed a model which contains three dimensions to be explored in such situations: the extent and nature of the power of the social worker in relation to the client, the duration of services, and the clarity of termination and the likelihood of further professional contact.[32] He suggests that the three dimensions be examined within a five step process: 1) assess the current relationship; 2) assess the contemplated relationship; 3) examine both relationships for role incompatibility; 4) obtain a consultation with a colleague; and 5) discuss the dilemma with the client. Using this assessment process, the client in the following situation appears to be at a low risk for potential harm in the event that the social worker decided to accept the invitation:

> A single female social worker provides bereavement counselling to a single male who is mourning the death of his father. After three sessions, he is better able to cope with the loss and does not see the need to continue. Three months later, they meet at a ski lodge and discover that they enjoy each other's company and have a lot in common. On the following week-end, he asks her to go skiing.

Here the therapeutic relationship, focussed on a situational problem that has been resolved, is brief. For this reason, it is likely that the power differential between the social worker and client is minimal; the power of the social worker tends to be greater in long-term, therapy-oriented relationships. In this case, the therapeutic relationship has been terminated, but, although it seems unlikely that services will be needed, that possibility always exists. There does not appear to be role incompatibility since there are few expectations remaining in the role as social worker and the power differential between them is minimal.

It is useful to discuss dual relationships with a colleague or supervisor.

When the possibility of conflict between differing relationships arises, the social worker should discuss the dilemma with the client as well.

Guidelines for Record Keeping

Social workers have a legal and ethical responsibility to maintain an accurate record of their contact with clients. The social work record is a measure of professional and organizational effectiveness. In most cases, a file will be maintained on each person coming to the agency, with variations in the recording requirements and expectations. Although the file is the property of the agency, the social worker has a legal and ethical obligation to allow the client reasonable access to it.

The record is important in coordinating services and keeping track of referral sources. Also, when workers become ill or leave their position, thorough note-taking will ensure that important information is not lost when another worker takes over and that there is as little disruption as possible. Further, file records are a useful source of data for program evaluation, advocacy for specific social concerns, and supervision.

Records are shaped by agency guidelines and expectations. The client's file usually contains signed consent and release of information forms; an intake form; a complete social history and assessment; a client contract or action plan; progress notes or case-notes (from individual, family or group sessions); and a summary of involvement, which includes the focus of the work, the number of sessions, an evaluation of the goals set, and the reason for ending the service. In recording a group session, a summary of the focus of the group and some specific information about the client's participation will usually suffice. Social workers ought also to document meetings and communications they have with their supervisor and/or other professionals and/or family members regarding the client.

The notes should be descriptive and provide details on what the client said or did, as well as the client's feelings. Objective information, such as a description of behaviour and the inclusion of direct quotes, is particularly important when reporting alcohol or drug use or other activities that may have illegal connotations. Care ought to be taken to accurately document the situation, commenting on the client's strengths and resources, as well as the difficulties and limitations the client may face. The record should be completed as soon after the intervention as possible while specific details are fresh. Assessments and progress notes ought to provide concrete information based on the social worker's observations and obtained from the client or others. Sufficient information is needed to outline clearly the presenting concerns, the actions of the social worker, and the practice intervention. Any correction or alteration to the record should be done by leaving the original legible with a line drawn through it and the correction initialed, signed, and dated.

The social worker must document with the view that the record may one day be subpoenaed in court: a complete and detailed record will assist the social worker's testimony. The documentation will create the impression of the social worker as a practitioner and as a credible witness. The general court position is that if an event or statement is not recorded in the case record, it did not occur.

> A social worker's credibility in court or before a tribunal may be influenced by the state of the record. If the record is accurate, objective and complete, the social worker will probably be perceived as organized, methodical and conscientious. Conversely, a sloppy record creates the impression of a social worker who is careless and unconcerned about the client's well-being, whether or not this is actually the case.[33]

For example, when Angie Martin, a Toronto CAS social worker, was charged with criminal negligence when infant Jordan Heikamp died, her case notes were used as evidence during the proceedings and the coroner's inquest.[34] In some situations—i.e., sexual assault cases, documentation found in records may be used against the victim by defense lawyers to discredit her. It is for this reason that workers in sexual assault and rape crisis centres often oppose the release of records of sexual assault survivors.

Agencies usually have policies, often called critical incidents, about the documentation of unusual occurrences and high-risk situations. Examples include situations when a client has been violent, threatening, or suicidal; the client has been threatened or assaulted; or the client reports witnessing child neglect and/or abuse. Critical incidents are documented immediately and reported to a supervisor.

In the context of reduced funding to agencies and growing social work case-loads, social workers are finding that they have little time to keep up their records. The situation is compounded by reduced clerical support, the introduction of detailed assessments, and computerization with its expectation of more documentation. In her research, Jill Doner Kagle found that 78 per cent of social workers surveyed reported that they did not have enough time for record keeping or that the requirements for documentation were unrealistic. Further, she found that computerization actually increased the time social workers were expected to spend on record keeping.[35] For example, in Ontario there has been a 100 per cent increase in children brought into care by Children's Aid Societies, with the result that workers spend 70 per cent of their work time on documentation, recording, legal paperwork, and report writing, leaving only 30 per cent of their time for providing front line services.[36] This is an example of how government decisions and policies may not be compatible with social work ethical standards and make it difficult for social workers to provide accountable and ethical services.

Ethical Responsibilities to the Workplace

Social workers have an ethical obligation to advocate for workplace conditions and policies that contribute to well-being of the client. The NASW Code of Ethics (3.09d) clearly states that "Social workers should not allow an employing organization's policies, procedures, regulations, or administrative orders to interfere with their ethical practice of social work." The CASW Code of Ethics states that a social worker shall advocate for workplace conditions and policies that are consistent with the code (8.0). However, what is a social worker's recourse in the event that her responsibility to the workplace comes in direct conflict with her obligation to the client? Malcolm Payne voices the concern that social workers are becoming "more subject to the authority of employers rather than being directly accountable to clients for their decisions."[37] The CASW Code of Ethics (8.0) recognizes this dilemma and directs the social worker to bring the situation to the attention of the employer and, if that is unsuccessful, to the attention of the professional association and the regulatory body. However, it is unclear how these actions are likely to result in supporting the client or the social worker.

In Situation #3, the social worker was fired for ignoring a government directive in accordance with the code of ethics that dictated his first responsibility was to the community he served. The manager's notification to his employer of the harmful impact of the policy on the community was dismissed, despite supporting documentation from a noted physician and other professionals in the community. While the provincial social work association actively supported the social worker, the national association was silent. All attempts at mobilizing a community response were unsuccessful in reversing the government decision and in averting the serious issue facing the Aboriginal community.

Situations such as this may become more prevalent and more acute as the reduced funding to social programs and policy changes place the social worker in the position of policing those who rely on dwindling resources. Governments increasingly espouse the view that social welfare recipients take advantage of social welfare provisions and implement punitive measures for social welfare recipients suspected of infractions.

What recourse does a social worker have in situations where social policies are unjust and come in conflict with the goals and ethical standards of the profession? There is the possibility of mobilizing for collective action, of which the professional association would hopefully be a part. Several other options are possible. The social worker could bend the rules and err on the side of generosity, since rules and policies often have some leeway and flexibility in implementation. The social worker could also assist the client in an appeals process. Although not always effective, as Situation #3 demonstrates, the social worker could mobilize other agencies and organizations to pressure for policy changes. For example, when the Ontario government set up "welfare snitch" phone lines in the province in order to encourage the public to monitor persons receiving social welfare, a coalition of social workers successfully organized to close down the line in Sudbury District.[38]

Ethical Responsibilities for Social Change and Social Justice

While the social work codes of ethics are a contradictory blend of conservative and liberal elements, they do emphasize the social worker's ethical responsibility for social change and the promotion of social justice.[39] The NASW Code says that social workers "should advocate for living conditions conducive to the fulfillment of basic human needs and should promote social, economic, political, and cultural values and institutions that are compatible with the realization of social justice" (6.01). NASW is also explicit regarding the social worker's role in social and political action: "Social workers should engage in social and political action that seeks to ensure that all people have equal access to the resources, employment, services, and opportunities they require to meet their basic human needs and to develop fully"(6.04 a). Social workers are also expected to "act to prevent and eliminate domination of, exploitation of, and discrimination against any person, group, or class on the basis of race, ethnicity, national origin, color, sex, sexual orientation, age, marital status, political belief, religion, or mental or physical disability" (6.04 d). Similarly, the CASW Code says that a social worker shall "identify, document and advocate for the elimination of discrimination" (10.1); advocate for the equal access of all persons to resources, services and opportunities (10.3);advocate for a clean and healthy environment (10.4); and promote social justice (10.6).

While social work codes of ethics clearly state that social workers have a responsibility to social change and social justice, there is little guidance on how this responsibility is to be put into operation, nor is there support to do so. Situation #3 is clearly one of injustice. In cases such as this, how are social workers to balance their responsibility to their employer with that for social justice? Merely reporting an injustice to the manager and the professional association is not actively addressing the injustice.

Given the attention to social justice in the codes of ethics and given that both the International Federation of Social Workers and the International Association of Schools of Social Work have acknowledged the importance of a global human rights perspective, it is surprising that the profession does not consistently incorporate human rights as a factor in social work practice, research, and program priorities.

In regards to evaluation research, Stanley Witkin urges us to expand our understanding of accountability to include a response to injustice:

> Some alternative ways to measure accountability might include the extent to which one's practice challenges existing forms of oppression within the social order, treats clients with dignity and respect (for example, by validating their life experiences, honoring their language, and working with them as collaborators), uses a strengths rather than a pathology perspective ... engages in emancipating practices (for example, by helping clients see themselves within a broader historical and social context, helping them identify options to change that context, and facilitate action towards those changes), and is grounded in fundamental human rights.[40]

In order to establish social justice and human rights as a foundational principle for social work theory and practice and as ethical standards, intense discussion is needed regarding the concepts and how social workers are to meet their obligation to social justice and social change.

NOTES

1 Adapted from Larry W. Applewhite and M. Vincentia Joseph, "Confidentiality: Issues in Working with Self-harming Adolescents," *Child and Adolescent Social Work Journal* 11.4 (August 1994): 280.

2 Adapted from Sharon Taylor, Keith Brownlee, and Kim Mauro-Hopkins, "Confidentiality Versus the Duty to Protect," *The Social Worker* 64.4 (Winter 1996): 9.

3 Lundy and Gauthier 190–94.

4 Frederic Reamer outlines the changes in the NASW code of ethics over the years in Frederic G. Reamer, *Ethical Standards in Social Work: A Critical Review of the NASW Code of Ethics* (Washington, DC: NASW Press, 1998). The 1997 Code of Ethics is almost twice as long as the one accepted in 1979.

5 Frederic G. Reamer, *Ethical Standards in Social Work: A Critical Review of the NASW Code of Ethics* (Washington: NASW Press, 1998); David Watson (ed.), *A Code of Ethics for Social Work: The Second Step* (London: Routledge and Kegan Paul, 1985).

6 Sophie Freud and Stefan Krug, "Beyond the Code of Ethics, Part 1: Complexities of Ethical Decision-Making in Social Work Practice," *Families in Society: The Journal of Contemporary Human Services* 83.5/6 (2002) 474–82.

7 Canadian Association of Social Workers (CASW), *Social Work Code of Ethics* (Ottawa, ON: CASW, 1994) 5.

8 CASW, *Social Work Code of Ethics* 5.

9 Frederic G. Reamer, *Ethics Education in Social Work* (Alexandria VA: Council on Social Work Education, 2001) 122.

10 Freud and Krug.

11 Adapted from Frederic G. Reamer, *Social Work Values and Ethics*, 2nd ed. (New York, NY: Columbia University Press, 1999) 76–77.

12 A. Rossiter, Richard Walsh Boweres, and Isaac Prilleltensky, "Learning From Broken Rules: Individualism, Bureaucracy and Ethics," *Ethics and Behaviour* 6.4 (1996): 307–20.

13 The principles of and laws guiding consent for this section are summarized from Robert Solomon and Dawn A. Dudley, *A Legal Survival Guide for Social Workers* (Toronto, ON: Family Service Ontario, 1996) Chapter 1.

14 *Substitute Decisions Act*, 1992, c.30, s.45.

15 See, for example, Ontario Ministry of the Solicitor General and Correctional Services, "Implementation of the 'Interim Accountability and Accessibility Requirements for Male Batterer Programs'"(Toronto: Ministry of the Solicitor General and Correctional Services, March 1994); "A Review of Standards for Batterer Intervention Programs" in the US. http://www.vaw.umn.edu/vawnet/standard.htm.

16 Sandra Kopels, "Confidentiality and the School Social Worker," *Social Work in Education* 14.4 (October 1992): 203–04.

17 Sidney Kardon, "Confidentiality: A Different Perspective," *Social Work in Education* 15.4 (October 1993): 249.

18 Applewhite and Joseph 289.

19 The information on the case was summarized from Frederic G. Reamer, *Social Work Malpractice and Liability: Strategies for Prevention* (New York, NY: Columbia University Press, 1994).

[20] Frank Bruni, "Child Psychiatrist and Pedophile," *The New York Times* 19 April 1998: 35, 40.

[21] C.D. Kain, "To Breach or Not To Breach: Is That the Question? A Response to Gray and Harding," *Journal of Counseling and Development* 66.5 (1988): 224–25.

[22] A.K. Harding, L.A. Gray, and M. Neal, "Confidentiality Limits with Clients Who Have HIV: A Review of Ethical and Legal Guidelines and Professional Policies," *Journal of Counseling and Development* 71.3 (1993): 297–305; Jill Donner Kagle and Sandra Kopels, "Confidentiality After Tarasoff," *Health and Social Work* 193 (1994): 217–22.

[23] F. Reamer and S.R. Gelman, "Is *Tarasoff* Relevant in AIDS-Related Cases?" *Controversial Issues in Social Work*, ed. E. Gambrill and R. Pruger (Boston, MA: Allyn and Bacon, 1997), 342–55.

[24] In Ontario this is required under the *Child and Family Services Act*.

[25] CASW Code of Ethics, Limits on Professional Relationship 4.0: 13.

[26] NASW Code of Ethics, Ethical Standard 1.06 (c): 6.

[27] Frederic G. Reamer, *Tangled Relationships: Managing Boundary Issues in the Human Services* (New York, NY: Columbia University Press, 2001) 194.

[28] Ofer Zur, "Guidelines for Non-Sexual Dual Relationships in Psychotherapy," http:drzur.com/dualrelationships.html; see also Arnold Lazarus and Ofer Zur (eds.), *Dual Relationships and Psychotherapy* (New York, NY: Springer, 2002).

[29] Karl Tomm, "The Ethics of Dual Relationships," Lazarus and Zur 33; emphasis in original.

[30] Miriam Greenspan, "Out of Bounds," Lazarus and Zur 427.

[31] Reamer, *Tangled Relationships* 15.

[32] M.C. Gottlieb, "Avoiding Dual Relationships: A Decision-making Model," *Psychotherapy* 30.1 (1993): 41–48. Also available at http://kspope.com/gottlieb.html.

[33] Solomon and Dudley 23.

[34] In the spring of 1997 Jordan Heikamp, 4 pounds, six ounces, was born to a 19–year-old single woman. Thirty-five days later he died of starvation while living with his mother at a shelter for Aboriginal women and under the supervision of the Toronto Catholic Children's Aid Society. He was 4 pounds, 2 ounces. Both his mother, Renee Heikamp, and the social worker, Angie Martin, were charged with criminal negligence causing death. The case was dropped due to insufficient evidence. On April 11, 2001 the Ontario coroner's jury ruled that his death was homicide; however, no one was prosecuted.

[35] Jill Donner Kagle, "Record Keeping in the 1990s," *Social Work* 38.2 (March 1993): 190–96.

[36] "Child Welfare Time Lost on Paperwork, Report Says," *Globe and Mail* 25 February 2002: A1.

[37] Malcolm Payne, "The Code of Ethics, the Social Work Manager and the Organization," *A Code of Ethics for Social Work: The Second Step*, ed. David Watson (London: Routledge and Kegan Paul, 1985) 104.

[38] Marge Reitsma-Street and Jennifer Keck, "The Abolition of a Welfare Snitch Line," *The Social Worker* 64.3 (Fall 1996): 35–66.

[39] CASW, *Social Work Code of Ethics*, Section 10 (Ottawa, 1 January 1994) 24; NASW Code of Ethics, Section 6.0.

[40] Stanley Witkin, "If Empirical Practice is the Answer Then What is the Question?," *Social Work Research* 20.2 (June 1996): 73.

CHAPTER 6

THE HELPING PROCESS: ASSESSMENT AND INTERVENTION

S ocial workers practice in varied and diverse settings such as family agencies, hospitals, prisons, schools, group homes, shelters, and community centres. Regardless of the practice setting, the social worker engages in a helping process with individuals and their families and, in most cases, assesses the situation, resources, and support networks; negotiates a plan of action or therapeutic contract; and offers support in the work ahead.

Agency Context

Whatever the practice context, it is essential that the setting be accessible with enough space to offer privacy and a certain degree of comfort. An inviting and inclusive atmosphere can be created in an agency by providing coffee, tea, or water; arranging comfortable chairs in conversational settings; decorating the space with plants and pictures; and offering information on community resources in various languages. For example, placing a rainbow flag in an agency window and arranging a display of pamphlets, magazines, newspapers, and notices that address concerns of gay men and lesbian women communicates that gay and lesbian persons are welcome and that culturally sensitive services are located there. Similarly, an assortment of toys, books, and drawing supplies will help keep a small child entertained and be welcomed by parents looking for help.

Individuals and families approach social work agencies when they do not have the personal or material resources to adequately respond to difficulties on their own or when they are legally mandated or directed to seek professional assistance. They do not make a decision to seek help easily and often are tense and apprehensive on arrival at the agency. Asking for assistance and revealing intimate and personal information to a complete stranger is intimidating and difficult for most people. Therefore, since the receptionist is the first contact for individuals and their families, he or she ought to be welcoming and respectful.

Personal and Political Tuning-In

Tuning-in is a preparation process by which the social worker gets in touch with personal biases, feelings, and concerns regarding the person(s) and problem situation. William Schwartz introduced the term "tuning in" as an approach for developing preparatory empathy.[1] Anticipation of how the interview may unfold can prepare the social worker to be a more sensitive listener and effective practitioner.

The effectiveness of the tuning-in process and the intervention that follows will be enhanced by a general understanding and knowledge of a person's experiences as they relate to ethnic/cultural background and customs, geographical setting(s), and the person's overall social and economic position in society. Faith Nolan emphasizes the importance of such an understanding in her song "If you don't know my people, you don't know me."[2]

For example, when providing help to an Aboriginal person, it is important to have a general knowledge about the history of Aboriginal people in Canada, the effects of colonization, and the ongoing struggle to reclaim languages and culture. If a social worker is about to see a Somali family recently arrived in Canada, the tuning-in process may include thinking about the traumatic conditions under which many people fled Somalia and the difficulty in adapting to a new culture and country, one which at times may not be very welcoming.

Helping is not a neutral act. Social workers, like other professionals, have likely developed biases and internalized the dominant messages embedded in the institutional fabric of our society. If social workers do not challenge the existing social structures and exploitative social relations, they implicitly support and maintain them. In cases of woman abuse, the concept of neutrality clouds the fact that abusive men frequently deny and/or minimize the forms of power and control they exert over their partners and poses the risk that the social worker will collude with the man in implicating the woman in her own battering.[3]

During the tuning-in process, social workers reflect on their own professional skills and experience and on personal factors such as ethnicity/race, gender, sexual orientation, and age. Reflecting on the differences and commonalities between oneself and the person one is about to see prepares one to effectively respond to possible difficulties and to build a connection. For example, while some people may feel more comfortable initially with a social worker who shares a similar culture and background, they may also feel anxious about disclosing personal information to someone from the same cultural community.

Individuals and families may seek assistance with varying degrees of ambivalence. "A part of the person is always reaching out for growth and change," explains Lawrence Shulman, "but another part is pulling back and holding onto what is comfortable and known."[4] While people want to move ahead to confront difficulties and to make changes in their lives, they may be reluctant to discuss the details of situations that they find painful. They may be embarrassed and not know even how to begin explaining their situation to a stranger and may be fearful that the social worker may not understand them and will blame them for their difficulties. It is likely that these doubts and fears may be more prevalent among members of marginalized groups who have experienced alienating circumstances.

The Helping Relationship

All social work helping takes place in the context of a therapeutic relationship between the social worker and the client. The social worker who is most likely to develop a positive relationship is one who is "respectful, attentive, interested, caring, trustworthy, friendly, genuine, unpretentious, sympathetic, warm, concerned, empathetic, accepting, compassionate, understanding, supportive, reassuring, patient, comforting, solicitous."[5] Shulman stresses the importance of authenticity and being a real person. "As we demonstrate to our clients our humanness, vulnerability, willingness to risk, spontaneity, honesty, and our lack of defensiveness (or defensiveness for which we later apologize), we will be modeling the very behaviours we hope to see in our clients."[6] These qualities contribute to an effective working alliance in which the client has the opportunity to explore the issues that are of concern and to receive support and resources to make the necessary changes.[7]

The first few minutes of the initial meeting are very important ones in the development of the relationship. During the greeting and introductions, the client will be closely observing to see whether or not the social worker is someone whom she can trust to help her. Therefore, rather than wait for the person or family to be ushered into the office by a secretary, it is preferable that social workers go to the waiting area, introduce themselves, warmly greet clients, and invite them in. The social worker who is seeing a family can begin by connecting with each person, finding out their names and what they would like to be called, and taking time to learn the correct pronunciation.

The client/worker relationship is unequal since social workers practice from a position that carries legal as well as professional influence, authority, and power. People are coming in search of help and, in order to be considered eligible for much-needed resources, must disclose personal information and open their lives to the scrutiny of the social worker and the state. A social worker's position constantly signals that she is the expert with power to deny resources and make judgments. At times, however, the client's situation requires that the social worker take on control functions and make decisions that are counter to what the client wants but are in the best interests of more vulnerable members of the family and/or the wider community.

The goal is to create a relationship based on dialogue and in which the helping relationship is demystified, the social worker's power is diminished, and the client's power is increased. Using a first name, soliciting and respecting the client's views, providing information, and working in partnership can all assist in reducing, as much as possible, the social worker's power.

Clarifying The Social Work Role and the Process of the Interview

Usually in the first interview, after the introduction, a social worker informs the client about the agency and what can be expected from the service provided: "Before I begin to hear from you about your concerns, I would like to take some time to discuss the agency, how we work, and what you can expect from us." The social worker then describes his or her role in the agency and, if appropriate, provides information about the agency, the resources available, and the client's rights and entitlements. This is particularly important when working with people who are newcomers to Canada and who may not be accustomed to seeking help outside the family for personal issues. Clients ought to be informed about the records that will be kept on the service provided and the access that they will have to their files. An opportunity for questions should be provided, and the use of jargon and complex terminology avoided.

The service contract is the initial agreement that clarifies the agency's obligation and the relationship of the client with the agency. The client is told about the length of each appointment, the fees for service, and the agency's hours and relevant policies. The service contract is usually completed at the time of intake or prior to the first interview.[8] The limits to confidentiality must be discussed with the client early in the interview (see Chapter 5).

Once these preliminary matters are discussed, the process of assessment begins. The social worker begins with a short summary of what is known about the situation and invites the person to begin to talk about why she is seeking help at this time. The social worker may say something like "The intake worker has indicated that you have come for some help to cope with a recent divorce. Where would you like to begin?" Or, if meeting with a couple or family, the social worker could say "Who would like to begin?"

The Assessment

The primary task of the first interview is to become familiar with the situation facing the person or family and to initiate a problem-solving process. The social work assessment begins during the first few minutes of contact and may take place on the phone, face-to-face during a scheduled appointment, or during a crisis situation; it can take from 15 minutes to more than an hour. The assessment process will vary depending on the practice setting and whether the social worker is meeting with one person, a couple, or a family.

The social worker provides an opportunity for the person to tell his story in order to gain an understanding of his situation and difficulties, as well as his resources and strengths. The social worker has the responsibility for respectfully guiding the interview and maintaining a focus on the purpose, whether it is to explore a young person's difficulty with drug overuse or to assess the ability of an elderly person to live independently. Individuals often find that it is difficult to invite a complete stranger to listen to the private and personal details of their lives. The interview belongs to the one receiving the help, not to the one giving it, and it is important that social workers "begin where the client is" and respond to the client's concerns. While this seems obvious, in his research Lawrence Shulman found that workers related to client's concerns only 60 per cent of the time.[9]

Although assessments may vary depending on the practice setting, there are a number of tools that are useful in gathering information and in situating the person and his or her concerns. While an assessment tends to take place at the beginning of the process, in fact it continues throughout. The process of helping consists of assessment and action, action and reflection, and again assessment. While there is a tendency to focus on gaining a history of "the problem" during the assessment phase, it is equally important to identify strengths and focus on solutions, those which have been successful in the past and those that might be possible in the future. A social worker's analysis of the difficulties facing the clients who come to the agency guides both the assessment and the intervention. How a social worker views the situation is reflected in the questions she poses and the direction the interview takes. At some point while seeing an individual, the social worker may suggest that friends or family members be included. This is usually the case when the difficulty and/or solution involves others.

During the assessment, the social worker gains entry into the lives of troubled individuals and families. We all have intimate knowledge of at least one family, the family or families in which we have lived or are currently living. One of the best ways to begin to understand family structure and family functioning in light of social, political, and economic conditions, is for social workers to spend some time reflecting on their own families or a family grouping with which they are intimately acquainted. This process of examining their own family can prepare them to understand individuals and families who will come to them for help (see Appendix D).

Human Needs and Human Rights

Often the difficulties that individuals and families are experiencing are related to basic human needs: *material needs* for food, clothing and shelter; *social and psychological needs*, such as loving and respectful social relationships, a sense of belonging and acceptance, and a sense of self-worth; *productive needs*, such as meaningful work and opportunities to contribute to society; *safety needs*, which include living without fear for one's life and a high degree of uncertainty; *self-actualization needs*, which involve developing one's potential.[10] These needs are interrelated and connected. In Canada, a family that lacks the "basic needs" (food, shelter, and clothing) is considered to be living in poverty.[11]

However, attention to human needs without also considering human rights is a shortcoming in social work approaches.[12] Both David Gil and Stanley Witkin refer to the 1948 *Universal Declaration of Human Rights*, adopted by the United Nations, which includes social, political, and economic rights. A discussion of human rights situates human needs within a political context. "Everyone has a right to a standard of living adequate for the health and well-being of himself and his family, including food, clothing, housing, and medical care and necessary social services, and the right to security in the event of unemployment, sickness, disability, widowhood, old age or other lack of livelihood in circumstances beyond his control" (*Universal Declaration of Human Rights*, Article 25.1, Appendix A).[13] An understanding of poverty that holds that people have a *right* to food, clothing, and shelter has a different connotation than one that states that people *need* food, clothing, and shelter. Reference to need implies that people are somewhat responsible for their own situation and places them in a situation of asking for help. However, when we speak of rights, we begin to see the injustice inherent in the conditions facing people who come for help, and, along with providing immediate resources, we are also led to seek a political solution.

As social workers listen to the accounts of people and their life experiences, they can begin to assess the degree to which their human rights are being violated. The struggle to survive during social and economic crises can have an impact on one's relationships, health, and self-worth. Virginia Satir, a social worker and family therapist, suggested four areas of difficulties that can be experienced by troubled families,[14] areas that can be related to their basic human needs and rights. Below is an expansion of these four areas:

1. *Communication.* How do family members communicate with each other? How do they discuss differences and express anger, affection, joy, and sadness? How are decisions made?
2. *Links to and place in society.* How are family members connected to other people, institutions, and material resources? What is their social and economic position in society, their social class, ethnic background, and experiences of discrimination?

3. *Rules.* Within families there are expectations of behaviour. What are the family rules? Who makes them? Who enforces them? What happens when a member acts outside of the expectations? Identify rules which enforce inequality within the family.
4. *Self-worth.* How do family members think about themselves?

Assessment Format

Most agencies have a required format for documenting demographic data and conducting an assessment of the presenting concern. Closely adhering to the agency format and asking question after question can appear bureaucratic and intrusive and result in a scripted and mechanical interview. An alternative is for the social worker to become familiar with the areas that are to be covered and to proceed in a more spontaneous and responsive manner. The social worker can notify the client that questions will be asked in different areas in order to understand the situation and that a few notes may be taken during the interview. Although the assessment can vary greatly, information is generally gathered in the following areas.

1. Presenting concerns. The social worker begins by gaining an understanding of the reasons the client has come for help at this time. This involves exploring how long the situation has been present and the attempts at solving it. Often such an inquiry highlights the person's strengths and resources and the times when the situation is better or non existent.[15]

2. Family and support network. Exploration of the client's support network is based on an inclusive definition of the "family." Families differ culturally and ethnically and include same-sex partners, as well as single parent mothers or fathers, who live with or without children. In a client's view the family may include extended family, friends, and any other persons to whom he or she is most closely connected. It is important not to assume that a client is heterosexual because he or she has children. The assessment tools described below (see pp. 120–23) are useful in constructing visual maps of the client's networks and the nature of the relationships.

3. Immigration/refugee conditions, and status. All families have a cultural heritage and, unless of Aboriginal origin, have a history of immigration to Canada. People entering Canada as Convention refugees have left their country of nationality because of fear of persecution for reasons of race, religion, nationality, political opinion, or membership in a particular social group; they are eligible for government assistance upon settlement. These refugees have left war-torn countries and/or are fleeing persecution and may arrive with a history of torture and trauma and be divided from family members who have relocated to other countries. They may also have family members who remain in the home country or who have been killed.[16]

There are two general categories of immigration: economic and family. Those entering under an economic class must demonstrate that they are able to establish themselves successfully by having sufficient financial resources to either set up a business or to establish, purchase, or invest in a business. In the category of family class, a family member sponsors the person and signs a commitment to undertake financial responsibility for up to ten years. Landed immigrants are eligible to apply for citizenship after three years residence in Canada. People can also enter Canada with a student visa or employment visa, both of which are issued for a limited period of time under specific terms and conditions.

The immigration category offers important information regarding eligible resources and the stability of the person's status. Whether the immigration occurred in past generations or in recent years, the time, circumstances, and conditions of the client's relocation will help the social worker better understand the situation. Memories, history, and culture influence the daily lives of all family members. Inability to speak either English or French, essential for integration and full functioning in Canadian society, will impede the client from fully participating in daily life. Also, adaptation to a new country and culture is often easier for younger members of the family than the elderly.

4. Work and education. A person's education and work experience influences his or her ability to be economically secure, to connect with others, and to contribute to society. Inquire about paid and unpaid work. If the person is employed in the workforce, assess the nature of the work and the working conditions (hours of work, health and safety concerns, whether or not the job is unionized). In the case of unpaid work, explore the demands of domestic work and child and/or elder care. For students, inquire about academic and social performance in school.

5. Housing/living arrangements. Inadequate housing conditions can have a negative impact on social relationships, safety, and health. Are the living arrangements adequate, accessible, and affordable for all members of the family?

6. General physical and emotional health. At times a person or his or her family members may experience health problems or concerns. Do family members have nourishing food, adequate clothing, and money for medications and other health care costs, and do they live in a healthy environment? Does the client demonstrate any high-risk behaviours such as suicidal thoughts, eating disorders, overuse of alcohol or other drugs, and/or abusive and controlling actions?

7. Present or previous social work/ counselling services. It is not unusual for someone seeking help to be also receiving related services from another professional. If so, the social worker might suggest that the client consents to the sharing of information when it is necessary and beneficial.

8. Summary. The summary of the assessment clearly identifies the major areas of concern and recapitulates strengths, concerns, support system, and recommendations/action plan.

Assessment Tools

A number of assessment tools have been developed to assist people in discussing their family relationships, social networks, and major life events. The use of a family tree or genogram, ecological map (eco-map), social network map, and life line are helpful visual tools for assessment and intervention. They also become a valuable component of the client's record and can assist in communicating information to other service providers.

Family Tree/Genogram

The family tree or genogram is an assessment tool that assists in gathering and organizing information about family members. It provides a visual record of both the relationships of current family members who are living together as well as looking back over several generations and major life events such as retirement, immigration, marriages and divorces, and births and deaths. Over the years it has been widely used by practitioners in their work with both individuals and families. While it can be completed by an individual, family members find that documenting their history together is a particularly rewarding exercise.

There are standard symbols that have been used to communicate the social data collected in the genogram (Figure 6.1). Males are generally indicated by a square and females by a circle, and the birth date, age, occupation, and name of the person are placed in the centre. A straight line connects two people who are a couple. Separation is noted with one slash across the line, divorce by two slashes. Children are placed below their parents according to age with the oldest first. If there is conflict between two members, a squiggly line connects them. The death of a member is indicated with an X through the figure. Dates for life events such as deaths and marriages/partnerships can also be added. The family members who are currently living together are identified by placing a broken line around them.

FIGURE 6.1 The Family Tree/Genogram

Anna Wiley is the sole parent of 3 children, ages 15, 12, and 8. She has come to the Family Service Agency to get help with discipline and parenting of her children. The 15-year-old daughter Laurie refuses to listen to her and is influencing her 12-year-old brother Jeff to do the same. Laurie is also overusing alcohol and doing poorly in school. The 8-year-old daughter, Krista, is very close to her mother and does not get along with either her brother or sister

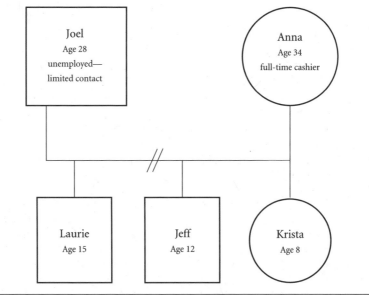

The genogram can be adapted to best illustrate the complexity and diversity within families and provides a visual understanding of family structure, including alliances and tensions among family members. For example, if there has been illness in the family, the health conditions of family members can be added and will enhance awareness of the stress on the family, as well as the possibilities of common sources for the illness, whether genetic or environmental. The genogram can also emphasize existing and potential resources and the strengths of the family members by shifting attention away from the nature of the current difficulties to an exploration of the possible solutions.[17]

Ecological Map

The eco-map was developed by Ann Hartman in the late 1970s as a visual tool to situate and record individual and family relationships within a social context.[18] This tool assists social workers during assessment and intervention in exploring how a family is connected to others on a regular basis. The symbols of the genogram are used to depict the immediate family

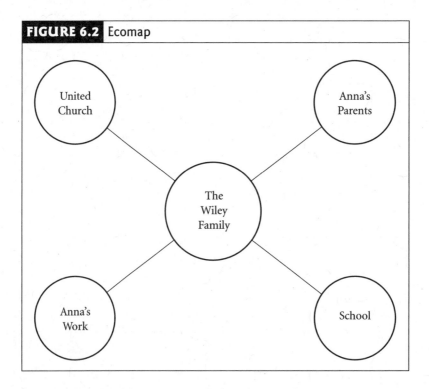

FIGURE 6.2 Ecomap

members. The nature of the relationship, whether conflictual and stressful or supportive, is indicated with broken lines or solid lines accordingly.

The completed eco-map provides a snapshot of the family and can have an impact as members see either their isolation and lack of a support network or the family and friendship networks available to them.

Social Network Map

Similar to the ecological map, the social network map was developed as part of a family support research project in order to collect information on the extent of the person's network, the support provided, and the nature of the relationships.[19] While the eco-map depicts the family's relationships with individuals outside of the family unit, it is often difficult to determine the function of these relationships. The social network map gathers information on members of the person's network in seven areas: (1) those living in the household; (2) other family members and relatives; (3) friends; (4) colleagues from work or school; (5) people from recreational, social, and religious groups/organizations; (6) neighbours; and (7) other social agencies. The length and closeness of these relationships and the degree to which they offer support should also be recorded.

Life Line

A life line records major life events organized chronologically on a horizontal line. This visual tool invites a person or family to explore and assess their situation and to understand how events in their lives have been supportive and/or challenging. The life line in Figure 6.3, illustrates a

FIGURE 6.3	The Life Line			
Parents divorce	Mother is Depressed	Move to Timmins	Mother has new partner	Move to Ottawa
Age 10(1997)	Age 12 (1999)	Age 13 (2000)	Age 14 (2001)	Age 15 (2002)
Living with mom, limited contact with dad.	On my own a lot.	New school and friends, some alcohol use, angry outbursts, conflict with mom, grades slipping.	Isolated, alcohol use ++, trouble sleeping, failed grade 8	Anxiety attacks, Hanging out with rough crowd, bullying.

chronological accounting of major events in the life of a troubled adolescent. Laurie, age 15, was referred to the school social worker by her teacher because she was failing her courses and was angry and aggressive in her interactions with peers. During the first meeting Laurie began talking about how her life "sucks" and that it started falling apart five years ago.

Constructing a life line with Laurie helped both her and the social worker document the major events in her life and quickly highlighted how she had coped with many stressful changes. After her father left and ceased contact and as she and her mother kept moving, Laurie said that she started to shut people out. She found it too painful to get close only to be hurt again. As the interview continued, Laurie also talked about how her use of alcohol had increased and that she had trouble sleeping and was experiencing anxiety attacks. These were all placed on the life line so that the progression could be recorded. It became clear to Laurie that some of her survival strategies were now working against her.

The Contract

In most helping relationships, a therapeutic contract is useful in guiding the helping process by identifying realistic and achievable goals. It becomes a working tool that is referred to and changed over the course of the helping relationship. Once the initial assessment is completed, the therapeutic contract or counselling plan is developed to guide the work to follow towards specific concerns and goals.[20] For example, Laurie identified four major concerns on which she wanted to work. While she recognized that her use of alcohol was a problem, she was not prepared to stop completely, since she relied on it to help her sleep and to calm her nerves. The social worker agreed to her plan to cut down and monitor her use. They also discussed whether the inability to accomplish this goal meant that she needed to quit entirely. The social worker and Laurie discussed how the alcohol use was a strategy to respond to her other problems, but that alcohol can also contribute to sleep disturbances, anxiety, and aggressiveness. Laurie also wanted to get closer to her mother and hoped to improve her school performance.

FIGURE 6.4 The Contract		
Concern/Problem	Goals: What you would like to happen	The Plan: Steps/Action Outcome
Overuse of alcohol.	Cut down.	1. Not drink from Monday–Thursday 2. No more than two drinks at a time. 3. Keep a journal.
Not spending time with mother.	Have more time together.	1. Plan two activities each week-end. 2. Share a meal together each evening.
Trouble sleeping.	Sleep at night.	1. Walk home from school. 2. Go to bed at 10 p.m.
Failing grades.	Pass her courses.	1. Speak with the teacher. 2. Go to all the classes. 3. Do homework.

When clients are mandated by law to receive social worker services, the development of the therapeutic contract becomes more difficult. Social workers often are placed in positions of policing and controlling clients in order to protect the most vulnerable members of society or the clients themselves.[21] This is the case for social workers who work with children in need of protection, women who are abused, men who are violent, and clients who are suicidal or homicidal. In such situations, the unnegotiable aspects of the contract such as reporting to a probation officer need to be openly discussed.

Scaling questions are useful for evaluating progress and determining outcomes for the agreed-upon goals. For example, the person could be asked to indicate on a scale of zero to ten, where zero is terrible and ten is terrific, how they would rate the progress that they have made on each of their goals. The meaning of the numerical indicator is then explored. What happened or did not happen to produce a three? As a way of building on strengths, the person could be asked what they did to not slide to zero.

Ending the Interview

It is useful to allow from 10 to 15 minutes at the end of the interview for winding down and summarizing the concerns that have been raised, the plan of action, and the next steps. The social worker can alert the client that the interview is coming to the end by saying "In the 15 minutes remaining, I would like to summarize what we have accomplished and where we go from here." This is also a time for both the person and the social worker to reflect on the interview and evaluate the time spent together. At times, a person may disclose a new concern just as the interview is closing. If the social worker determines that it is not an urgent issue, it is still important to validate the concern and place it on the agenda for next time. For example, the following response is appropriate: "You have just raised a very important issue, and we don't have the time to talk about it. I think you have made a good start in raising it now, and we can begin there at the next meeting."

If the initial interview and assessment have been successful, the client ought to leave feeling supported and understood, less overwhelmed, and more hopeful. If this is the case, the helping relationship is off to a good start.

NOTES

1   Lawrence Shulman, *The Skills of Helping: Individuals, Families, and Groups* (Itasca, IL: F.E. Peacock, 1992) 56. Shulman provides a number of examples of tuning in.
2   Faith Nolan, "Nobody Knows My People," *Africville*, 1986.
3   Deborah McIntyre, "Domestic Violence: A Case of the Disappearing Victim," *Australian Journal of Family Therapy* 5.4 (1984): 253.
4   Shulman 105.
5   Alfred Kadushin and Goldie Kadushin, *The Social Work Interview: A Guide for Human Service Professionals*, 4th ed. (New York, NY: Columbia, 1997) 103.
6   Shulman 27.
7   One of the most comprehensive texts on the social work relationship is by Helen Harris Perlman, *Relationship: The Heart of Helping People* (Chicago, IL: University of Chicago Press, 1979).
8   Juliet Cassuto Rothman, *Contracting in Clinical Social Work* (Chicago, IL: Nelson-Hall, 1998).
9   Shulman 114.
10 Adapted from Chapter 10, "Intermediate Needs," of Len Doyal and Ian Gough's *A Theory of Human Need* (New York, NY: Guilford Press, 1991) 191–221; A. Maslow, *Toward a Psychology of Being* (New York, NY: Van Nostrand, 1962). Maslow's framework for understanding human needs and his five levels of basic human needs required for healthy functioning (physiological,

safety, love and belonging, self-esteem, and self-actualization), are well-known to human service workers. Maslow believed that a person's most basic physiological needs had to be met before
the others could be fulfilled.

[11] Any family spending 56 per cent of gross income on the basic necessities (food, shelter, and
clothing) is considered poor. Kazemipur and Halli 19.

[12] Stanley L. Witkin "Human Rights and Social Work," *Social Work* 43.3 (May 1998): 197–201;
David G. Gil, *Confronting Injustice and Oppression: Concepts and Strategies for Social Workers*
(New York, NY: Columbia University Press, 1999).

[13] The reference only to the male gender reflects the time period in which the document was
created.

[14] Virginia Satir, a social worker and family therapist, emphasized the importance of communication in influencing and resolving family difficulties. Her "growth model," influenced by
humanistic psychology and the work of Fritz Perls, Carl Rogers, and Eric Berne, avoided
labelling and diagnostic categories. She influenced many social workers during the 1970s,
including Maurice Moreau. See for example, Virginia Satir, *Peoplemaking* (Palo Alto, CA:
Science and Behavior Books, 1972).

[15] Steve de Shazer, et al., "Brief Therapy: Focussed Solution Development," *Family Process* 25.2
(1986): 207–21.

[16] Convention refugees meet the definition of "refugee" in the UN Convention Relating to the
Status of Refugees, which has been incorporated into the Immigration and Refugee Protection
Act. See Citizen and Immigration Canada at http://www.cic.gc.ca.

[17] Marilyn R. Zide and Susan W. Gray, "The Solutioning Process: Merging the Genogram and
the Solution-Focused Model of Practice," *Journal of Family Social Work* 4.1 (2000): 3–19.

[18] Ann Hartman, "Diagrammatic Assessment of Family Relations," *Social Casework* (October,
1978): 465–76; Ann Hartman and Joan Laird, *Family-Centered Social Work Practice* (New York,
NY: The Free Press, 1983). The eco-map is found on page 160.

[19] Elizabeth M. Tracy and James K. Whittaker, "The Social Network Map: Assessing Social
Support in Clinical Practice," *Families in Society: The Journal of Contemporary Human Services*
(October, 1990): 461–70.

[20] Gilbert Greene, "Using the Written Contract for Evaluating and Enhancing Practice
Effectiveness," *Journal of Independent Social Work* 4.2 (1990): 135–55.

[21] Wise 236–49.

CHAPTER 7

FACILITATING EMPOWERMENT AND CHANGE

S ocial workers endeavour to guide clients in a helping process that will lead to empowerment and change. As the previous chapters have emphasized, social work practice is informed by ideology, values, and theories and is guided by ethical and legal considerations. In this chapter we focus on a structural approach with its various practice elements and skills that promote individual and social change through a process of empowerment.

Social workers, for the most part, offer help to people who are experiencing a loss of control over their lives, are isolated and marginalized, and often need basic resources. Those coming for help may not have adequate housing or sufficient food and may experience despondency and a loss of dignity as they unsuccessfully search for employment. Others may live in fear and uncertainty as they face violence in their personal lives and/or encounter institutional and personal forms of racism, homophobia, and sexism. There are also those who are coping with physical or mental health concerns.

Empowerment

Although the term "empowerment" is thought to have been introduced by Barbara Solomon in her 1976 book *Black Empowerment: Social Work in Oppressed Communities*, the concept has a century-long tradition in the field.[1] Currently, the term is widely used and has been incorporated into the lexicon of most practice approaches. At times it is even referred to as a distinct practice approach.[2]

Within a structural approach to social work practice, empowerment is viewed as both a goal and process and has an action component. The concept refers to the act of acquiring a critical awareness of one's situation and an increased capacity to act on that awareness. This process helps a person to gain a greater degree of control over his or her life through personal and social change. The action component is important since awareness on its own without action can leave people feeling despondent.

Power and Powerlessness

Since power is defined as "the capacity to influence the forces that effect one's life space for one's own benefit,"[3] then powerlessness can be understood as the inability to directly influence one's life. Prolonged periods of powerlessness often can result in an oppressed consciousness or a "colonization of the mind," through which individuals understand themselves and their troubles as those in power define them. If someone is a member of a group that has been historically and/or systematically exploited and discriminated against, there is the possibility that he or she may to varying degrees internalize the damaging messages and in the process feel powerless to change the situation. Sustained feelings of powerlessness, uncertainty, and loss of control over decisions that influence one's life create high levels of damaging stress that impact negatively on mental and physical health. "Chronic stress is expected to increase the rate of premature death directly through the immune and neuroendocrine systems and indirectly through adverse behavioural responses such as smoking, excessive drinking, and violence."[4]

Awareness of the impact that stress can have on an individual can be achieved by remembering a personal experience of powerlessness. For instance, sometimes one can feel that decisions have been made without one's own input, or errors have been made by others that have made one's life difficult, or that a misunderstanding has occurred with no opportunity to offer clarification. One can ask the following questions: "What was I thinking at the time? What was I feeling? What changes in my physical health and general functioning did I notice? What did I do? In what way is this situation of powerlessness structural or social in origin?"

Empowerment can involve both an individual and collective process. Many situations of powerlessness are based on structural problems and require collective solutions to promote social change.[5]

The Change Process

The anticipated outcome of social work practice, whether with individuals, groups, families, or communities, is positive change. The challenge for social workers is to understand the broader political context and organization of society while responding directly to the immediate concerns and needs of those who seek help. This type of analysis focusses on the socio-economic or structural context of individual problems and the power arrangements and the economic forces in society that create and maintain social conditions that generate stress, illness, deprivation, discrimination, and other forms of individual problems. This means developing an awareness of the ways in which individuals and their families adapt and conform to their social and material conditions, as well as the ways they resist and challenge them.

In order to practice from a social change perspective, social workers must be critical thinkers and engage in exposing the contradictions between how things ought to be and how they are in reality.[6] If social workers fail to see the contradictions within agencies and the welfare state, they may question their abilities and those of the people they are helping.

For example, social workers in a child protection agency who felt that they were not coping adequately with their caseloads requested some skill-based continuing education workshops in order to increase their effectiveness. During the workshops, the social workers were asked to describe the nature of their work and their caseload. This exercise quickly revealed their vast experience and competence and brought into focus the conditions under which they were expected to work. Although they were responsible for an ever-expanding caseload of children and their families, they had few resources since many worked in isolation in remote areas. Not surprisingly, they had come to believe that they were at fault for being unable to cope with these difficult conditions. Through an exchange of information and experience, they gained a critical awareness of the context of their practice and developed both a greater sense of their competencies and an ability to act on their own behalf in order to gain more control of their working conditions.

Critical thinking of this nature contributes to an awareness of the conditions under which we all live day to day and the ways in which personal troubles are connected to broader social forces. As social workers engage in the helping process and utilize a critical analysis they make the connection between the material reality (economic, social, political, legal) and personal reality (self-concept, emotional life, personal troubles) of those seeking assistance (Figure 7.1).

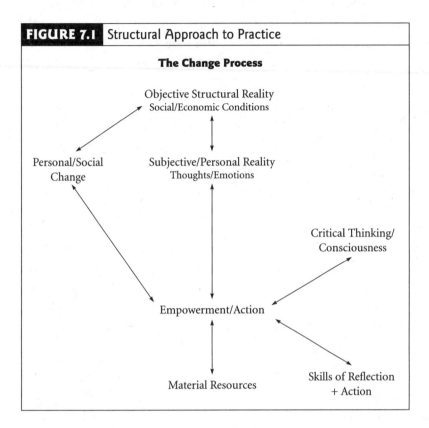

FIGURE 7.1 Structural Approach to Practice

The Change Process

Central to helping is an understanding of the influence of objective reality and social/economic conditions on one's subjective/emotional reality. Equally important is the role of ideology in shaping the way in which individual and social problems are perceived and defined by society, as discussed in Chapter 3. Also involved is a critical awareness of the role of social work and the delivery of social services and how they are situated within a political context.

Connecting the Structural and the Personal

There is a direct connection between people's economic and social position in society and their emotional and physical health. Poverty, gender, and racial discrimination contribute to a sense of profound alienation, "a pervasive tendency to feel estranged from—rather than a part of—one's work, other people, the established society, and aspects of oneself."[7] Living with the reality of economic uncertainty produces stress in people's lives. Lillian Rubin, in her study of working-class families, documents how parents struggle to nurture and maintain family members. She found that the lack of both time and money "combine to create families that are both frantic and fragile."[8] While families offer emotional as well as material support to their members, at times they are also the source of tension, stress, violence, and neglect.

It is then reasonable to expect that the degree to which people are exploited and marginalized because of their status in society, based on factors such as social class, race, disability, gender and sexual orientation, influences the degree of oppression and alienation they experience.

> Oppression can be seen as taking two forms, both overlapping in an intricate weave. On the one hand, there's the external oppression of laws, institutions and other social structures that reinforce the principles of inequality—namely that certain people are inferior and therefore deserve less than their "betters." And on the other hand, there's internalized oppression in which we come to believe in our own inferiority, worthlessness and powerlessness, both as individuals and as a group. Whenever we act out negative messages against ourselves and each other, internalized oppression is at work.[9]

How a person sees herself reflected in society, whether in the media or in history books or among professionals such as teachers, doctors, and lawyers, has an impact on her perceptions of self-worth and ability. Stephen Rose reminds us that oppression is not some distant structure but integral to our social relations with others and is experienced in the activities of daily life.[10]

Whether situational or chronic, a high level of stress impacts negatively on general health and contributes to hypertension, depression, anxiety, and anger. Examining these "symptoms" of anxiety, sadness, and anger by exploring the context of peoples lives offers a clearer picture of the situation.

Miriam Greenspan examines how various practice approaches differ in their focus:

The traditional therapist listens for pathology. The humanist therapist listens for self awareness. The feminist therapist listens to the connection between the personal and political in women's stories.[11]

If the focus is on psychopathology and weaknesses, the tendency is to decontextualize client concerns and remove them from the social, political, and economic context in which they develop.[12] Central to the change process, as illustrated in Figure 7.1, is the client's empowerment, increased consciousness, and access to resources. As we gain a critical awareness of our situation, and have the necessary resources, we can act to change our circumstances, and, in the course of that activity, we become changed people. Or as Jeffry Galper said in 1975, "A new society will create new people, but must be brought about by people in the process of becoming new."[13]

Critical Thinking and Consciousness-raising

In his seminal work, *The Pedagogy of the Oppressed*, Paulo Freire introduces scholars and practitioners to the concept of conscientization, by which one becomes aware of, and resists, the social, political, and economic conditions that oppress people.[14] Without critical thinking, people often "view social changes or political decisions as somehow mystically removed from their own existence, they frequently turn inward, focussing exclusively on their private lives."[15] Generally, this is reinforced by traditional helping where client problems and behaviour are given diagnostic categories and viewed as pathological.[16] Once behaviour or problems are labelled in a way that emphasizes personal deficiency or malfunction, individuals are "treated" as ill, or less than whole, and can begin to feel unsure of themselves, perhaps assuming total responsibility for their situation. The process of consciousness-raising is fundamental in the work of moving from a position of powerlessness, internalized oppression, and alienation to one of empowerment and individual and social change. If people have internalized a view of themselves as not equal and not worthy, then it is likely that they will assume complete responsibility for the problem situation. Once they have a critical understanding of their situation, they are better able to engage in a process of individual change as well as confront the unjust and alienating circumstances of their lives.[17]

Our consciousness of who we are, in relation to others, is rooted in the social and material conditions in which we live.[18] Critical consciousness is essentially an educational process that helps individuals to uncover the source of their difficulties within the context of a dialogic relationship and a commitment to both individual and social change.[19] Consciousness-raising involves both reflection on and an understanding of dehumanizing social structures and includes action directed at changing societal conditions. Central to the consciousness-raising process is critical thinking, a way in which individuals situate the circumstances of their lives within the broader social context.[20] Such a process contextualizes the individual's experience and assists in reducing self-blame. Rather than emphasizing only personal and interpersonal dynamics, material conditions and social relations are also considered. It is a process whereby people develop sufficient trust to articulate their views about matters of personal concern, and then, through a dialectic expression of reflection and action, they relate these personal interests to similar concerns of others. The process of uncovering the nature of one's oppression and strengths is believed to increase self-concept and lead to empowerment. An awareness and understanding of daily events is energizing and can lead to organized resistance and social change.

The change and empowerment process, as outlined in this section, includes an education and critical thinking component, the connection of the personal and political, and the mobilization of material and interpersonal resources. Lee Staples adds that "the capacity for effective action is an essential component of any meaningful conceptualization of empowerment."[21]

Skills of Reflection and Action

While social workers practicing from a structural approach utilize many of the traditional helping skills, the goals of empowerment and reducing power between the social worker and person coming for help are foremost in their application. What follows are seven key helping skills that facilitate a process of empowerment and the engagement in individual and social change.

1. The Skill of Empathy

The skill of empathy—the ability to feel what the client is going through, to reflect upon the situation, and to communicate that understanding —has long been viewed as essential to the development of a helping relationship and involves both cognitive and emotional responses. It was initially identified with the client-centred counselling of Carl Rogers whose humanistic approach offered an alternative to Freudian psychology. Social workers, too, have recognized the importance of the skill of empathy. Thomas Keefe views it as central to a helping process that is liberating and empowering and believes that "critical consciousness grows from and requires empathy."[22] Recently, the skill of empathy has been extended to include the ability to empathize not only with the person individually but also with the social context of a person's experience. This skill—"social empathy"—was developed by Janis Fook, an Australian social worker, and requires a critical awareness of the social and economic context of a client's problem.[23] For example, in the case of newcomers to Canada, demonstrating knowledge about their country of origin and culture and the general difficulties that occur during the settlement process can offer reassurance that their particular concern is understood.

Empathic responses come most naturally after an expression of feeling or statement of fact. It is important that the social worker listen carefully and hear what the person is saying, asking for clarification and elaboration when necessary. The understanding is then reflected back to the client in brief statements. Often empathic statements begin with "I see that ...," "It sounds like ...," "You look ...," "You sound ...," "It's difficult to," and so on.

The following vignette illustrates how one moves from empathy to consciousness-raising.

Woman: Mike came home drinking. I was angry and asked him where he had been. We started to argue. He pushed me and I fell over the coffee table, hit my head, and fell to the floor. He was over me pulling my head up and banging it on the floor... I thought he was going to kill me.

Worker: How frightening! [empathic response, calm voice of concern]

Woman: I really should know better than to ask him where he's been when he's drinking.

Worker: As women we often take responsibility for the actions of others. I think that it is important to remember that no matter what you said or did he is responsible for his violence.

Here the social worker initially responds with empathy by acknowledgaing how fearful the woman must have been. In response to the woman's next comment, the worker shifts to helping the woman see that she is not to blame for her partner's abuse and thereby begins the process of consciousness-raising. The worker also normalizes the situation by using the phrase "as women we...." This connection also equalizes the power between them and normalizes the client's behaviour. The social worker could also reinforce the idea that the woman has a right to personal safety and could comment on the severity of the situation she has described.

Social workers often find that empathy for those who have harmed another person does not come easily. In these cases, it is helpful to empathize with the social and economic context of the person's life and gain an awareness of what the person is going through. The challenge is to communicate empathy while at the same time emphasizing accountability and responsibility.

2. Posing Relevant Questions

The helping process is guided by questions posed by the social worker. The questions assist the client to focus and tell his or her story, generate important information about the client's situation, and can influence the client to think about his or her situation in a different way. The choice of questions and tone of voice reflect the social worker's theoretical framework, the assumptions and ideology she uses to consider the client's situation. After all, how we understand the problem guides our response, our helping. However, the questions can either facilitate or halt the interview process. For example, if a social worker interviewing a woman who comes to the emergency room because she was raped asks "Why were you out so late?" and "Why did you ask him into your apartment?," she is implying that the woman is to blame for her situation. Such questions will create distance between the social worker and client, as well as be destructive to the helping process. It is preferable to avoid "why" questions because they sound, and often are, judgmental. What follows are some basic guidelines to posing questions that will move the interview along and contribute to an effective empowerment and change process.

While some closed questions may be necessary during the interview, generally open-ended questions generate a more detailed response that includes factual and emotional content. For example, "Is your job stressful?" may solicit a response such as "Yes" or "Isn't everyone's?" On the other hand, the client may respond to the question "Tell me a bit about the nature of your job—your working conditions?" by talking about job hours, shift work, colleagues and boss, stress, and fears about getting laid off in the next downsizing.

It is also important to avoid leading questions such as "You're not married, are you?" Such a question may deter someone from talking about an important relationship that does not have legal sanction. Better questions are "Do you have a partner?" or "Tell me about the people that are most important to you?"

Questions that are only problem-focussed and aimed at exploring individual deficiencies and limitations can leave the client feeling despair, whereas questions that assist clients in further understanding their situation and their individual and social resources can strengthen and empower them. Paulo Freire believes that people have the right to fully understand their environment —to go beyond "the *common sense* in order to discover the *reason* for the facts."[24] While it is common for people to fully accept their reality as "the way things are," at times they also think critically about their lives. Social workers can facilitate this process by posing critical questions to assist clients in uncovering truths and understanding the sources of their problems. The following situation illustrates a problem-posing question.

> During the Depression years of the 1930s, cookery classes were being organized for women in poor communities in an attempt to help them provide nutritious meals for their families despite their low incomes. One particular evening a group of women were being taught how to make cod's head soup—a cheap and nourishing dish. At the end of the lesson the women were asked if they had any questions. "Just one," said one member of the group, "whilst we're eating the cod's head soup, who's eating the cod?"[25]

The "critical question" posed by the woman in the class reflects honest questioning of the instructions she was receiving—she did not want to know how to do something without also understanding why she must do it in the first place. Her question has the potential of moving the discussion to a deeper level, which may assist in linking poverty to a broader context. A response to the question quickly uncovers structural inequalities and the inequitable distribution of the necessities of life. Such an awareness of the structural context assists both the social worker and the client in avoiding a victim-blaming response.

The Milan Associates, a group of Italian family therapists, based their approach on the concept of "new epistemology," understanding the knowledge and beliefs family members held rather than analysing their behaviour.[26] They introduced *circular questioning,* the use of questions which enable families to see their problems differently by highlighting differences among family members and clarifying relationships. For example, take a family in crisis: the father is overusing drugs, and the 17-year-old son wants to leave home, quit school, and find work. The social worker might ask, "Who would miss the son most if he were to leave home?" Or the father might be asked to describe the relationship between his son and daughter or to speculate how an absent member of the family might respond to the question.

Michael White introduced "landscape of action" questions to explore unique outcomes and shift away from "problem-saturated" stories that he believed got people mired in repeating mistakes. For example, he might pose the following series of questions to someone who has just made a change in his or her life: "Just prior to taking this step did you nearly turn back? If so, how did you stop yourself from doing so? Looking back from this vantage point, what did you notice yourself doing that might have contributed to this achievement?"[27] These questions promote identification of client strengths and strategies.

Similarly, coping questions, popular among solution-focussed practitioners, assist clients in exploring the factors that have contributed to a change that they have made.[28] Examples include: "How did you manage to reduce your drug use, what did you do?" or "It is wonderful that you and your daughter are talking more. How did that happen?"

3. Self-Disclosure/Sharing a View

Sharing a personal expression of the social worker's own feelings, ideas, attitudes, and experiences with the client often reduces the power differential and builds a more egalitarian relationship. An essential skill is for social workers to present themselves as real human beings, not clinical, detached, distant professionals. Such involvement and disclosure has been called "unprofessional" by more traditional workers; however, if we do not synthesize "professional" with "personal," spontaneity is lost, and we become robotic in our responses, mechanical social workers who fail to connect on a human level.

It is important to share perceptions without imposing them on the client. The purpose of offering a personal view should be for the benefit of the client, to contribute to problem-solving, empowerment, and lessening the distance between the social worker and the person seeking help. It can improve the client's self-esteem, validate the experience of someone who is seeking help, and/or offer an alternative way of understanding an issue. The focus remains on the client and his or her needs when social workers select what to disclose from their own experience.

In Larry Shulman's research on social work practice "sharing worker's feelings skills," and the direct expression of the worker's real feelings (anger, fear, love, and ambivalence) were rated the most important. Shulman suggests that this skill "effectively strengthens the working relationship (the process) while contributing important ideas for the client's work (the content)."[29] Self-disclosure can also collectivize dilemmas and foster hope. It is most effective if it is meaningful in both content and context.

4. Reframing/Restorying

Often people are constrained by the beliefs they have or the stories they carry. When someone is in the middle of the forest, only the surrounding trees are visible, not the entire area. Decisions are often made based on limited information and do not provide a complete understanding. Clients may be very hard on themselves for the situations they find themselves in. The social worker can engage the client in a process of reexamination, draw on the client's strengths, and offer another way a situation can be viewed (reframing). Suggestions ought to be made tentatively. For example, a social worker might say "Another way of looking at it might be ..." or "I see it as ..."

The following is an adapted example of reframing from an abused women's group.[30]

Woman: I am as much to blame for the violence. I help cover up for him by lying to his mom about my bruises.
Worker: What would happen if you told her the truth?
Woman: He'd get mad at me and beat me up again.

Worker: That's right. Your covering up for him was a way to help you survive.

Deconstructing, revisioning, and restorying has a similar outcome to reframing. The goal of narrative approaches is to help people become authors of their own stories and to deconstruct and revise old problematic stories. The premise is that people are troubled because "They continue to be constrained by the power of an old story that enabled them to survive what was then a harrowing childhood, but is of no value for adult living...."[31] Stories that are retold in the family often serve to keep the family history alive and speak to the strengths and limitations of the members and their place in the family. Unfortunately, in some cases, these stories are selective and damaging and do not reflect a person's potential.

Another popular technique among narrative therapists is to externalize conversation so that clients are encouraged "to provide an account of how the problem has been affecting their lives and their relationships."[32] In these conversations the problem is viewed as external to the person, not an intrinsic part of his or her identity; in the process, "the problem is to an extent disempowered, as it no longer speaks to persons of the truth about who they are as people, or about the very nature of their relationships."[33] The person is freed from the problem and is able to develop an identity separate from the problem. During this process, it is best if the externalization of the problem is put in the client's own words. For example, a client may refer to depression as "the blue meanies,"[34] waiting for a call as "life glued to the phone," or criminal behaviour as "career of crime." In some ways externalizing the problem and reframing assist the client to see the problem differently.

Deconstructing is a questioning of assumptions about traditional roles, practices, and beliefs, similar to the consciousness-raising widely used by the women's movement.

5. Identifying Strengths

There is a growing literature on strength-based, solution-focussed practice.[35] Identifying strengths and recognizing how people have coped with and survived difficult situations facilitates empowerment and change. In most cases, they have done the best they could given the available resources. In the following example, during the beginning of the interview a woman speaks of the years of abuse she endured at the hands of her husband. She speaks of how hard it was to keep going and be a mother to her three children.

> Woman: I don't know how I survived. You know, I've never been suicidal even after all I've been through....
>
> Worker: Well, you're a pretty amazing person to be going through all that and still be functioning and being a good provider for your children. Sounds like you're really there for them.

Later on, the woman wonders if her partner is serious about stopping the abuse. The social worker helps her to rely on her own knowledge.

> Woman: I'm battling between whether he's really changing or if he'll be abusive again ... like I'm worried and still afraid of him. Like I don't know if I should be scared of him ... I want to find out.
>
> Worker: What does your gut feeling tell you?
>
> Woman: I guess I'm not feeling sure about him.
>
> Worker: I think if you are feeling unsure it is important to pay attention to your feelings. You probably are the best person to know. And from what you have said, it sounds like you have recognized some controlling behaviour. Pay attention to things like that. I think it is always important to listen to yourself.

In this situation the social worker links current feelings and behaviour to the immediate context and encourages the woman to allow her own knowledge to guide her. In working with people who have experienced trauma, reach for the strengths that have supported their survival. Dr. Rosemary Meier, a psychiatrist who works with survivors of torture, suggests asking questions such as "Through all this, what sustained you, what kept you going?" or "You've obviously been through something I can hardly imagine, but I hear how you kept going and survived...."[36]

6. Communicating Effectively

Several communication skills are essential to a social worker in the task of helping clients "to tell their story." Listening to someone is an act of respect and acknowledgment and requires time, concentration, and a genuine interest and concern for the teller. Attentiveness and encouragement provide an atmosphere in which someone can feel comfortable expressing thoughts and feelings. Clients frequently have disturbing experiences and gauge the social worker's reaction and responses to what they are saying in order to determine if the social worker is prepared to hear the worst.

Providing an opportunity for people to talk about their situations, responding appropriately, and keeping a focus are the responsibility of the social worker. While there are a number of authors who address interviewing skills, one of the most comprehensive texts is *The Social Work Interview: A Guide for Human Service Professionals* by Alfred Kadushin and Goldie Kadushin. The following skills are among those they recommend in order to be an effective interviewer:

Exploring. As the interview progresses, social workers gather more specific information by exploring and asking for further details. Questions such as "How did you respond?," "And then what happened?," or "What did she say exactly?" move the interview along.

Clarifying. At times social workers will ask for clarification so that they can fully understand the situation. "When you say that she is out late all the time, what do you mean?" Reach for specifics behind the general comments: "Will you say more about that?"

Paraphrasing. When the person has given a detailed account of a situation, it is often useful to capture the main message by paraphrasing what you have just heard, including emotions. "Your son Tom has been getting more and more dependent on pot. It sounds like you are worried about both his drug use and his grades in school." When paraphrasing, it is important that the social worker not impose personal ideas and feelings.

Summarizing. As the interview moves from one area to another, it is useful to summarize before changing focus: "We just discussed the difficulties and stress associated with your job. You have identified how the long hours and unpredictable demands are affecting your health. Now I would like to focus a bit on your family life and relationship with your partner and children."

7. Presenting a Challenge

At times individuals may lack an awareness of the contradictions in their lives and the obstacles in their path to personal change. Challenging ought to take place only in a helping relationship in which the client feels understood and respected and can tolerate some discomfort. Since a challenge can be difficult for someone to hear, be direct, clear, constructive, and caring rather than punitive. Challenging brings the client face-to-face with reality and generally is used when there is a discrepancy between a client's comments and behaviour or what the client is saying and the social worker's perception of the experience: "Oh, I'm fine, just great" (while looking weary and tense). The social worker might respond, "I sense that it has been a difficult week for you."

In this example, a man in group session began to speak in abstract and general terms about why men are abusive. The group leader attempted to get him to focus:

Group leader:	Can I give you a suggestion: speak of your own experience rather than general information about men.
Group member:	OKAY I'll shut up if that's what you want.
Group leader:	Just a minute ... something just happened here. [Looking at other group members] Did I ask Joe to shut up?

Challenging comments that assist the person to take a closer look and reexamine beliefs and behaviours can be very effective. While the person may find it difficult to have an action or statement challenged, if done effectively, the result can promote critical awareness and growth. One man after leaving a group said, "I learned the most from what I liked to hear the least."

The empowerment and change process is the core of all social work intervention and is facilitated by a number of essential helping skills. The process that is suggested in this chapter can not only facilitate problem-solving, but also contributes to the development of a critical consciousness and client empowerment.

NOTES

[1] Barbara Bryant Solomon, *Black Empowerment: Social Work in Oppressed Communities* (New York, NY: Columbia University Press, 1976). Barbara Levy Simon has documented the history of the empowerment tradition in social work in her book *The Empowerment Tradition in American Social Work: A History* (New York, NY: Columbia University Press, 1994).

[2] Stephen M. Rose, "Advocacy/Empowerment: An Approach to Clinical Practice for Social Work," *Journal of Sociology and Social Welfare* 17.2 (1990): 41–51; Ruth J. Parsons, Lorraine M.

Gutierrez, and Enid Opal Cox, "A Model for Empowerment Practice," *Empowerment in Social Work Practice: A Sourcebook,* ed. Ruth J. Parsons, Lorraine M. Gutierrez, and Enid Opal Cox (Pacific Grove, CA.: Brooks/Cole Publishing, 1998) 3–51; Wes Shera and Lillian M. Wells, *Empowerment Practice in Social Work* (Toronto, ON: Canadian Scholars Press: 1999).

3 Elaine B. Pinderhughes, "Empowerment for Our Clients and for Ourselves," *Social Casework* (June 1983): 332.

4 North York Health Network, *Inequality is Bad for Our Hearts: Why Low Income and Social Exclusion are Major Causes of Heart Disease in Canada* (Toronto, ON: North York Health Network, 2001) 25. The full report can be found at http://www.yorku.ca/wellness/heart.

5 Lee H. Staples, "Powerful Ideas About Empowerment," *Administration in Social Work* 14.2 (1990): 37.

6 Stephen Brookfield, *Developing Critical Thinkers: Challenging Adults to Explore Alternative Ways of Thinking and Acting* (London: Jossey-Bass Publishers, 1987).

7 Arthur Maglin, "Alienation and Therapeutic Intervention," *Catalyst* 2 (1978): 70.

8 Lillian B. Rubin, *Families on the Fault Line: America's Working Class Speaks About the Family, the Economy, Race and Ethnicity* (New York, NY: Harper Collins, 1994) 101.

9 Pam Trevithick, "Unconsciousness Raising with Working-class Women," *In Our Experience: Workshops at the Women's Therapy Centre,* ed. Sue Krzowski and Pat Land (London: Women's Press, 1988) 72.

10 Stephen M. Rose, "Reflections on Empowerment-Based Practice," *Social Work* 45.5 (October 2000): 403–12.

11 Miriam Greenspan, *A New Approach to Women and Therapy,* 2nd ed. (Bradenton FL: Human Services Institute, 1993) 233.

12 Eleni E. Skodra, "Counselling Immigrant Women: A Feminist Critique of Traditional Therapeutic Approaches and Reevaluation of the Role of Therapist," *Counselling Psychology Quarterly* 2.2 (1989): 185.

13 Galper, *The Politics of Social Service* 185.

14 Freire, *Pedagogy of the Oppressed* 19.

15 Brookfield 54.

16 See, e.g., Mary Sykes Wylie, "Diagnosing For Dollars?," *Networker* (May/June 1995): 23–33, 65–69.

17 John F. Longres, "Marxian Theory and Social Work Practice," *Catalyst* 20 (1986): 30.

18 See, e.g., Leonard, *Personality and Ideology.* Peter Leonard places emphasis on the dialectical relationship between consciousness and material existence.

19 Scott Bock, "Conscientization: Paulo Freire and Class-based Practice," *Catalyst* 6 (1980): 5–25.

20 Brookfield.

21 Staples 38.

22 Thomas Keefe, "Empathy Skill and Critical Consciousness," *Social Casework* (September 1980) 393; Thomas Keefe, "Empathy: The Critical Skill," *Social Work* (January 1976): 10–14.

23 See Fook, *Radical Casework.*

24 Brenda Ball, John Gaventa, John Peters, Myles Horton, and Paulo Freire, *We Make the Road by Walking: Conversation on Education & Social Change* (Philadelphia, PA: Temple University Press, 1990) 157; emphasis in original.

25 Jennie Popay and Yvonne Dhooge, "Unemployment, Cod's Head Soup and Radical Social Work," *Radical Social Work Today,* ed. Mary Langan and Phil Lee (London: Unwin Hyman, 1989) 140.

26 See, e.g., M. Selvini-Palazzoli, L. Boscolo, G. Cecchin, and G. Prata, *Paradox and Counter Paradox* (New York: Jason Aronson, 1978).

27 Michael White, "Deconstruction and Therapy," *Therapeutic Conversations,* ed. Stephen Gilligan and Resse Price (New York, NY: Norton, 1993) 41.

28 See, e.g., Insoo Berg, *Family-Based Services: A Solution-Focused Approach* (New York, NY: Norton, 1994).

29 Shulman, *The Skills of Helping* 137.

30 Pam A. Brown and Claire E. Dickey, "Facilitating Critical Thinking in an Abused Women's Group," *Proceedings* Eleventh Annual Symposium of the Association for the Advancement of Social Work with Groups, Montreal, 26–29 October 1989, 450.

31 Parry and Doan 40.

32 Michael White, *Re-Authoring Lives: Interviews and Essays* (Adelaide: Dulwich Centre Publications, 1995) 21.

33 White, *Re-Authoring Lives* 23.

34 Perry and Doan 87.

35 Steven de Shazer, *Keys to Solution in Brief Therapy* (New York, NY: Norton, 1985); M.D. Selekman, *Solution-Focused Therapy with Children: Harnessing Family Strength for Systemic Change* (New York, NY: Guilford Press, 1997); Berg, *Family Based Services.*

36 Karen Price (ed.), "Doing the Right Thing: Suggestions for Non-Medical Caregivers: An Interview with Rosemary Meier," *Community Support for Survivors of Torture: A Manual.* (Toronto, ON: Canadian Centre for Victims of Torture, n.d.) 82.

CHAPTER 8

USE OF GROUPS FOR EMPOWERMENT AND SUPPORT

G roup work is a powerful means for offering support, increasing awareness, and influencing change. The sense of belonging that develops in groups—the "we're all-in-the-same-boat" phenomenon—can be empowering. Members experience being part of a collectivity and come to realize that others not only share their struggles and experiences but can also offer assistance in finding solutions. As a result, problems become less overwhelming. For those who are isolated, alone, or marginalized, the group can offer a support network and a sense of hope.

Group work may combine the goals of individual change, mutual aid, and social change.[1] (The combination of mutual aid with a community development component is discussed in the next chapter.) It is an effective method for helping people with a variety of concerns, from healing from traumatic situations such as illness, a death in the family, or physical and sexual assault to addressing problems in professional and personal relationships. An increased awareness of one's situation and access to resources all contribute to problem-solving and empowerment. Group members, once they have gained a sense of competency, begin to make changes in their lives.

The role of the group facilitator is to create a process that encourages members to identify common ground and purpose and to respond to concerns raised in the group. The social worker's understanding of these concerns will be reflected in her responses, the issues she chooses to highlight or to set aside, and the various paths she suggests for resolution. She provides some of the structure and guidelines for the group as well as uses her knowledge and practice skills to situate the personal troubles of individuals within a broader context of social structures and unequal social relations based on class, gender, race/ethnicity, and sexual orientation.

Most people have been part of a group in school, the workplace, or the community. Some may recall a positive experience, while others may remember feeling misunderstood, anxious, and uncomfortable. Simply having people come together does not naturally create a supportive and therapeutic environment. All members entering a group bring with them differing viewpoints, biases, and ideas about the source of their concerns, possible solutions, and ideas about how the group will work. Facilitating a successful group takes careful planning.

Planning the Group

Usually the idea for developing a group emerges from a need that has been identified. In some cases an agency has a long-standing mandate and receives funding in specific areas, such as intervention for women who have been sexually abused as children or for men who are perpetrators of violence against their partners.

A social worker may recognize a common concern among those she is seeing on an individual basis and decide to invite them to meet as a group. For example, as a social worker in a community counselling centre, I noticed that several women were coming for help about how to live on their own for the first time in many years. They agreed to meet as a group and were open to inviting others as well. This resulted in an ongoing group for "Women Who are Alone" either by choice or circumstance. Members included women who had been recently widowed or separated. One woman came because her partner was dying and she wanted to prepare for being alone.

Personal Preparation

The social worker does not have to be an all-knowing expert with all the answers. While it is important to be responsive in an authentic way to the experiences being shared by group members, she is not expected to do this flawlessly. Larry Shulman, a seasoned group worker, believes that effective practice is "shortening the time between making and catching a mistake."[2] A belief in, and commitment to, the group process, as well as a willingness to risk and admit mistakes and to be fully present for group members are essential qualities for a group leader.

Group members often speak openly about their situation and the social worker's role is to join with them in trying to understand the problems they face and to search for solutions. While professional experience contributes to group work skills, the social worker's personal life experience is also important in responding to group members. "It is important that you acquire knowledge of how groups function, learn the necessary skills and techniques to implement your knowledge in actual group work, and do so in such a way that your techniques become an expression of your personal style and an extension of the unique person you are."[3]

At the time I facilitated the group for women living alone, I myself was a woman living on my own. While this was helpful, it was not necessary. However, in some situations, such identification is important; for instance, a gay or lesbian social worker is best suited to facilitating a group for gay or lesbian persons who are "coming out."

Group Structure

Some groups are closed: all its members come in at the same time and no new members are invited to join. The result is cohesiveness and a sense of safety, and it works well for those who feel particularly vulnerable and are struggling with sensitive concerns—for instance, survivors of violence such as childhood sexual abuse, woman assault, or torture. A fixed membership is also desirable for groups with an educational focus and a structured content delivered over a limited number of weeks. Groups to stop smoking and anger focus groups are examples of the latter.

Closed groups usually have a set time frame (eight to 12 weeks) with a planned agenda. The time boundary creates a sense of urgency and helps members focus quickly and maintain purpose and direction, although its closed nature means that members cannot be replaced if they drop out. In an open group, members enter and leave at different times. In residential settings, such as a group home or drug rehabilitation program, whoever is in residence is expected to attend the group.

Some groups for abusive men are open-ended and are up to 24 weeks in length. The content is planned in such a way that no matter when a man enters, he will rotate through all topic areas in the course of the six months. While new members are always being integrated into the group, its strength is in its older members who are there as role models and to challenge and offer feedback. Because many men who have been abusive tend to enter a group full of denial and minimizing the abuse they have done, it is very helpful for them to be challenged by other members.

Open-ended groups offer new members encouragement as they see others who have made important changes leave; some senior group members may achieve a sense of growth and accomplishment. However, for some, entering a pre-existing group may be stressful, and some existing members may resent time taken with a new member. One solution to these problems is to introduce three or four new members at a time so that they feel they belong to a cohort.

The frequency and duration of the group must be decided in advance. Many groups tend to meet weekly for two to three hours. In some residential programs, such as those for alcohol and other drug problems, groups often meet daily. Generally, groups for children are shorter in duration because of their limited attention span.

The size of the group depends on its purpose. Small groups of seven to ten members offer greater opportunity for individual work, while at the same time they have greater expectations for participation. Smaller groups are disadvantaged when members are absent. Large groups of 15 or more work well when the purpose is primarily educational.

While some groups are structured and cover particular content (abused women, drug addiction, or assertiveness training), others are more focussed on process and depend on the material that emerges from members. At any rate, groups tend to centre around a common need.

Group Membership

Often groups are organized around a common need or concern. Therefore, it is important to decide on the purpose of the group and on any restrictions on membership; for instance a group may consist of all women, women over 55 years of age, or lesbian women who are recovering from an addiction. The group may be for male survivors of childhood sexual abuse or for people who are living with HIV disease.

Group members who are diverse in regards to age, social class, gender, race, and ethnicity may have more difficulty coming together. However, sharing a common problem can minimize such differences, and "as a rule of thumb members usually tolerate and use greater diversity when common interests and concerns are expressed intensively."[4] While diversity is expected, it can be difficult if a group member is the only representative of a particular group—the only woman in a group, the only Aboriginal person, or the only gay man.

Once the structure of the group has been put into place, the next task is the recruitment of members. Potential participants ought to have information about the purpose of the group and the expectations for membership so that they can make an informed decision about attending. Members can be recruited from existing caseloads, from the agency as a whole, or from the community. For some groups, members are invited, while for others they are referred or decide on their own to join. In the case of abusive men, they are frequently mandated by the court to attend.

Often advertising assists with recruitment. For example, a notice announcing a group for men who are partnered with survivors of childhood sexual abuse can be placed on bulletin boards of a family agency. In this way, workers within the agency can refer prospective members from their own caseloads. Notices can also be placed in community centre newsletters or posted in the centres themselves. It is important to include all the relevant information so that someone can make an initial contact knowing the purpose of the group, the time and place, and cost, if any.

In situations where a particularly isolated population (i.e., sex trade workers, homeless youth at a drop-in) is to be reached, active recruitment might include personal contact. The provision of day care and/or transportation costs insure that low-income women and men will not be excluded.

Meeting individually with each prospective group member before the group starts can be helpful in clarifying both the structure and purpose of the group and expectations of membership. The individual meeting also provides an opportunity to assess the appropriateness and readiness of the person for group membership and whether or not the group will be able to meet his or her needs. During the interview the social worker can begin the therapeutic relationship by identifying the client's concerns, how these concerns have been handled, and what are the goals. During this time the social worker can address any special needs before the group meets. Pre-group meetings reduce anxiety, enhance participation, and prepare the member for the group.[5]

Limits to confidentiality ought to be clearly stated. It is helpful to have information about the group in writing and to offer information about the group leader(s). Potential members, having gained a sense of the leader's

personality and qualifications and the expectations about their participation, are better able to make an informed decision about joining.

In some settings, such as hospitals and residential programs, where
everyone in a particular unit/ward will be expected to attend the group,
pre-meetings will not be necessary.

Location and Time of the Group

Meeting with people in a familiar and convenient location can encourage
participation. The social worker may decide to hold the group in a local
community centre or within a major housing development. The building,
the group room, and the rest room ought to be wheel chair accessible. The
room itself should fit the size of the group, have comfortable chairs that
can be placed in a circle, and provide a quiet and private place to meet.

Evening groups are preferable for those who are working during the
day, while afternoon groups may suit those who are primary caregivers
of school-age children, are unemployed, or who work during the evening
or night. If meeting in the evening, women, the elderly, and people with
disabilities will appreciate a well-lit parking lot and entrance way and
attention to concerns regarding personal safety. The location should be
on regular bus routes.

Working With a Co-facilitator

Working with another person in the group, sharing responsibility for
responding to all issues that may arise, can be a source of support and
feedback. Also, co-leadership offers the assurance that groups will not
have to be cancelled if one of the group leaders becomes ill; in addition,
it provides excellent opportunities for training and skill development for
students and volunteers.

Two leaders offer alternate role models for group members. For example, it is recommended that groups for abusive men be co-led by a man
and a woman. Co-leaders who differ culturally will be able to offer diverse
perspectives and a welcoming environment. Also, when possible, "it is
helpful to a minority member to have at least one worker of similar sex
and/or ethnicity."[6]

Of course, matching leaders for groups requires some care. Qualities
such as mutual respect and trust are important for cooperative work,[7] as

are a common theoretical approach to the analysis of problems, approaches to group practice, and leadership styles. While co-facilitators do not need to be identical in their views, it is essential that they are complementary. A group leader who is highly directive and confrontational will not be well-matched with someone who is low-profile and interested in engaging group members.

Group leaders who work well together usually have established an excellent process of communication and clarity regarding the division of responsibilities and roles. It is important that both workers are committed to being involved in the myriad tasks and planning details required to insure a successful group. These include setting up the room, preparing materials, primary facilitating, post-group reflection and feedback, recording group notes, and follow-up of absent members.

Attending to Special Needs

Some members may require assistance in order to be full participants in the group. If using written materials, it is important to be aware of members who are illiterate, have low reading and writing levels, or whose first language is not English or French. On a number of occasions I have had members approach me outside the group, fearful that I will call on them to read something, or ask them to write on a flip chart, or complete written homework.

Written material should be clearly and simply written, and assistance should be provided outside the group to members who require it. Alternatively, films can be used to stimulate discussion and provide information. Popular education methods, such as having members draw a picture to describe something and then to speak from their drawing, are very effective.

Getting Started

Everyone participates in the first group session with a degree of dread, as well as a sense of excitement. Members wonder what will be expected of them and who the others are. A minority member may feel particularly vulnerable. It is likely that there will be distrust, defences, and a certain degree of caution. Often group leaders are apprehensive about their ability to facilitate a therapeutic group process. Certain tasks and aims are crucial to set the tone at the first meeting and to insure a sound beginning for the group.

Personal/Political Tuning-In

Before the group meets, the social worker engages in tuning-in to the personalities of the members, to the issue(s) they have in common, and into how group members may be feeling. If it is an ongoing group session, she reflects on the members and the previous work that has taken place in the group and identifies possible areas of conflict, hostility, and/or disengagement among members. The tuning-in process heightens responsiveness and can result in increased empathy and more effective intervention.

Introductions

Getting to know each other is the most important goal of the first meeting. It is helpful to have participants put their name on a file card bent in half and placed on the floor in front of each chair. This facilitates a quick learning of names, and the file cards can be retrieved at the end of each group. The group facilitator may decide to be the first to introduce herself and can begin by saying something about who she is professionally, her interest in the group, and how she is feeling at the first session: "I'm Nicole, and I'm a social worker here at the agency. I have been involved in couple groups for the past five years. I've already spoken to all of you, and I am excited that we're finally here as a group."

There are a number of ways in which members can be asked to introduce themselves. In a simple go-around everyone says their name and a little about why they came to the group. Members can also interview and introduce each other. Emphasis can be placed on goals by having each member complete a sentence such as, "What I want most from the group is..." or introduce themselves as the person they want to be when they leave the group. Completing sentences like "A fear I have about being in the group is..." raises concerns early so they can be addressed. If the members are from different geographical areas, a world map can be very useful: each member pins his or her name tag on their country of origin.

Whatever form the introductions take, when everyone has finished, the facilitator's role is to summarize her observations by noting the similarities, the common experiences, anxieties, and difficulties. Such feedback will help begin connecting the group members in developing common ground, and will demonstrate that she has been listening.

In open-ended groups, one or two members may be joining everyone else who are already familiar with each other. These new members should be invited to say a few words about why they decided to come to the program and what they hope to get out of it.

Guidelines and Ground Rules

Whether someone is attending group for the first time or has had other group experiences, some basic guidelines for participation and group functioning are essential in assisting members to participate and to enhance feelings of safety and security.

Some recommended guidelines include:

1. Keep names and personal information heard in group confidential. In the group setting, both the social worker and the group members are obligated to honour confidentiality. Generally, group members are told that information shared in the group stays in the group. If members want to speak about their group experience to others, they ought to talk only about what they are learning or the changes they are making. Members often want to know what they should do if they see each other on the street or how the facilitator will respond to them outside the group. While there is no firm protocol, one suggestion is that group members not openly acknowledge each other in the presence of friends, family, employers, etc. This is important for group members who may not wish others to know that they are attending a group and don't want to be placed in the situation of explaining who is greeting them. The facilitator also reminds members of the limits to confidentiality that professionals must follow (as outlined in Chapter 5).

2. Arrive on time or call if absent. The expectation that the group will begin on time respects the busy schedules of members and their efforts to attend. At the same time it is important to understand when members are unavoidably late due to unreliable or missed buses and paid work and domestic responsibilities.

Group members should be informed that their absence will be noticed and that an explanation will reduce the concern of the group facilitators and members. In some cases, there may be a guideline about absences; i.e., after three unexplained absences, a member will be asked to leave the group. Absences due to illness, vacation, and crises in the family ought to be accepted; however, at some point the social worker will have to decide how many absences can be accommodated. The person may be better off rejoining another group at a later time if they cannot attend regularly. At times members will be unable to come to group because they don't have bus fare or resources for child care, and advocacy on the part of the social worker will be necessary.

3. No eating in the group. While coffee or juice are often provided during group sessions, eating can be a distraction.

4. No alcohol or illicit drugs on the day of the group. The personal work that takes place in group requires the full presence of participants, and the use of substances can cloud perceptions and effect judgment. If the facilitator suspects that someone has arrived at the group under the influence of drugs, her response will vary depending on the situation. If the person has "had a beer," the facilitator can talk to her prior to the group, remind her of the agreement, and continue with the group as usual. If, on the other hand, the group member has had "several beers" and is noticeably effected, the social worker may choose to remind her of the agreement, restrict her group participation to listening, or arrange for her to get safely home. In the case of someone who is attending a group because of her problem with alcohol and has a goal of abstinence, the decision to drink or use other drugs will require special consideration.

It is advisable to explore the possibility of substance use in a non-threatening and supportive manner, preferably in private. The social worker can begin with an observation, posing questions such as "I smell alcohol—have you had a drink before group?" and "You appear very drowsy tonight—is everything OKAY?" At times the behaviour the social worker observes may be the effects of prescribed drugs such as tranquilizers, anti-depressants, or analgesics, and the group member may need encouragement to approach a physician to speak about side-effects.

It is always possible that something else is contributing to the signs of intoxication other than alcohol or other drug use. For example, on one occasion, I observed reddened eyes in a young male group member. Suspecting marijuana use, I commented on this. His response was, "Yea, I've been hanging drywall all day."

5. One person speaks at a time. Group members may need to be reminded not to interrupt when another group member or the group facilitator is talking.

6. Give feedback to each other; express oneself, one's thoughts and feelings, in a respectful way. Speak directly to the person. The strength of the group is in the feedback given to one another.

7. Respect difference and be open to hearing different ideas and views. Group members represent differing views and cultures and are expected to respond to each other in a respectful manner. As the facilitator and other group members respond to comments in group in a respectful manner, they become models for others.

8. Do not leave group for unscheduled breaks unless absolutely necessary. The coming and going of members while the group is meeting is disruptive.

It is helpful to encourage discussion on the guidelines and to ask if there are others that members would like to see. It is useful to record the established guidelines and to provide a copy for all members. At times throughout the course of the group, the guidelines should be revisited and revised as needed.

The Group Session

The group leader maintains the focus while facilitating participation, attending to both content (the topic of discussion) and process (responses of group members). The core communication skills, relationship-building, and problem-solving skills discussed in previous chapters are essential to the task. During the initial stages of the group, the social worker strives to connect members and to build cohesion among them.

According to Lawrence Shulman, two themes present in every group to some degree are authority and intimacy.[8] The authority theme refers to the relationship between the social worker, who leads the group, and the group members. Some members who are court mandated or pressured to attend the group may directly challenge the social worker's authority. For instance, in group work with abusive men, I found that men reacted to the imposed service and the fact that it was delivered by a woman. The intimacy theme reveals itself in the way group members develop relationships with each other and disclose personal details of their lives. As an effective group process is established and group members gain trust and begin working with each other, the facilitator becomes viewed less as an authority.

Group sessions often have an overall structure to them. It can be helpful to have opening and closing rituals. At the beginning of open group sessions, various "housekeeping" tasks take place, such as introduction of a new member or farewell to an old. The group facilitator may want to briefly check with a member who achieved some progress the previous week or offer some personal reflections.

In highly structured groups centred on a specific topic, the agenda may be prearranged and leader-focussed. Such groups offer new information and promote learning. In other groups the focus emerges from the members themselves, often prompted by a question such as "Who needs some time tonight?" Members, knowing that they will have an opportunity to speak up in the group, come prepared to work on their issues. Two or three members may raise their hands, thus giving the session structure. Instead of a show of hands, members as they arrive write their names and the amount of time they need for discussion on a flip chart. The list, reviewed at the start of group and changes made if necessary, can be part of the agenda for the evening. Once feedback and some closure has come to one member's concern, the social worker moves on to the second person who wanted some time by saying "Is it okay if we move on to Marie now?"

Helping Members Tell Their Story

The group facilitator has two clients, the group member who is raising a concern and the remaining group members.[9] While the focus may be on one member and his or her issue, the facilitator observes other members and attempts to include them in the process to discover common ground. Questions such as "Has anyone else shared Bob's fear of being on his own after many years of marriage?" or "Who else has difficulty expressing their feelings?" invites others to connect with these experiences. Often group members are very unfocussed and go on at great length. The social worker must listen carefully during these situations. She can then pose questions for clarification or offer a succinct summary in order to assist the group member to focus. Careful listening also communicates that the group member's story is important.

At times members can begin to talk about other people in their life and how they have to change. For example, it is common for men who have been abusive to focus on what their partner said or did, not on their own actions. Redirecting attention to how the actions of others affected them or to how they responded can be helpful and emphasize that the group can help only the group member, not friends and family.

Use of Contracts

The contract offers a focus and purpose for attending the group and contains goals for personal change, actions that will meet those goals, and the outcomes of these efforts. Effective contract goals are specific, stated in terms that can be assessed and that are achievable. For example, the action plan below records the goals, actions, and outcomes of a group member in a program for abusive men.

FIGURE 8.1 Action Plan
I am in the New Men program to make some positive changes in my life. There are specific behaviours and attitudes that I want to change so that I stop my abuse and begin to respect and support my partner. I want a relationship based on equality.

Action Plan			
Date	Behaviour/attitude	Action	Outcome
	(What I want to change)	(What I will do)	(The results)

The goals and outcomes of group members can be reviewed on a regular basis in the group.

Use of Homework

Assigning a structured activity to be completed in between group sessions assists members to continue to work on the agreed-upon goals. Expectations for homework are an integral component of re-education programs for abusive men. One assignment is to log any abusive behaviour (the Abuse Log); this helps the men to identify and to examine their controlling actions and to realize that they occur in a context, are connected to beliefs, and are purposeful. The Abuse Log below was adapted from the one initially developed in the Duluth program and is designed to assist men in the development of critical thinking. The Log assists men to examine their own violence and guides them through a process of naming the problem, critically reflecting on the impact on others, and taking action to change.[10] This counters the common view that men abuse because they lose control and shows instead how abuse is based on an intention to gain control—to stop their partner from saying something or doing something.

FIGURE 8.2 Abuse Log

Name_____

Date_____

ABUSE LOG

1. The Situation: A brief description of the incident that I responded to in an abusive way.
2. My Feelings: What I felt.
3. My Actions: A description of what I did, what I said, my facial expressions and tone of voice.
4. My Intent: What did I want to happen.
5. My Self Talk: What I was saying to myself just before and during my actions.
6. My Beliefs that support my actions.
7. The Effects of My Actions on:
   a) my partner
   b) others, including children
   c) myself.
8. What I can do differently: It would have been better if I ......

The journal is another useful tool sometimes recommended to group members as a way to develop self-awareness.

Giving Feedback

The feedback that members give each other is a vital aspect of helping in groups. The following guidelines are useful to assist group members in giving feedback:

1. Use I statements: "I think you..."
2. Be specific: "When you ...it reminded me of..."
3. Be tentative: "I have a hunch..."; "I'm wondering if..."
4. Connect to personal experience: "When I first came to the group I felt the same way."

If the feedback is challenging, a group member may begin to deflect what is being said and counter each point. Instead of listening, he may be actively constructing a response. In this case it is helpful to ask the member to listen silently while a number of people give feedback. Then ask him what he has heard and what has been helpful.

Use of Structured Activities

There is often a tendency when first starting out to highly structure the group and control the content. This offers a sense of security to a new group leader. However, with experience, the social worker soon discovers that much of the material comes from the group. Nevertheless, structured exercises can be very useful in assisting group members to express themselves. All participation in such activities ought to be voluntary. Members should have the option of passing or declining.

1. The check-in. A common practice in working with groups is to begin with a "check-in," a go-around in which each member summarizes the week or speaks about their current feelings. In working with men who are abusive, one of the objectives is to increase their sensitivity and understanding towards partners. Thus, George checks in as his partner Alice and speaks about how it was living with George in the past week. The group leader and the members then have an opportunity to ask Alice questions. This manner of checking tends to elicit far more information and also provides men with an increased awareness about their partners' lives.[11]

Sometimes going around is done by passing around a "talking stick" or an object such as a seashell or stone. Only the person who holds the object can speak. When that person is finished speaking, she passes it to the one next to her. The passing continues until no one has any more to say, and the object completes the circle without anyone saying anything.

2. Role plays. At times the social worker will invite a group member to role play. This is particularly important when a member is facing a difficult situation and would benefit from a practice session. A woman who wishes to talk to her 15-year-old daughter about expectations for curfew and household responsibilities and the consequences for not complying is very hesitant to do so because in previous attempts the daughter has been hostile and left the room. The group leader asks group members how they would respond to such a situation and then invites the woman to play out one of these suggestions; another member is asked to volunteer to play the role of the daughter. After the role play, the group leader asks both the "mother" and "daughter" what they learned from the exercise and asks group members for their feedback.

Critical Thinking and Problem-Posing

Critical thinking is central to consciousness-raising as individuals place the events of their lives within a social, political, and economic context and identify ways that they can work to change that context.[12] Rather than emphasizing personal and interpersonal dynamics only, material conditions and social relations are also considered. This process of consciousness-raising helps clients to move from a position of powerlessness, internalized oppression, and alienation to one of empowerment and liberation. The assumption is that once clients reach a critical understanding of their situation, they are able to more effectively engage in personal change as well as confront inadequate social and economic conditions.

In the group process, the group facilitator asks a number of questions of group members, some of which elicit more information than others. For example, open-ended questions generate a richer response than closed questions. Questions can also help a group member reach for deeper meaning and understanding.

Problem-posing is an approach that structures dialogue and advances critical thinking in a group process.[13] Introduced by Freire, problem-posing has been adapted to the university classroom, including schools of social work[14] and ESL classes in North America.[15] The dialogical approach invites group members to enter the process of learning "not by acquiring facts, but by constructing their reality in social exchange with others."[16] For example, many abusive men are aware of the "facts" of abuse and read newspaper accounts about the prevalence of male violence in intimate relationships, but they have seldom considered or connected their own thoughts and actions to these events.

In groups for abusive men, the use of codification or codes help to stimulate problem-posing, structure and focus the discussion, and assist men in examining their beliefs and feelings about their violence. A code is a depiction of reality, a physical representation of an issue, concept, or theme that has emerged from the group. Codes can take the form of video vignettes, photographs, poems, drawings, comics, newspaper clippings, or a song. In groups for men who are abusive, the code externalizes actions of abuse so that they can be examined and connected to personal experiences.

The video vignettes and power and control wheel, developed by the Duluth program and now used in countries around the world, are the result of women coming together in focus groups and speaking of their experiences of violence.[17] By portraying several minutes in a relationship when a man is abusive, each vignette focusses and grounds the work of the group.

In order to move the discussion of a code to critical analysis and action, Wallerstein suggests using the following questioning process:

1. Describe what you see.
2. Define the problem(s).
3. Share similar experiences.
4. Question why there is a problem.
5. Strategize what you can do about the problem.[18]

This process examines situations that directly impact on the lives of the members; it may lead to consciousness-raising and personal and social action. The abuse logs described earlier reflect a similar questioning process.

In my own groups, I have suggested that members draw a picture of a situation in which they used violence. Many of these pictures portray the man as larger than everyone else and holding his fist in the air; his partner has a look of horror and pain; and there are often children hovering in the background. This has proved to be a particularly moving experience for men as they describe their picture to the group.

Ending the Session

The group facilitator must set aside time to bring the session to a close and the work of the group together by pointing out connections among the issues discussed and identifying issues for the following sessions. A final go-around to all group members creates closure. For example, a group for abusive men could close with a round of commitments: the men identify something they will put into practice, some action they will take in the week to come toward their goal of equality with their partner. Occasionally, an issue may arise during the go-around that appears to be something on which one member needs to work; that member is encouraged to take group time in the following week for the issue.

Challenges in Group Work
Lack of Participation

There are many reasons why someone may not fully participate in group. A member may be reluctant to talk about a part of her life that is very painful and/or that she may feel guilt or shame about. While a part of her may want to move ahead, another part may fear change. She may fear being rejected or misunderstood or may think that the social worker and other members have nothing of importance to contribute. In the case of mandated group attendance, group members may be angry and be taking the only control over the process they believe they have: "You can force me to be here, but you can't make me listen." Another reason for a member's silence could be cultural differences and/or language difficulties. It may take some members longer to trust the group because of some past vulnerability. Fully acknowledging a problem in group means doing something about it.

Instead of pressuring quiet members to talk about a particular problem, it is often helpful to ask them to talk about what makes it difficult to share. Regular go-arounds in which all members are given an opportunity to say a few words are helpful in assisting those who tend to be quiet.

In a group for abused women, a member talks about wanting to leave her husband but feeling frightened and insecure about being alone with two children. In order to draw out other members, the social work might respond, "It's very difficult thinking of being on your own, yet you're feeling very unsafe living with your husband. Who can relate to what Elaine is saying?" It is important to collectivize the work—to search out a common ground between the individual and the group as a whole—without denying the uniqueness of the member's problem. Moving around the circle to scan members' faces and reactions will give the facilitator a sense of how the members are responding.

Another strategy to draw out quiet members is to recognize their nonverbal communication and invite them to comment. If one member nods her head while another speaks, the facilitator could say, "Nora, you seem to be connecting to what Connie said," thus linking the experience of members together.

Promoting Cooperation

It is common for group members to be reluctant to acknowledge difficult situations in order to begin the process of change. At times members
enter the group against their will. When the service is imposed, the social
worker may find that the group members may defy guidelines, challenge
the leadership, and refuse to participate. This is a common occurrence
in groups for men who are abusive, where the men are there involuntarily as the result of legal or non-legal pressure to attend, or are court-
mandated or partner-mandated. Men's reluctance to participate in this
case may be termed "resistance," and the frustrated facilitator may demand
participation, impose group content, and engage in harsh confrontation.
Such a response shows disrespect, violates the dignity of group members,
and may encourage others to rally in support of the member(s) under
attack. In this situation, a more effective response is to recognize that the
member is more than the abuse that he has done and to engage him as a
whole person. While men are held responsible for their actions and their
violence, they should not be viewed "as demonic beings out to inflict pain
and suffering but as people who are acting from a set of beliefs that are
harmful and make stable and loving relationships impossible."[19]

Diversity and Conflict

At times actions of group members will reflect their prejudice and beliefs
regarding gender, ethnicity, sexual orientation, and social class. Sandra
Butler and Claire Wintram discuss this in their book *Feminist Groupwork*:

> J, for example, had ended a lesbian relationship and was now caring
> for her elderly father at home. After several months of hearing other
> women in the group talk about their heterosexual partners and their
> child-rearing practices, she suddenly shouted out that she was sick
> of women making heterosexist assumptions about the 'normality'
> of sexual relations with men, that she felt excluded, and that it was
> further assumed that choosing to have a child-free life made her
> incomplete. For months she had felt marginalized and oppressed by
> other women because of inferences with which she was surrounded.[20]

It appears that the group leaders had been unaware of the degree to which
this woman felt alienated and alone. Since this had gone on for "several

months," it is possible that the leaders too are practicing with a heterosexual bias. In responding to this woman's outburst, it would be critical for the group leaders to acknowledge what she has said and to join with the other women as they begin to address their exclusion of her experience.

The following is an excerpt of a facilitator responding to racist language from Ellen Pence and Michael Paymar's book *Education Groups For Men Who Batter*:

> Bill: She's going out with this gook.
>
> Facilitator: Why do you use the term "gook"?
>
> Bill: It's a term for Vietnamese—you know, I think of them as gooks. You would too if you'd been to Nam.
>
> Facilitator: Bill, let's finish what we were talking about, then I want to go back to this discussion about Vietnamese as gooks. OK?
>
> Bill: Yeah, anyway, she's going out with this Vietnamese guy...

After the discussion on why Bill was following his ex-wife, the facilitator turned to the use of the term "gook."

> Facilitator: I want to talk a few minutes about the words that we use for people based on their race, like the word "gook" or the terms used in World War II for Japanese people, and look at why it's important to objectify the enemy in war and how and why we do that in civilian life too.[21]

The response of the group leader in this situation is respectful: he acknowledges what he has heard, flags it for later, and continues with the situation the member has started to talk about. Later he gets back to the comment and invites group members to think critically about what may seem as everyday thinking.

Group Closure

Whether the entire group is coming to an end or an individual is leaving an open group, the social worker should mention the ending at least two weeks before. It is not unusual for participants to want to disregard or deny their leaving. Generally, we have not learned to say good-byes very easily and often find it easier to just slip out the back door. The group leader can provide a model for ending relationships.

The last group meeting should provide an opportunity for members to express their feelings and thoughts about the group experience and their time together. Facilitating a "talking circle," as described above (see page 160), offers an opportunity for all to fully contribute and creates a symbolic closing.

Comments from members inevitably are a combination of humour, memories of high points in the group, and moving accounts of the impact of the group on their lives and the changes they have made. In one group a member said, "I have been in Canada for 12 years, and this group is the first time I have socialized with Canadians, and now I know that I can do that." Members also express sadness to see the group end and resolve to keep in touch and to continue with the changes they have made.

NOTES

[1] Marcia Cohen and Audrey Mullender, "The Personal is Political: Exploring the Group Work Continuum from Individual to Social Change Goals," *Social Work with Groups* 22.1 (1999): 13–31.
[2] Lawrence Shulman, "Group Work Method," *Mutual Aid Groups and the Life Cycle*, ed. Alex Gitterman and Lawrence Shulman (Itasca, IL: F.E. Peacock, 1986) 25.
[3] Gerald Corey, Marianne Scheider Corey, Patrick Callanan, and J. Michael Russell, *Group Techniques*, 2nd ed. (Pacific Grove, CA: Brooks/Cole Publishing, 1992) 12.
[4] Alex Gitterman, "Developing a New Group Service: Strategies and Skills," *Mutual Aid Groups and the Life Cycle*, ed. Alex Gitterman and Lawrence Shulman (Itasca IL: F.E. Peacock, 1986) : 53–71.
[5] Hannah Patricia, "Preparing Members for the Expectations of Social Work with Groups: An Approach to the Prepatory Interview," *Social Work with Groups* 22.4 (2000): 51–66.
[6] Allan Brown and Tara Mistry, "Group Work with Mixed Membership Groups: Issues of Race and Gender," *Social Work with Groups* 17.3 (1994) 14.
[7] Marianne Schneider Corey and Gerald Corey, *Group Process and Practice*, 4th ed. (Belmont, CA: Brooks/Cole, 1992).
[8] Shulman, "Group Work Method."
[9] Shulman, *Skills of Helping Individuals, Families and Groups*.
[10] The Duluth program spearheaded education groups for abusive men and introduced the use of tools such as the abuse log, now adapted in programs around the world. See, e.g., Ellen Pence and Michael Paymar, *Education Groups for Men Who Batter: The Duluth Model* (New York, NY: Springer, 1993). This version was created with colleagues while I was facilitating groups in the New Directions program for abused men in Ottawa, Canada.
[11] This exercise was developed by Mark Holmes, Coordinator of the New Directions Program in Ottawa, Canada.
[12] Freire, *Pedagogy of the Oppressed*.
[13] Ira Shor, "Education is Politics: Paulo Freire's Critical Pedagogy," *Paulo Freire: A Critical Encounter*, ed. Peter McLaren and Peter Leonard (London: Routledge, 1993) 25–35; Ira Shor, *Empowering Education: Critical Teaching for Social Change* (Chicago, IL: University of Chicago Press, 1992).

14 Bonnie Burstow, "Freirian Codifications and Social Work Education," *Journal of Social Work Education,* 272 (1991): 196–207.

15 Nina Wallerstein, "Problem-Posing Education: Freire's Method for Transformation," *Freire for the Classroom,* ed. Ira Shor (Portsmouth, MA: Boynton Cook/Heinemann, 1987) 33–44.

16 Wallerstein 34.

17 Fernando Mederos, " Batterer Intervention Programs: Past and Future Prospects," *Coordinated Community Response to Domestic Violence: Lessons from the Duluth Model,* ed. Melanie F. Shepherd and Ellen L. Pence (Newbury Park, CA: Sage, 1998) 127–50.

18 Wallerstein 38.

19 Mederos 132.

20 Sandra Butler and Claire Wintram, *Feminist Groupwork* (Newbury Park, CA: Sage, 1992) 76.

21 Pence and Paymar 82.

CHAPTER 9

COMMUNITY-BASED SOCIAL WORK PRACTICE

T he social work profession has a long history of working within communities to create social, economic, and political changes. Although community work was widely practiced by social workers in the settlement houses during the early part of the last century, it was not acknowledged as a primary area of social work practice by university schools of social work until the 1930s. This is not surprising because of the emphasis at the time on individual problems and advancing the theory and practice of casework. Another factor contributing to the lack of recognition of community practice was the early tension between professionalization and social and political activism. However, the high levels of unemployment and poverty during the Depression years drew attention to the importance of community-based social work practice. The social movements of the 1960s contributed to a redefinition of community work with a focus on creating community-based services and the inclusion of a social action component.[1]

This chapter provides an overview of social work practice in communities and suggests strategies for joining with community members to strengthen and restore their communities. Most social workers, regardless of where they work, extend their practice into communities. For example, those who offer agency-based services to individuals, families, or groups also identify areas of concern for which a community-based solution is needed. Others who are employed in community-based programs, such as community health centres, neighbourhood community centres, and shelters, work with community members to identify resources and needs and organize to change the conditions that produce social inequalities and injustices.

The relevance and importance of community practice during times of economic hardship, poverty, homelessness, and unemployment cannot be overstated. Currently, as federal and provincial governments privatize services and shift the responsibility for social welfare provision to municipalities, more and more pressure has been placed on local communities to provide for their members. Decreasing employment and family incomes have resulted in growing numbers of impoverished families and have intensified the social needs, social divisions, and conflict in communities. The result has been a particularly high concentration of poverty in neighbourhoods with a high percentage of people of visible minority origins.[2] In such neighbourhoods, or ghettos as Kazemipur and Halli refer to them, poor families only have a connection to other poor families and end up separated from society generally. In their analysis of the situation, Kazemipur and Halli report that this over-representation is due to ethnic poverty, the kinds of jobs that are available to these residents, and residential segregation.

Within this context a revitalization and rethinking of community-based social work practice is taking place. It has even been suggested that the very survival of social work requires a reclaiming of community practice.[3] "The challenge for the social work profession is to respond to these changing conditions in ways that are proactive, advocate for vulnerable populations, and emphasize and expand skills in community-focussed practice that connect empowerment strategies with social and economic development."[4]

Approaches to Community-Based Practice

A number of models have been proposed for social work community organizing activities. The three forms of community development proposed by Jack Rothman over 30 years ago—locality development, social planning, and social action— still capture the specific social work practice activities in the community today.[5] Rothman suggested that community practice involves mixed models and a combination of these three strategies:[6]

1. Locality development. The primary method used in settlement houses focusses on building community capacity: members of a defined locality or neighbourhood are supported in identifying problems and/or common concerns and discovering solutions. Capacity building as a goal involves increasing community resources, increasing member involvement and local leadership, and enhancing community functioning. Neighbourhood-based services improve accessibility and solve transportation difficulties. They are also likely to offer culturally relevant and appropriate services in a number of languages or through translation.

2. Social planning. Social planning councils and task forces place emphasis on specific tasks and goals for information-gathering, analysis, and the identification of solutions. The outcome might be a brief to the municipal government on concerns such as homelessness, illicit drug use, or hate crimes.

3. Social action. The organized resistance and response of community members intends to force concessions and achieve institutional and structural social change in policies or laws and power distribution. When the source of community concerns is situated within unequal power relations and unequal material conditions, social action is a necessary part of social work practice. The social action approach, according to Rothman, requires that the social worker act as an advocate and activist with "a disadvantaged segment of the population that needs to be organized, perhaps in alliances with others, in order to make demands on the larger community for increased resources or treatment more in accordance with social justice or democracy."[7] Such activity can lead to the development of alternative services, and program and policy changes.

Elements of Rothman's models are evident in current social work practices in the community such as "community organizing," "community development," "community action," "building community capacity," and "restoring communities." While the language has changed, the actual practices reflect his original formulation. For example, community development, as defined by Felix Rivera and John Erlich, combines locality development and social action and refers to "efforts to mobilize people who are directly affected by a community condition (that is, the 'victims,' the unaffiliated, the unorganized, and the nonparticipating) into groups and organizations to enable them to take action on the social problems and issues that concern them."[8] However, Rivera and Erlich are critical of Rothman's models because they do not acknowledge the racial, ethnic, and cultural diversity of community members and the role of religion, language, and kinship patterns in community building.

In their book *Community Action*, Henri Lamoureux, Robert Mayer, and Jean Panet-Raymond emphasize the importance of mobilizing community members and suggest that the process of community organizing:

1. brings together people who directly or indirectly have common interests;
2. utilizes a democratic process for decision-making and participation;
3. engages in an educational process that builds on existing knowledge and skills of members;
4. brings about "change, to reduce or eliminate exploitation, oppression and alienation."[9]

A feminist understanding of community work has further transformed community practice. Women's organizing expresses their standpoint and grows out of specific issues that are impacting their lives. While working towards empowerment through consciousness-raising, such organizing concentrates on bridging differences and building solidarity. Marilyn Callahan describes feminist community organizing as including all of the traditional activities; however, she finds that what distinguishes feminist community organizing from other approaches is the inclusion of gender analysis, alongside that of class and race and its commitment to helping women to identify their needs and to organize for solutions in their communities.[10]

Assessment and Strategies for Change

Often the term "community" refers to residents in a geographic area, including their diversity and subgenres. There are also communities of individuals who have common interests based on culture, ethnicity, disability, sexual orientation, or gender. For the most part, community practice and organizing takes place in neighbourhoods that include "a majority of workers, welfare recipients, the unemployed, the elderly, and the young, and a minority of petty bourgeois, which includes artist and organizers."[11] These communities may have fewer resources and greater social concerns, little space or opportunity to come together to create and sustain a sense of community, and serious environmental pollution.

Entering the Community

Researching the community is an essential component of community work and prepares the social worker for the process ahead.[12] If a social worker does not live in the community, the first task is to learn about its history and geographic boundaries; the diversity among the residents; their strengths; the available social, educational, and health resources; and local primary industries and employers. The depth of the social worker's knowledge and sensitivity will influence the working relationship that follows. All communities have both specific problems and conflicts as well as strengths, resources, and existing leaders. The social worker generally begins by identifying these community leaders and connecting with local organizations. Recognition of current strategies and programs established by committed community workers and agencies will facilitate the full and meaningful participation of members and relevant community strategies.

Since geographic communities are not homogeneous, members are diverse based on their identification with ethnicity/race, age, gender, sexual orientation, and/or ability. When working in ethnically mixed communities the uniqueness of diverse groups and the economic and political realities in each community must be taken into account. The relationship of the specific community with the wider community and the political and economic factors that are impacting on its members is another consideration. For example, after the September 11, 2001 terrorist attacks on New York City and Washington, DC, there has been an increase in racism against persons of Arab and Muslim backgrounds in both Canada and the US. Discrimination against and injustice experienced by specific groups in society generally thus may be reflected in the smaller community.

Identifying Concerns/Needs and Social Action

The common goal of community approaches is to work collectively and engage members of the community in the task of identifying concerns or needs and in improving social, political, and economic conditions. This practice facilitates communication among members, enhances knowledge and skills, contributes to improved individual and community functioning, and fosters empowerment through consciousness-raising. Through effective participation and control of the process and decision-making, social relationships and organizational structures in the community are strengthened. Particular attention is placed on creating bridges among diverse ethnic groups, fostering positive relationships and engaging members who have systematically been disadvantaged.

Community organizer Joan Kuyek, in her book *Fighting for Hope: Organizing to Realize Our Dreams,* suggests an exercise called "community mapping" to assist members in the assessment of their community.[13] In the exercise, the social worker provides pencils, crayons, or markers and a piece of paper for each participant and divides people into groups of four to five members. Each participant is asked to draw a picture of their community including the geographic area, friends, workplace, or organizations. Then the members come together as a larger group and discuss the major concerns facing their communities, their strengths and sources of hope, as well as the limitations and sources of despair. The social worker can assist community members to compile a list of concerns and prioritize them, identify goals and resources, and create a plan of action.

Community activists in Toronto also suggest an educational process as a means to strengthen the ability of community members to identify concerns and to engage in collective struggle towards social change. The popular education tool called the "spiral model" is an action and reflection model that guides the process of social action (Figure 9.1).

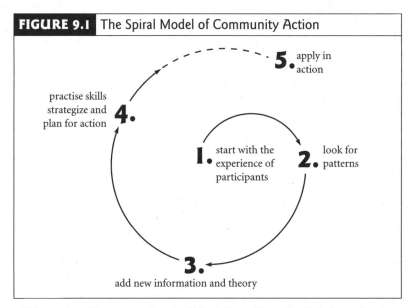

| FIGURE 9.1 | The Spiral Model of Community Action |

5. apply in action

practise skills strategize and plan for action 4.

1. start with the experience of participants

2. look for patterns

3. add new information and theory

"The spiral model of community action" Margie Bruun-Meyer/Art Work, from *Educating for a Change* by Rick Arnold, Bev Burke, Carl James, D'Arcy Martin, and Barb Thomas (Between the Lines, 1991.) Reproduced by permission.

The beginning point is the concrete experiences and past actions of the concerned community members; from these, a problem, need, or identified injustice may emerge. The members begin to reflect on their experiences, to identify patterns in what they have reported, and to discern commonalities and differences. New information and theory builds on the experiences and helps to understand them, leading to further debate and discussion. The members apply what they have learned in order to develop a strategy, a plan of action based on their knowledge and experience. Finally, the plan is implemented and a process of praxis—reflection, action and reflection—takes place. Strategies may be revised and members may move through the cycle again.

Bernard Wohl offers the following example that reflects the spiral model and education process. A youth group in a New York settlement house organized a social action project called the "Nike 'Give-Back' Campaign."[14] It began with a discussion among the members about how brand name sneakers, particularly Nike, are coveted but too expensive for them and many other poor young people. Working with staff, the young people researched the corporate exploitation of workers and the high price of the sneakers in the US and wrote letters to the company's president and to Michael Jordan, the basketball star who endorsed the product. When they did not receive adequate answers to their questions, they began to organize a "sneaker give-back" action. They were able to mobilize youth from 11 other settlement houses to travel by bus to Niketown in New York City to demonstrate and give back bags of worn Nike sneakers. In the process they increased their understanding of the globalization of poverty and social injustice, developed organizing skills, and gained a realization of their collective capacity to carry out a plan of action.

Mutual aid groups often have a community development component and follow a process similar to the spiral model, as evident in this experience of the Canadian Centre for Victims and Torture.[15] One young Muslim woman disclosed to a worker that she had been raped while in a Somali prison and was ashamed to tell anyone. She experienced serious physical trauma not only from the rape but from earlier ritual female genital mutilation. Workers soon became aware of other women with similar experiences who shared a profound sense of physical, psychological, and social isolation. A weekly mutual aid group was formed to help these women make new friends connected by these common experiences. The women quickly identified basic survival needs—housing, food, clothing, job and

English language training, and their rights as refugees—as their primary concerns. At the time Metro Toronto Housing Authority had refused to accept applications from refugees for subsidized housing. The women decided to form a Somali Women's Advocacy Group and successfully challenged the housing policy under the Canadian Human Rights Code. The direct involvement of the women and their collective action demonstrated their potential and prepared them for more involvement.

Community Functioning

Communities differ in their level of functioning, their resources, and their strengths. Therefore, a community assessment inevitably leads to questions about why the disparities exist in the first place. The promotion of critical thinking assists members in gaining an understanding of the inequities facing them.

The task of the social worker is to engage community members in order to advance the goal of enhancing overall community functioning in economic terms (work and income) and in areas such as mutual support. Members of the community must be able to find assistance in extreme circumstances or emergencies; this requires a process for communication among members and between them and the wider community. Through such communication, a forum for expressing ideas and concerns develops.[16] Building capacity in communities in this way helps members to take control of their communities, establishes local leadership, and lays the groundwork for much-needed community resources.

One example of a community-driven and controlled community centre that has enhanced community functioning is the Debra Dynes Family House in Ottawa.[17] The Family House, directed by social worker Barbara Carroll, is situated in one of the town houses in a low income social housing neighbourhood of 800 people living in 183 homes. The highly diverse community population consists of families from 25 nations, many of whom are recent immigrants and refugees who have arrived in Canada from war-torn countries. The Family House is the centre of the community and provides a food bank, educational programs such as English as a second language and sewing classes, day care services and an after-school program for children, access to computers and the internet, support for job hunting, and a drop-in area to socialize and connect with others. People are often isolated from their extended families and benefit greatly from organized community support. In communities such as Debra Dynes, social work practice is based on capacity-enhancement and the recognition that there are personal and social resources in the community. Such an approach strengthens and unifies communities, particularly those that consist of groups from different ethnic and cultural backgrounds.[18]

Community gardens are another example of strengthening mutual support and promoting participation from a cross-section of the community. The garden itself provides food and many learning opportunities. Coordination and cooperation are needed to make decisions regarding the space, preparation of the soil, planning the garden itself, the ongoing upkeep, and the harvest. It can become a focal point of the community and a source of pride as a vacant lot or unkept field is transformed into a productive space. The garden is perceived as a safe and neutral place in which to interact.

Murals generate a sense of community pride and can also serve as a strategy for conveying a message. Posters, banners, and buttons all educate and mobilize community members around an issue. In Ottawa in the 1970s a group of activists living in a low-income community produced a button that said "Pierre Trudeau [the Prime Minister at the time] lives in public housing" in order to dispel the myth that only they were receiving direct support from the government.

Empowerment Through Participation

Community members gain the most for their communities when they participate in decision-making at all levels of the process of organizing. Table 9.1, adapted from the work of George Brager and Harry Specht,[19] demonstrates the differing degrees of community participation in various organizing strategies.

In any form of community practice, there is the danger of community members losing their voice as community practitioners take the lead and neglect to involve them in the process. In her discussion of feminist organizing, Joanna Brenner points out how feminist activists have shifted from organizing to advocacy and how there has been " a displacement of goals in which feminists aim to get something from the state for women rather than to encourage the self organization of women."[20]

If the goal is to work in partnership with community members in achieving a better functioning community, as is argued here, emphasis must be placed on the knowledge and skills of community members, as

TABLE 9.1 Degrees of Participation of Community Members	
Degree of Participation	Organizing Strategy
None	Community not informed
Receives information	Present a completed plan to community members with expectation of compliance.
Is consulted	Present a completed plan and asks for support.
Offer advice	Present a plan and invites feed-back/ contributions
Some decision-making	Identify and present a problem to the community and request decisions be made in a number of defined areas.
Has control	Assist the community in identifying the problem and generating solutions/ goals and a means to meet them.

well as on their full participation in decision-making both in their communities and in society generally. While advocacy may continue to be a social work activity, it should not occur without a community organizing component and community involvement. In this way the process of community change is not imposed from the outside but created, owned, and controlled by the community members. Otherwise, community members become passive recipients of service rather than actors in the change process.

As members participate in the act of acquiring resources for themselves and their community, they also become empowered and have improved functioning. Si Kahn reminds us that the process and content of our organizing activities very much influences the outcome:

> Through the organizing process, people are supposed to become empowered. Because knowledge is power (and because lack of knowledge is in and of itself disempowering), people also need to become knowledgeable. They need new information, and new interpretations of old information, along with the tools to acquire and interpret information in the future. But they need to learn all this in ways that are themselves empowering. If the content of what they

learn is contradicted by the way(s) in which they learn it, the organizing and empowerment process undercuts itself and dies.[21]

Through direct involvement to bring about change, community members
gain awareness of their existing and potential resources and strengths
and, in the process, become empowered to act on their own behalf.

At times grass-roots community responses to problems are both initiated and controlled by community members. For example, in Harlem a
mutual support approach to communal living was organized by drug
users themselves in order to provide services to both those who are active
drug users and those who have stopped and are in recovery. "Stand Up
Harlem" has around 30 people living and working out of three houses.
They work in partnership with those who are experiencing drug-related
harm, homelessness, hunger, and ill health and offer them a meal, shower,
clean clothes, and a safe environment. By providing a place where survival
needs can be met, the staff support people in their choices while opening up other options to drug use. As "Stand Up Harlem" demonstrates:
"What works for many is a community-based response that provides
social networks, services, and medical intervention that allow individuals to make choices and to reclaim their lives." [22]

Art and Performance in the Disability Community

In an innovative community outreach program, Alan Shain, a social
worker, disability activist, and performer has brought the art of dance to
the disability community by integrating their issues into a community
development framework.[23] In the context of a graduate field placement
at The Ottawa School of Dance, Shain was co-creator and co-facilitator
of creative movement programs for people with disabilities. External
funding for the project ensured that community programs could be
offered for a reduced fee at the school itself, as well as on-site in group
homes, community organizations, and day programs. Information pack-
ages were developed and sent to organizations of people with disabilities, and the mail-out was followed with emails and telephone calls. This
outreach strategy generated considerable interest within the community.
A planned event to spotlight the new program drew over 100 people and
showcased a performance by two dancers with disability from Toronto.
Shain contacted the media, issued press releases, and offered interviews.

The active and well-planned outreach component successfully captured the attention of the community.

Weekly workshops involved improvisation exercises with live music accompaniment and explored different techniques to link music, space, anatomy, and energy to dance. Alan Shain describes how he used movement and dance as a source of creative expression:

> Dance therapy focuses on unlocking individual emotions. While this was partly what our workshops involved, we were also working on building concrete skills in using dance as artistic expression that sometimes involved analysis/commentary on the part of the participants. We were also developing participants' skills in using dance as a way of working with others and of working within a larger group context.[24]

Using the concepts of community and isolation to create a dance piece, Shain incorporated the meaning these concepts had for group members and developed a series of movements to express what these concepts meant to the participants. "In practice," Shain explains, "I learned how to use movement and dance to bring out people's own ideas about the world around them."

> The challenge is to make dance and creative movement relevant to the lives of people with disability. This requires adapting exercises and techniques to allow people to explore movement on their own terms. But this initiative is not merely about adapting techniques. Participants will be creating new dance and new ways of moving. These workshops will be changing the meaning of dance itself.[25]

On a personal level, participants report improved balance, coordination, and fitness and increased confidence. In turn, social work practice is advanced, and the art of dance is being enriched and transformed.

Fighting for Social Justice

Community-based social work practice cannot be separated from the political context and, at times, is controversial. On occasion, community members will decide that they have "had enough" and that an organized protest or mass defiance is the only avenue open to them. "Disruptive dissensus," as Richard Cloward and Frances Fox Piven refer to it, is a mass action that is often unlawful and institutionally disruptive;[26] disruptive protests, such as strikes, pickets, and civil disobedience, have been effective strategies to communicate concerns and gain concessions throughout the history of community organizing in Canada and the US. Cloward and Piven note that, in the US, substantial gains, preceded by disruptive protest, were made in labour rights, social welfare legislation, and civil rights during the periods of 1933–37 and 1963–67. They conclude that "poor people's organizations have a dependent, even parasitical relation to the very disruptive protest that they disparage; they form and thrive during periods when there is a surge of political energy from the bottom, only to wither and disappear when the energy subsides."[27] The organizing efforts of social workers therefore are influenced by the political climate and the readiness of citizens to act on their own behalf.

Social workers have fought for both a community service and their own employment. For instance, in 1990 the already meagrely funded Women's Programme of the Secretary of State was targeted for cuts in funding to women's publications and 80 women's centres across the country. This prompted an organized resistance from women, particularly centre workers and grass-roots activists. That spring, women in St. John's, Halifax, and Vancouver occupied Secretary of State offices to protest the elimination of operational funding to women's centres. While police removed women in Halifax and Vancouver within a few hours, the St. John's occupation lasted five days and received solid support from the wider community. The resistance resulted in a reinstatement of funding to all the centres.

Increasingly, social workers are realizing the importance of coalition and social movement building in order to gain a more powerful base and a greater voice. Coalitions are able to quickly mobilize large numbers of people for marches and advocacy campaigns. In recent years, anti-poverty activists have been most active and visible. The Ontario Common Front (OCF) was formed to mount a militant resistance against the attack on poor people that followed from the Conservative government's drastic dismantling of social programs and reduction of social assistance. The Ontario Coalition Against Poverty (OCAP), a province-wide alliance of anti-poverty activists, advocates for the poor and actively opposes evictions and police mistreatment of the homeless. In June 2000 an OCAP protest at the Ontario Legislature in opposition the Conservative government's policies and against the growing crisis in homelessness and poverty drew 1500 marchers, including a delegation of poor and homeless people. Police in riot garb and on horseback charged the crowds, and a melee ensued. Dozens of charges were laid, and three leaders of OCAP were handed particularly serious charges. The activists believe that these actions are intended to intimidate those who are part of an effective protest.[28] Similarly, in the US, the Coalition on Human Needs is an active anti-poverty coalition of national and grassroots organizations, including the National Association of Social Workers.[29]

While some social workers do become involved in "disruptive dissensus," others may feel more comfortable in exerting pressure on decision-makers through other tactics such as organizing petitions, leafleting, and letter-writing.

Whether situated in family agencies, schools, hospitals, or community centres, when social workers focus on the community, they become aware of the strengths and resilience of community members and the difficulties facing them on a daily basis. Community work inevitably includes strategies to promote social change and social justice.

NOTES

[1] George Brager and Harry Specht, *Community Organizing* (New York, NY: Columbia University Press, 1973).

[2] Kazemipur and Halli, *The New Poverty in Canada.*

[3] Ken Barter, "Reclaiming Community: Shaping the Social Work Agenda," *Canadian Social Work* 2.2 (Fall 2000): 6–18.

[4] Marie O. Weil, "Community Building: Building Community Practice," *Social Work* 41.5 (September 1996): 481.

[5] Jack Rothman, "Three Models of Community Practice," *Strategies of Community Organization*, 2nd ed., ed. Fred Cox et al. (Itasca, IL: F.E. Peacock, 1974) 22–39.

[6] Jack Rothman, "Approaches to Community Intervention," *Strategies of Community Intervention*," 5th ed., ed. J. Rothman, J.L. Erlichs, and J.E. Tropman, with F.M. Cox (Itasca, IL: F.E. Peacock, 1995) 26–63. Cited in Weil, 491.

[7] J. Rothman, "Three Models of Community Practice" 24.

[8] Felix G. Rivera and John L. Erlich, "A Time of Fear; A Time of Hope," *Community Organizing in a Diverse Society*, 3rd ed., ed. Felix G. Rivera and John L. Erlich (Toronto, ON: Allyn and Bacon, 1998) 3.

[9] Henri Lamoureux, Robert Mayer, and Jean Panet-Raymond, *Community Action* (Montreal, QC: Black Rose Books, 1989) 7.

[10] Marilyn Callahan, "Feminist Community Organizing in Canada," *Community Organizing*, ed. Brian Wharf and Michael Clague (Don Mills, ON: Oxford University Press, 1997) 183.

[11] Lamoureux, Mayer, and Panet-Raymond 30.

[12] Lamoureux, Mayer, and Panet-Raymond 62.

[13] Joan Newman Kuyek, *Fighting for Hope: Organizing to Realize Our Dreams* (Montreal, QC: Black Rose Books, 1990) 82.

[14] Bernard J. Wohl, "The Power of Group Work with Youth: Creating Activists of the Future," *Social Work with Groups* 22.4 (2000): 3–13.

[15] Jill Blakeney, Fadumo Jama Dirie, and Mary Ann MacRae, "Empowering Traumatized Somali Women: A Support Group Model for Helping Survivors to Cope," Price, *Community Support for Survivors of Torture*, 50–58.

[16] Antonia Pantoja and Wilhelmina Perry, "Community Development and Restoration: A Perspective and Case Study," *Community Organizing in a Diverse Society*, ed. Felix G. Rivera and John L. Erlich (Toronto: Allyn and Bacon, 1998) 220–42.

[17] For a detailed report on activities see "Humble Computer Station Links Global Village," *Ottawa Citizen* 16 October 2001: 13.

[18] Melvin Degado, *Community Social Work Practice in an Urban Context: The Potential of a Capacity-Enhancement Perspective* (New York, NY: Oxford University Press, 2000).

[19] Adapted from: Brager and Specht 39.

[20] Brenner 262.

[21] Si Kahn, "Leadership: Realizing Concepts Through Creative Process," *Community Practice : Models in Action*, ed. Marie Weil (Binghamton, NY: The Haworth Press, 1997) 110.

[22] Kelly McGowan and Nancy McKenzie, "A Community Response to the Needs of Drug Users, Stand Up Harlem," *Health/PAC Bulletin* (Winter 1993): 13.

[23] Alain Shain is committed to the power of performance in transforming the social experience of disability. Through his company, Smashing Stereotypes Productions, he performs across Canada and around the world at festivals and comedy clubs, as well as for schools and community events. He can be reached at alanshain@yahoo.ca.

[24] Alan Shain, personal interview, 1 April 2003.

[25] *Dance Network News* 9.35 (Winter-Spring 2002) 4.

[26] Richard A. Cloward and Frances Fox Piven, "Disruptive Dissensus: People and Power in the Industrial Age," *Reflections on Community Organization: Enduring Themes and Critical Issues*, ed. Jack Rothman (Itasca, IL: F.E. Peacock Publishers, 1999) 165–193.

[27] Cloward and Piven, "Disruptive Dissensus" 188–89.

[28] E.g., see Bryan Palmer, "Repression and Dissent: The OCAP Trials," *Canadian Dimension* (May/June 2003); http://www.canadiandimension.mb.ca.

[29] http://www.chn.org/humanneeds/.

CHAPTER 10

THE WORKPLACE, PROFESSIONAL ASSOCIATIONS, AND UNION MEMBERSHIP

T hese are difficult times not only for those who seek help from belea-guered social agencies, but also for those who work in these agen-cies. Funding cuts and expanding caseloads mean that social workers are experiencing tremendous stress both from the nature of people's social and personal problems, inadequate resources, and the structure of social welfare delivery, and from the tension between their role as social work-ers and the mandate of the agency and the needs of the client. This chap-ter examines the working conditions of social workers and the role of professional associations and unions in advancing social work practice.

The Workplace

Along with a declining commitment by governments to the welfare state, which has resulted in dwindling resources, social workers face increased bureaucratization of the workplace, greater control from funding sources, and lack of autonomy and consequently reduced ability to make deci-sions that directly affect policy and practice. They witness the impact on people of inadequate social welfare programs and suffer a greater feeling of helplessness and frustration. Those who work with victims of torture, physical, and sexual violence may begin to experience symptoms of trauma themselves, such as emotional numbing, sleep disturbances, and fear for their own safety and the safety of family members.[1]

Worsening economic and social conditions, compounded with the absence of workplace autonomy and organizational support, contribute to burn out and impact negatively on the physical and mental well-being of social workers. A 1999 survey by the Canadian Union of Public Employees (CUPE) found that an increase in workload among Ontario social service workers in Development Services, Worker's Compensation, and Children's Aid Societies has an alarming impact on their well-being. Of the social service workers who responded, 87 per cent reported an increase in work-load with a negative toll on their overall health (Figure 10.1). Of the survey respondents, 50 per cent reported that their physicians also suggested that their symptoms were connected to their work. Social workers also deal with actions that pose a threat to their personal safety. Close to three-quarters (71 per cent) of the workers said that they were subjected to physical assaults, verbal abuse, or threats at work, and, of the CAS workers, 50 per cent were threatened with assault by a client. Acts of violence against social workers are often perpetrated by clients who are in desperate situations, who have exhausted all possibilities, who feel power-less, and who are reduced to vicious expressions of legitimate rage.

FIGURE 10.1	Impact on Workers' Health

- 94% reported feeling run down
- 89% reported having headaches
- 87% reported feeling exhausted
- 86% reported muscle or joint pain
- 84% reported sleeping difficulties
- 80% reported anxiety
- 65% reported change in appetite
- 60% reported indigestion

Adapted from Ontario Services Work Environment Survey, *Overloaded and Underfire* (Ottawa, ON: Canadian Union of Public Employees, 1999).

Although social welfare agencies operate under a clear mandate, they often fall short of meeting their objectives. For example, Children's Aid Societies are mandated to protect children who are being abused and/or neglected, but funding levels prohibit the agencies from hiring a suffi-cient number of social workers to meet the demands for service. At the same time as social welfare services are cut, and the cost of housing and food rise, more and more parents find the struggle to provide adequate care to their children a more onerous one. Recently, the Ottawa CAS reported a 20 per cent increase in caseload over a two-month period, far exceeding the existing resources.[2] As a result, 400 reports of abuse or neglect were waiting investigation, potentially placing children in jeopardy. Such situations create anxiety among social workers, in part because they are aware of the possibility of being blamed and charged in the event of traumatic occurrences among children on their caseload.

Tragic outcomes such as the Ontario case of Jordan Heikamp, a 37–day old infant who starved to death at a women's shelter in Toronto, are on every child protection worker's mind. Although both Jordan's mother and the social worker were charged initially, these charges were dropped at the inquiry as the judge, lawyers, and CUPE attributed the baby's death to an inadequate social service system.[3] However, press coverage of the case denigrated the social worker and called into question the profession's educational standards by suggesting that a province-wide, public review of social work education in Ontario ought to be conducted.[4] The media coverage prompted the Ontario Association of Social Workers to release an "opinion article" on March 26, 2001, speaking out against the vilification of the social worker and the profession by the media.[5]

Child protection workers, in particular, are expected to assume the contradictory and difficult roles of both compassionate individuals concerned mostly with social care and agency bureaucrats who must enforce rules and take on the function of social control. For example, in their work, they offer support to families while, at the same time, they use their authority to monitor and police parents and make decisions regarding children. A social worker interviewed by CUPE offers a list of the changing working conditions and policies in child welfare that make the work more difficult and stressful: "Over the last four or five years in child welfare, things are in a constant state of change—new legislation, changes in job expectations, new paperwork formats, increased reliance on computer technology. Staff shortages, lack of resources for referring clients, changes in client procedures, significant delays in matters moving through court process, reduced availability of at-school programs for children with special needs—The list is endless."[6] A workload study of CAS workers in Ontario found that 70 per cent of workers' time is spent on paperwork, leaving a mere 30 per cent for the children and families they are mandated to help.[7] Recently, a child protection worker interviewed by the author summed up the difficulties of working under these kind of conditions by stating, "When you go home you have this pain in your stomach."

Organizational Analysis

One of the first tasks of social workers is to gain familiarity with the stated goals of the agency in which they work and to understand the policy and procedures that are in place to meet these goals. Much of this information is available in annual reports, staff manuals, and agency web sites, as well as being imparted by the agency to workers on the job. As social workers familiarize themselves with an agency's structure, programs, and policies, they invariably gain an understanding of the contradictions and conflicts within it. An organizational analysis, argues Joan Arches, assists social workers in understanding burn-out as a public issue rather than as private trouble due to individual deficiency. In a study of social workers, Arches found that the only statistically significant contributors to burn-out were bureaucratization, control from funding sources, and lack of autonomy in the workplace. In particular, social workers reported conflict between the policies of the organization and the professional judgments of agency employees. Arches emphasizes the importance of conducting an organizational analysis of workplace stress and to develop strategies for responding to it. She guides social workers in assessing sources of organizational conflict by examining four areas: (1) decision-making and the degree of input employees have in decisions that impact on their work; (2) the labour process itself, including the assignment of caseload and the determination of activities and tasks; (3) bureaucratization of the workplace; and (4) the connection between private individual issues and collective public issues and the isolation and powerlessness experienced by employees. All areas are important in understanding the current context of cuts to programs and restructuring of services. These questions will guide an assessment of agency bureaucratization and capture the workplace reality experienced by many social workers:

1. Are there too many rules and/or too long a chain of command to permit working in a way that feels clinically correct?
2. Do you feel that you cannot always carry out the professionally best type of intervention because of organizational constraints?
3. Do you often experience ethical dilemmas between agency policy and your professional judgment?
4. Are you spending too much time on paperwork? Does it help the client or others working with the client?
5. Are you encouraged or discouraged by supervisors/administrators from making changes in the way work is carried out?

6. Have you seriously discussed these concerns with others in your workplace, union, or professional organization? What other individuals and groups might be most receptive?[8]

Increased bureaucratization, whether imposed by agency administration or government policy, has a profound affect on the autonomy of social workers and their ability to be both ethical and caring in their practice. As suggested above, there are many challenges for social workers as needed welfare programs and resources are reduced. One of these is the difficulty of advancing a critical perspective without becoming isolated within one's agency. Colleagues and supervisors are more likely to respect a differing view, critique, or suggestion if they see the social worker as a valued member of the agency, a person who has demonstrated competence and commitment. However, gaining this acceptance often means tacitly accepting or not criticizing agency goals and practices. This is particularly true in the case of social work managers who are placed in the position of enforcing agency policy.

Social workers face a growing pressure and increasing dilemma as they experience the tension between practicing in an ethical and competent manner and implementing policies and program regulations in the context of program cutbacks and mean-spirited governments; sometimes, they decide that they cannot ethically follow agency or state directives. Using a fair degree of latitude in the interpretation of rules and regulations allows them to err on the side of generosity and maximize resources for the client. However, social workers who take a stand for their clients in opposition to the agency and employer often face dismissal.[9] As was discussed in Situation #3 in Chapter 5, a social worker manager and three workers refused to implement a provincial policy on the grounds that it was culturally inappropriate to the Aboriginal community they were serving, potentially harmful, and counter to the social work ethics of practice at the time which directed the social worker to "subordinate the employer's interests to the interests of the client."[10] They were dismissed by the employer and subsequently pursued legal action. The Supreme Court of Newfoundland supported the actions of the government. One of the social workers appealed, only to find the appeal dismissed by the Newfoundland Court of Appeal on the grounds that his "breach of duty was a fundamental breach of the master-servant relationship."[11] Despite the potential seriousness of the ethical dilemma between policy and their professional judgment neither the national office of CASW nor the union advocated on behalf of these workers.

The Professionalization and Regulation of Social Work

In the early years, one of the central tasks for social work was to gain recognition as a profession by establishing educational programs, a theoretical and practice base, a professional association, and a code of ethics. The purpose of the Canadian Association of Social Workers (CASW), formed in 1926, was "to bring together professional social workers for such cooperative effort as may enable them more effectively to carry out their ideals of service to the community."[12] The activities of the association included the promotion of professional standards, development of educational programs, public recognition of the profession, the production of an official publication, a professional employment service, and research.

In the early years branches were formed in provinces and regions. Initially they reported directly to the national office, but gradually provincial branches became autonomous organizations. In 1975 CASW became a national association by gathering these provincial associations under a federated structure.[13] Today CASW is the voice for 18,000 members out of the estimated 37,470 social workers in Canada.[14] However, the Ordre professionnel des travailleurs sociaux du Quebec (OPTSQ) has given notice to withdraw from CASW as of August 31, 2003 for budgetary reasons. At 5,841 members, the OPTSQ has the largest membership among the provincial/territorial associations.[15] Since CASW relies on membership fees for its revenue, the national association now faces a financial challenge. The loss of the representation and practice contributions from Quebec social workers will create a void in the profession of social work in Canada.

All provinces in Canada and all states in the US legally regulate the social work profession. Along with protecting the title "social worker" to gain public legitimacy, professional regulation is viewed as a way of protecting the public from incompetent practitioners by providing a structure to police those who call themselves social workers. It is also recognized that a consequence of giving the social work occupation credential is "to benefit the profession by limiting its practice to those who can establish their qualifications, thus providing a mechanism for professional identity and public recognition, social prestige, and financial rewards."[16] The nature of the regulation of the profession differs across the provinces and states.[17]

All the regulated provinces have an academic requirement and title protection as the basic control over who can use the title social worker. One exception is Manitoba where registration is voluntary, and, although the title "registered social worker" is protected, the term "social worker" is not. All provincial associations have responsibility for the regulation of social work practice, except for those in Ontario, British Columbia, and Prince Edward Island, where a college separate from the association has been formed. The proportion of social workers who belong to the association is considerably higher in those provinces where the association also regulates practice. For example, virtually 100 per cent of social workers in Newfoundland, Nova Scotia, and New Brunswick belong to the association, whereas in Ontario only 25 per cent do.[18] In Ontario membership in The Ontario College of Social Workers and Social Service Workers costs $370 while membership in the Ontario Association of Social Workers is $299. In the case of economic hardship, social workers are likely to give priority to the former since they must belong to it in order to use the title "social worker" and secure employment.

The Struggle for Regulation in Ontario

All provinces in Canada, except Ontario, had introduced regulatory legislation for social workers by 1966. It wasn't until 1998 that efforts by the Ontario Association of Social Workers (previously the Ontario Association of Professional Social Workers) and the Ontario College of Certified Social Workers (OCCSW) resulted in the government's Bill 76 to regulate the profession.[19] That it took well over 15 years of active lobbying reflects the opposing visions of social work and the diverse views of the role and practice of social work that have divided the profession itself as well as public and government attitudes towards it.

While the Ontario College of Certified Social Workers, formed in 1982, provided for voluntary certification, others argued that statutory legislation was needed to protect "clients of social workers in Ontario in respect to cases of alleged professional incompetence or misconduct."[20] Project Legislation, as it was named, consumed much of the energy and finances of both the members of the association and college in order to lobby the members of the Ontario Legislature, the media, senior bureaucrats of other professional associations, and the public. The decision to keep the college independent of the association had grave implications for the latter. "While the profession in Ontario may be capable of supporting two independent organizations, the viability of both may be endangered as they compete for members and resources. The future viability of OASW has significant implications for the support of CASW and consequently for the social work profession in Canada."[21] Those opposed to the legislation were not only concerned with the possible demise of the national voice provided by CASW since OASW represented 40 per cent of national membership but also took exception to the assumption that there was widespread malpractice by social workers and a need for a policing mechanism monitored by the state.

The central argument of those advocating for a legislated regulatory framework for social work was the need to protect the public from incompetent social workers. In support of this position, Shannon McCorquodale offered a summary of the kinds of complaints received by social work regulatory bodies across Canada that have presumably placed clients at risk. Included were a number of problems such as errors in judgment, incorrect assessments, mis-diagnosis, and employing inappropriate treatment.[22]

Many of the examples provided by McCorquodale inevitably raise questions about how workplace and working conditions impact on the delivery of services in an ethical and accountable manner. For instance, given the current conditions for child protection workers discussed earlier, it is imperative that social workers not have to carry full responsibility in situations where factors in their workplace are beyond their control. In most of these examples of "incompetent practice," the social and economic context has been stripped away. Ben Carniol (Ryerson) and Brigitte Kitchen (York University) agree that there is a crisis in the social services but argue that it is not a crisis caused by social work incompetence:

> Rather, it is a crisis of underfunding and of structures which perpetuate inequalities. It is a crisis experienced daily by social service clients who are not provided the means by which to escape poverty. As a consequence, child poverty, homelessness and hunger escalate to scandalous levels, even within prosperous Ontario.[23]

Harm to clients most likely results from punitive social policies and inadequate social welfare programs rather than from unethical social workers. Thus, an examination of the ethical practice of social workers cannot be separated from their working conditions. It has been my experience that social workers are extremely committed and work long hours in order to meet the needs of their clients. Judith Globerman, in her review of the literature, discovered little support for the premise that legislation protects the public and reduces unethical practice.[24] On the contrary, she found reports of a growing gap between the profession and clients, with less accountability to the public, more emphasis on self-interests, and a move away from social problems.

Some argue that the less visible agenda of government regulation is the pursuit of power, autonomy, and control by the established professions. Magali Sarafatti Larson in her study of professions examines how occupations organize as professions in order to attain power in the market. She defines professionalization as "the process by which producers of special services sought to constitute *and control* a market for their expertise. Because marketable expertise is a crucial element in the structure of modern equality, professionalization appears *also* as a collective assertion of social status and as a collective process of upward mobility."[25] Regulation and licensing offer authority and community sanctions, two of the attributes of a profession.[26] Paul Wilding argues that "professions are occupational groups that have been taken over by the state or have forged an alliance with it."[27]

The recent *Social Work and Social Service Worker Act* of Ontario marks a social work alliance with the Progressive Conservative government. The act, developed by the government, gives widespread power to the minister of community services who controls and directs the regulatory body, the College of Social Workers and Social Service Workers, which is governed by a Council of 21 people, with equal representation from social workers, social service workers, and members of the public appointed by the government. The minister has the power to review the activities of the Council and require it to provide reports and information, or do anything that the minister believes necessary or advisable to carry out the objectives of the College; in addition, under section 36 of the act, the minister may require the Council to make, amend, or revoke a regulation. Ironically, this is the same government that drastically cut social welfare programs, introduced workfare, passed anti-labour legislation, closed hospitals, and stopped building subsidized housing in the province. By dividing the college from the association and by legislating government influence on the college Council, social work practice in Ontario has been compromised. In particular, there is the danger of a weakened provincial association and the development of clinical social work practice at the expense of social action. The membership in the Ontario provincial association has declined—at 3,054, the membership now represents 17 per cent of the national membership, down from 40 per cent prior to regulation.

There has always been concerns that social work professionalization has been pursued at the expense of social action. In 1988 Paulo Freire commented on the political nature of social work practice at an address at the International Federation of Social Workers conference:

> ... the social worker, as much as the educator, is not a neutral agent, either in practice or in action. One of the inclinations that we sometimes have—and this is an offence, an illegality, that we imbibe in our technological society—is to think that the social worker is a very specialized person, a technician, who works in a compartmentalized technical area, and who has a sort of protection within this area, a sort of aggregate of rights, as a particular social group, to stand apart from the political battles of society. For me, this is impossible. It is an error. Social workers are compromised if they become convinced that they possess a technical expertise that is more defended than is the work of other workers.[28]

However, if social work practice is political as Freire argues, and if professional associations are to be active in supporting a social change agenda, support must be provided to social workers who challenge policies and programs in support of ethical and accountable social work practice. In turn, social workers need to support professional associations while working towards change within them. The profession's code of ethics provides the broad principles of social work practice; a strong and responsive professional association can offer a national voice for social workers and leadership in meeting the challenges that face the profession.

The Role of Unions

> Whether in factory or in social agency, the relationship between employer and employee is precisely the same.[29]

Like all wage earners social workers are experiencing the impact of restructuring and privatization of services and are fighting against roll backs in wages and benefits and lay-offs. While exact numbers are not known, it can be expected that the majority of social workers in Canada belong to public-sector unions such as the Canadian Union of Public Employees (CUPE), the Public Sector Alliance of Canada (PSAC), or the National Union of Public and Government Employees (NUPGE). However, there is little attention placed on the labour movement in social work curriculum or in social work journals.[30] While professionalism is promoted in social work courses and represented in social work publications, identification as a worker and as a union member is not.

In the first half of the twentieth century social workers in Canada and the US joined organized labour. In the US between 1931 and 1942, a group of politically progressive social workers organized the rank and file movement to become part of organized labour. The membership of the movement exceeded that of the national social work association of the time, the American Association of Social Workers (AASW). Rank-and-file social workers realized that they needed a collective voice in order to achieve job protection, benefits, and decent working conditions:

> Recognized by most historians of social work and social welfare as the most significant radical movement in social work history, rank and file social workers such as [Mary] van Kleeck, Harry Lurie (Director of Jewish Social Research, New York City), Gordon Hamilton (Professor, New York School of Social Work), Eduard Lindeman (Professor, New York School of Social Work), Ewan Clague (Director of Research, Community Council, Philadelphia), Bertha Reynolds (Assistant Director of Social Work, Smith College) and Jacob Fisher (Editor, *Social Work Today*) helped develop social work's first and most powerful unions in its history and forced the profession to examine its relationship with government, organized labour, and its own client base.[31]

The New York branch was the first to define the employer-employee relationship in social work, to fight for collective bargaining, and to organize mass meetings and petitions on various issues.[32] Members were very connected to prominent people on the left both at national and international levels.[33]

In Canada, it was not until the early 1940s that full attention was placed on collective bargaining and the formation of "staff associations." Nonetheless, those who led the movement made the connection between workers in the social welfare arena and workers in factories. It was felt that "Organized labour and organized social work had their origins in identical conditions, but they rose for different reasons and at opposite ends of the economic scale."[34] It was argued that both labour unions and social work emerged in response to the social injustice and inequality that accompanied capitalist industrialization—unions from class conflict, social work from charity. Social work's role in the early days of charity provision was seen as "minor benefits handed down, often through the medium of the church, by those who owned the wealth, to those who had helped create the wealth but who had no part in controlling it."[35] It was argued by some that the emphasis on professionalization, in some ways, came in conflict with the principles of unionization. "The concern with status not only prevents *alliances* with other workers or with clients. It also works as a preventive against unity—and the unionization—of professional workers themselves."[36]

There were also opponents. For example, a long-time board member of a number of social welfare agencies in Toronto felt that terms such as "collective bargaining" and "demands of employees" were "red rag words."[37] Others, while not opposed to staff associations, wished to separate social workers from factory workers on the basis that, "In Canada, with almost no fee-collecting agencies, social agencies have neither goods nor services to sell. The 'management group' is therefore not in direct competition with 'labour' in the distribution of income."[38] Past worker-management conflicts such as occurred in 1936 at the Ottawa Welfare Bureau where social workers were blamed for the high cost of relief and 40 female social workers were fired and replaced by a smaller number of men supported the more radical view.[39]

There has always been a reluctance by some social workers to actively support unionism. This position is often based on the view that social workers are "professionals," not "workers." Professionals have the expectation and belief that they are better able to negotiate working conditions and salaries on an individual basis and that the negotiation process will be a fair one. In a study of organized shelters, Joan Pennell found that while shelter staff initially joined unions to resolve labor-management conflicts and gain control in the workplace, they also realized the effectiveness of collective bargaining for increasing their wages, benefits, and job security.[40] Pennell also discovered that in some shelters where staff and management were committed to the same organizational goals, consensual bargaining was a possibility and was viewed as a synthesis of the collective manner in which women work and the traditionally male-dominated process within unions.[41] A partnership between management and worker within social agencies can be expected to be an uneasy one at best.

Since the right to strike is fundamental to the bargaining process, unionized social workers usually have the right to strike and withdraw their labour. The strike situation can present a major dilemma for many social workers, who realize that a disruption in services may have negative consequences for their clients and may conflict with professional ethics. While the Canadian Code of Ethics offers a set of principles for social workers, there is no specific guidance for social workers who face the possibility of a strike. Nor does the CASW have a policy or statement regarding strike action by members of the profession. However, the National Association of Social Workers (NASW) has acknowledged the importance of collective bargaining by taking a position to oppose any law or policy that prohibits strikes. The NASW Code of Ethics contains a section on "Labor-Management Disputes" (3.10) which affirms the right of social workers to engage in organized action and acknowledges that in a strike situation there may be differing views within the membership. The silence of the CASW on this matter may also be indicative of conflicting views within the profession. However, individual social workers have made their pro-union stand very clear. During the regulation process in Ontario, in the consultation paper written by the government, social workers commented on a query regarding labour action: "We expect [that] registered/certified social workers who are members of unions will develop an effective means of both maintaining their direct accountability to those served and their responsibility as a union member."[42]

In a survey of social workers in the United States, Alexander et al. conclude that, while unionism and professionalism are viewed as compatible, social workers disapproved of tactics such as strikes and slow downs.[43] This became evident in 1984 when social work staff in hospitals and nursing homes in the US went on a 47–day strike. Within the membership there was "substantial disagreement regarding the congruence and conflict between labor union activities and professional activities and responsibilities by professional social workers in a hospital."[44] Clearly collective

bargaining for unionized social workers is accepted, while use of the ulti-
mate weapon for unions—strikes—are a problem.

While some might question the ethics of strike action for a professional association, Howard Karger, drawing on major schools of ethical
theory, concludes that "the morality of action depends on the goodness
of consequences.... A short term strike—which may harm clients for
some limited time period—may be justified if it leads eventually to
improved care and quality of service."[45] In a study of Canadian social
workers, Ernie Lightman found that social workers were more likely to
strike to enhance client services than to improve their own wages and
benefits. Survey findings report that over three-quarters of the social
workers who responded approved going on strike as long as adequate
safeguards, such as emergency services, were provided for clients.[46]
Although the majority of social workers in Canada are members of unions
and a substantial number belong to their professional associations,
research on the effectiveness of both in contributing to the delivery of
ethical, accountable, and effective social work services is needed. The
working conditions of social workers is related integrally to the quality
of service that they are able to provide. There is evidence that increased
workloads and diminished resources impact negatively on both social
workers' ability to meet the expectations of their jobs and on the people
who are accessing the service. Unions play a critical role in not only
protecting job security, wages, and benefits but also in securing workplace conditions, caseloads in particular. Clearly, however, the militancy
of unionized social workers and the range of tactics they are willing to
use are affected by the position they occupy and the professional ideology and standards to which they adhere.

The Way Forward: Social Work and Social Justice

As outlined in Chapter 1, the current context of globalization and neolib-
eralism, with the accompanying erosion of federal support for social
welfare, is creating harsh social and economic conditions for citizens,
particularly working people. Since the role of a federally funded welfare
state is to redistribute resources in favour of the most vulnerable in society, advancing a social justice agenda under current conditions will not
be easy. However, it must be done, and social workers must be an integral part of the movement. For Michael Reisch, "the pursuit of social

justice in the twenty-first century requires social workers to acknowledge the political dimensions of all practice and to engage in multifaceted struggles to regain influence within the public arena."[47]

Sam Gindin suggests two essential components of an effective resistance against globalization and imperialism: the ability to have a vision and dream and to work internationally, yet to be rooted locally and nationally. A vision for a just society and the means to get there requires an informed analysis of the political context. For Gindin, our perception of social justice is affected by what we believe is possible:

> Social justice demands reviving the determination to dream. It's not just that dreaming is essential for maintaining any resistance, but because today, if we do not think big—as big as the globalizers themselves think—we will not even win small.[48]

The rich history of social work demonstrates the important position social workers hold within the social welfare arena and the potential the profession has for influence. This is the time for social work to renew its vision and visibility and to become active proponents of social justice. Reisch and Andrews remind us that this requires much more than written statements:

> In today's media-saturated age, it is enough, therefore, to use words like "empowerment," "multiculturalism," "oppression," and "social justice." The test of social work's commitment to its underlying values lies in the willingness to struggle on an often mundane, day-to-day basis to translate theses values into deeds, as our professional forebears did individually and collectively.[49]

Such an engagement will need to extend beyond the submission of briefs or letters to include advocacy, social action, and participation in collective mobilization.

However, social workers do not agree about the potential of social work, as it stands, to advance social justice. Some argue that the drive for professionalization has been a major obstacle to a progressive practice, while others believe that the two are compatible.[50] Fred Newdom argues that "Professionalization of social work has led to a deification of technique over social justice: a concern for protecting our professional status even at the cost of assigning client concerns a lower priority."[51] Neil Thompson believes the challenge for social work is to develop forms of professionalization based on partnership and a commitment to equality and social justice.[52] Although he does not develop the specific ways that this could occur, the idea is an important one for social workers to collectively pursue.

Central to the task is an acknowledgment of the political dimensions of social work practice. While social workers have an ethical responsibility to advancing social justice and social change, leadership, guidance, and support are needed from the professional associations in order to meet this mandate. Now is the time to strengthen, revitalize, and transform social work professional associations so that social workers collectively have both a local and a national voice in response to the current political and economic changes that are creating the crisis in social welfare and violating the human rights of so many. In addition, social work is a global profession. Social work associations and the trade union movement are both connected internationally. If the social work profession could capture the strengths and potential of both, it could become a vital force in the social justice movement, locally, nationally, and internationally.

NOTES

[1] Cheryl Regehr, "Secondary Trauma in Social Workers," *Newsmagazine: the Journal of the Ontario Association of Social Workers* 28 3 (2001): 11.

[2] Bev Wake, "CAS Workers Warn Child 'Disaster' Awaits," *Ottawa Citizen* 29 June 2001: A1,2.

[3] Wake A1, 2.

[4] Editorial, *Ottawa Citizen* 16 April 2001: A2.

[5] Brian R. Adams and Joan MacKenzie Davies, "Social Work Profession Speaks Out About Press Coverage of Heikamp Inquest," press release Ontario Association of Social Workers, 26 March 2001: 2.

[6] Canadian Union of Public Employees, *Overloaded and Under Fire*, Report of the Ontario Social Services Work Environment Survey (Ottawa: CUPE, 1999)5. http://www.cupe.ca/overloaded.html.

[7] Wake A1, 2.

[8] Joan L. Arches, "Burnout and Social Action," *Journal of Progressive Human Services* 8.2 (1997): 55.

[9] Lundy and Gauthier 190–94.

[10] Canadian Association of Social Workers, Code of Ethics, 1983, Section 8.2. This section of the Code was revised in 1993 to read: "Where a serious ethical conflict continues to exist after the issue has been brought to the attention of the employer, the social worker shall bring the issue to the attention of the Association or regulatory body."

[11] Newfoundland Court of Appeal, *Bown vs Newfoundland*, NFLD and PEI Reports, Maritime Law Book 54 (1985) 259.

[12] Maines 2.

[13] For a summary, see Juliet Foley, "Professional Associations in Canada," *Social Work Practice: A Canadian Perspective*, ed. Francis J. Turner (Scarborough, ON: Prentice Hall, 1999) 477–91.

[14] For a thorough portrayal of social work in Canada see *In Critical Demand: Social Work in Canada*, published by the CASW in 2001.

[15] Membership figures obtained from France Audet, CASW National Office, 13 June 2001.

[16] Bruce A. Thyer and Marilyn A. Biggerstaff, *Professional Social Work Credentialing and Legal Regulation: A Review of Critical Issues and An Annotated Bibliography* (Springfield, IL.: Charles C. Thomas, 1989) 4.

[17] For a summary of provincial regulation, see Shannon McCorquodale, "The Role of Regulators in Practice," Turner 462–76. Also see the CASW web site for a complete listing of regulation in all provinces. In the US the Association of Social Work Boards (ASWB), an association that coordinates regulation and develops and maintains the licensing examinations for all states except Michigan (which does not use an exam) and California, has a web site at http://www.aswb.org.

[18] Foley 477–91.

[19] The Ontario *Social Work and Social Services Act* can be found at www.e-laws.gov.on.ca.

[20] Frank Turner, "Legislative Protection Against Malpractice," *Canadian Review of Social Policy* 25 (May 1990): 63–64.

[21] OAPSW, Strategic Planning Committee, *Interim Report* (Toronto, ON: Ontario Association of Professional Social Workers, September 1987) 3.

[22] McCorquodale 472–73.

[23] Ben Carniol and Brigitte Kitchen, "OAPSW Proposal is a Disaster and Must be Defeated," *Canadian Review of Social Policy* 25 (May 1990): 62.

[24] Judith Globerman, "Regulating Social Work: Illuminating Motives," *Canadian Social Work Review* 9.2 (Summer 1992): 229–43.

[25] Magali Sarfatti Larson, *The Rise of Professionalism: A Sociological Analysis* (Berkeley, CA: University of California Press, 1977) xvi; emphasis in original.

[26] E. Greenwood, "Attributes of a Profession," *Social Work* 2 (1957) 45–55. Greenwood suggested that there were five attributes of a profession: systematic theory, authority, community sanctions, ethical codes, and a culture.

[27] Paul Wilding, *Professional Power and Social Welfare* (London: Routledge and Kegan Paul, 1982) 15.

[28] Freire, "A Critical Understanding of Social Work" 5.

[29] Ethel Jessel, "Staff Associations," *The Social Worker* 11.4 (May 1943): 20.

[30] Ben Carniol is one of the few who has contributed to discussions on social work and unions in Canada. See, e.g., "Social Work and the Labour Movement," Wharf 114–43; *Case Critical: Challenging Social Work in Canada*, 2nd ed. (Toronto, ON: Between the Lines, 1990).

[31] Patrick Selmi and Richard Hunter, "Beyond the Rank and File Movement: Mary van Kleeck and Social Work Radicalism in the Great Depression, 1931–1942," *Journal of Sociology and Social Welfare* 27.2 (June 2001): 76.

[32] Jacob Fisher, "The Rank and File Movement 1930–1936," *Social Work Today* 3.5–6 (February 1936); reprinted in *Journal of Progressive Human Service* 1.1 (1990): 95–99.

[33] For example, Florence Kelly, one of the social work leaders in the labour movement had a longstanding friendship with Frederick Engels. See Howard Jacob Karger, *Social Work and Labor Unions* (New York, NY: Greenwood Press, 1988).

[34] Hazel Wigdor, "Social Work and Trade Unions," *The Social Worker* 12.2 (November 1943): 18.

[35] Wigdor 18–19.

[36] Larson 236; emphasis in original.

[37] Catherine Canfield Elliott, "A Board Member Speaks out," *The Social Worker* 12.2 (November 1943): 15.

[38] Katherine Best, "Another Point of View on Staff Associations," *The Social Worker* 12.2 (November 1943): 16.

[39] "What Happened in Ottawa," *The Social Worker* 5.2 (November 1936): 1–8. Bessie E. Touzel , then supervisor of staff of the Ottawa Public Welfare Board, resigned in protest. "A Social Workers Protest," her address to the Board of Control and her resignation appear in the same volume.

[40] Joan Pennell, "Feminism and Labor Unions: Transforming State Regulation of Women's Programs," *Journal of Progressive Human Services* 6.1 (1995): 45–72.

[41] Joan Pennell, "Consensual Bargaining: Labor Negotiations in Battered Women's Programs," *Journal of Progressive Human Services* 1.1 (1990): 59–74.

[42] *Response to the Consultation Paper on Regulation of Social Workers and Other Social Service Practitioners in Ontario*, undated and no indication of authors. The consultation paper was published in 1989.

[43] Leslie Alexander, Philip Lichtenberg, and Dennis Brunn, "Social Workers in Unions: A Survey," *Social Work* (May 1980): 216–23.

[44] Dena Fisher, "Problems for Social Work in a Strike Situation: Professional, Ethical, and Value Considerations," *Social Work* 32.3 (1987): 252.

[45] Karger 141.

[46] Ernie Lightman, "Social Workers, Strikes, and Service to Clients," *Social Work* 28.2 (March-April 1983): 142–47.

[47] Michael Reisch, "Defining Social Justice in a Socially Unjust World" 351.

[48] Gindin 2.

[49] Reisch and Andrews 231.

[50] See Reisch and Andrews for an excellent discussion on this topic.

[51] Fred Newdom, "Progressive and Professional: A Contradiction in Terms?" *BCR Reports* 8.1 (1996): 1.

[52] Neil Thompson, "Social Movements, Social Justice and Social Work," *British Journal of Social Work* 32 (2002): 711–22.

UNIVERSAL DECLARATION OF HUMAN RIGHTS

On December 10, 1948 the General Assembly of the United Nations adopted and proclaimed the Universal Declaration of Human Rights the full text of which appears in the following pages. Following this historic act the Assembly called upon all Member countries to publicize the text of the Declaration and "to cause it to be disseminated, displayed, read and expounded principally in schools and other educational institutions, without distinction based on the political status of countries or territories."

Preamble

Whereas recognition of the inherent dignity and of the equal and inalienable rights of all members of the human family is the foundation of freedom, justice and peace in the world,

Whereas disregard and contempt for human rights have resulted in barbarous acts which have outraged the conscience of mankind, and the advent of a world in which human beings shall enjoy freedom of speech and belief and freedom from fear and want has been proclaimed as the highest aspiration of the common people,

Whereas it is essential, if man is not to be compelled to have recourse, as a last resort, to rebellion against tyranny and oppression, that human rights should be protected by the rule of law,

Whereas it is essential to promote the development of friendly relations between nations,

Whereas the peoples of the United Nations have in the Charter reaffirmed their faith in fundamental human rights, in the dignity and worth of the human person and in the equal rights of men and women and have determined to promote social progress and better standards of life in larger freedom,

Whereas Member States have pledged themselves to achieve, in co-operation with the United Nations, the promotion of universal respect for and observance of human rights and fundamental freedoms,

Whereas a common understanding of these rights and freedoms is of the greatest importance for the full realization of this pledge,

Now, Therefore THE GENERAL ASSEMBLY proclaims THIS UNIVERSAL DECLARATION OF HUMAN RIGHTS as a common standard of achievement for all peoples and all nations, to the end that every individual and every organ of society, keeping this Declaration constantly in mind, shall strive by teaching and education to promote respect for these rights and freedoms and by progressive measures, national and international, to secure their universal and effective recognition and observance, both among the peoples of Member States themselves and among the peoples of territories under their jurisdiction.

Article 1: All human beings are born free and equal in dignity and rights.They are endowed with reason and conscience and should act towards one another in a spirit of brotherhood.

Article 2: Everyone is entitled to all the rights and freedoms set forth in this Declaration, without distinction of any kind, such as race, colour, sex, language, religion, political or other opinion, national or social origin, property, birth or other status. Furthermore, no distinction shall be made on the basis of the political, jurisdictional or international status of the country or territory to which a person belongs, whether it be independent, trust, non-self-governing or under any other limitation of sovereignty.

Article 3: Everyone has the right to life, liberty and security of person.

Article 4: No one shall be held in slavery or servitude; slavery and the slave trade shall be prohibited in all their forms.

Article 5: No one shall be subjected to torture or to cruel, inhuman or degrading treatment or punishment.

Article 6: Everyone has the right to recognition everywhere as a person before the law.

Article 7: All are equal before the law and are entitled without any discrimination to equal protection of the law. All are entitled to equal protection against any discrimination in violation of this Declaration and against any incitement to such discrimination.

Article 8: Everyone has the right to an effective remedy by the competent national tribunals for acts violating the fundamental rights granted him by the constitution or by law.

Article 9: No one shall be subjected to arbitrary arrest, detention or exile.

Article 10: Everyone is entitled in full equality to a fair and public hearing by an independent and impartial tribunal, in the determination of his rights and obligations and of any criminal charge against him.

Article 11: (1) Everyone charged with a penal offence has the right to be presumed innocent until proved guilty according to law in a public trial at which he has had all the guarantees necessary for his defence.
(2) No one shall be held guilty of any penal offence on account of any act or omission which did not constitute a penal offence, under national or international law, at the time when it was committed. Nor shall a heavier penalty be imposed than the one that was applicable at the time the penal offence was committed.

Article 12: No one shall be subjected to arbitrary interference with his privacy, family, home or correspondence, nor to attacks upon his honour and reputation. Everyone has the right to the protection of the law against such interference or attacks.

Article 13: (1) Everyone has the right to freedom of movement and residence within the borders of each state.

(2) Everyone has the right to leave any country, including his own, and to return to his country.

Article 14: (1) Everyone has the right to seek and to enjoy in other countries asylum from persecution.
(2) This right may not be invoked in the case of prosecutions genuinely arising from non-political crimes or from acts contrary to the purposes and principles of the United Nations.

Article 15: (1) Everyone has the right to a nationality.
(2) No one shall be arbitrarily deprived of his nationality nor denied the right to change his nationality.

Article 16: (1) Men and women of full age, without any limitation due to race, nationality or religion, have the right to marry and to found a family. They are entitled to equal rights as to marriage, during marriage and at its dissolution.
(2) Marriage shall be entered into only with the free and full consent of the intending spouses.
(3) The family is the natural and fundamental group unit of society and is entitled to protection by society and the State.

Article 17: (1) Everyone has the right to own property alone as well as in association with others.
(2) No one shall be arbitrarily deprived of his property.

Article 18: Everyone has the right to freedom of thought, conscience and religion; this right includes freedom to change his religion or belief, and freedom, either alone or in community with others and in public or private, to manifest his religion or belief in teaching, practice, worship and observance.

Article 19: Everyone has the right to freedom of opinion and expression; this right includes freedom to hold opinions without interference and to seek, receive and impart information and ideas through any media and regardless of frontiers.

Article 20: (1) Everyone has the right to freedom of peaceful assembly and association.

(2) No one may be compelled to belong to an association.

Article 21: (1) Everyone has the right to take part in the government of his country, directly or through freely chosen representatives.

(2) Everyone has the right of equal access to public service in his country.

(3) The will of the people shall be the basis of the authority of government; this will shall be expressed in periodic and genuine elections which shall be by universal and equal suffrage and shall be held by secret vote or by equivalent free voting procedures.

Article 22: Everyone, as a member of society, has the right to social security and is entitled to realization, through national effort and international co-operation and in accordance with the organization and resources of each State, of the economic, social and cultural rights indispensable for his dignity and the free development of his personality.

Article 23: (1) Everyone has the right to work, to free choice of employment, to just and favourable conditions of work and to protection against unemployment.

(2) Everyone, without any discrimination, has the right to equal pay for equal work.

(3) Everyone who works has the right to just and favourable remuneration ensuring for himself and his family an existence worthy of human dignity, and supplemented, if necessary, by other means of social protection.

(4) Everyone has the right to form and to join trade unions for the protection of his interests.

Article 24: Everyone has the right to rest and leisure, including reasonable limitation of working hours and periodic holidays with pay.

Article 25: (1) Everyone has the right to a standard of living adequate for the health and well-being of himself and of his family, including food, clothing, housing and medical care and necessary social services, and the right to security in the event of unemployment, sickness, disability, widowhood, old age or other lack of livelihood in circumstances beyond his control.

(2) Motherhood and childhood are entitled to special care and assistance.

All children, whether born in or out of wedlock, shall enjoy the same social protection.

Article 26: (1) Everyone has the right to education. Education shall be free, at least in the elementary and fundamental stages. Elementary education shall be compulsory. Technical and professional education shall be made generally available and higher education shall be equally accessible to all on the basis of merit.

(2) Education shall be directed to the full development of the human personality and to the strengthening of respect for human rights and fundamental freedoms. It shall promote understanding, tolerance and friendship among all nations, racial or religious groups, and shall further the activities of the United Nations for the maintenance of peace.

(3) Parents have a prior right to choose the kind of education that shall be given to their children.

Article 27: (1) Everyone has the right freely to participate in the cultural life of the community, to enjoy the arts and to share in scientific advancement and its benefits.

(2) Everyone has the right to the protection of the moral and material interests resulting from any scientific, literary or artistic production of which he is the author.

Article 28: Everyone is entitled to a social and international order in which the rights and freedoms set forth in this Declaration can be fully realized.

Article 29: (1) Everyone has duties to the community in which alone the free and full development of his personality is possible.

(2) In the exercise of his rights and freedoms, everyone shall be subject only to such limitations as are determined by law solely for the purpose of securing due recognition and respect for the rights and freedoms of others and of meeting the just requirements of morality, public order and the general welfare in a democratic society.

(3) These rights and freedoms may in no case be exercised contrary to the purposes and principles of the United Nations.

Article 30: Nothing in this Declaration may be interpreted as implying for any State, group or person any right to engage in any activity or to perform any act aimed at the destruction of any of the rights and free-doms set forth herein.

CANADIAN ASSOCIATION OF SOCIAL WORKERS CODE OF ETHICS[1]

Definitions
In this Code,
Best Interest of Client

means
(a) that the wishes, desires, motivations, and plans of the client are taken by the social worker as the primary consideration in any intervention plan developed by the social worker subject to change only when the client's plans are documented to be unrealistic, unreasonable or potentially harmful to self or others or otherwise determined inappropriate when considered in relation to a mandated requirement,
(b) that all actions and interventions of the social worker are taken subject to the reasonable belief that the client will benefit from the action, and
(c) that the social worker will consider the client as an individual, a member of a family unit, a member of a community, a person with a distinct ancestry or culture and will consider those factors in any decision affecting the client.

Client[2]

means
(a) a person, family, group of persons, incorporated body, association or community on whose behalf a social worker provides or agrees to provide a service

    i) on request or with agreement[3] of the person, family, group of persons, incorporated body, associations or community, or

ii) as a result of a legislated responsibility, or

(b) a judge of a court of competent jurisdiction who orders the social worker to provide to the Court an assessment.[4]

Conduct Unbecoming

means behaviour or conduct that does not meet standard of care requirements and is therefore subject to discipline.[5]

Malpractice and Negligence

means behaviour that is included as "conduct unbecoming" and relates to social work practice behaviour within the parameters of the professional relationship that falls below the standard of practice and results in or aggravates an injury to a client. Without limiting the generality of the above,[6] it includes behaviour which results in assault, deceit, fraudulent misrepresentations, defamation of character, breach of contract, violation of human rights, malicious prosecution, false imprisonment or criminal conviction.

Practice of Social Work

includes the assessment, remediation and prevention of social problems, and the enhancement of social functioning of individuals, families, groups and communities by means of

(a) the provision of direct counselling services within an established relationship between a social worker and client;

(b) the development, promotion and delivery of human service programs, including that done in collaboration with other professionals;

(c) the development and promotion of social policies aimed at improving social conditions and equality; and[7]

(d) any other activities approved by CASW.[8]

Social Worker

means a person who is duly registered to practice social work in a province or territory or where mandatory registration does not exist, a person practising social work who voluntarily agrees to be subject to this Code.

Standard of Practice

means the standard of care ordinarily expected of a competent social worker. It means that the public is assured that a social worker has the training, the skill and the diligence to provide them with professional social work services.

Preamble
Philosophy

The profession of social work is founded on humanitarian and egalitarian ideals. Social workers believe in the intrinsic worth and dignity of every human being and are committed to the values of acceptance, self-determination and respect of individuality. They believe in the obligation of all people, individually and collectively, to provide resources, services and opportunities for the overall benefit of humanity. The culture of individuals, families, groups, communities and nations has to be respected without prejudice.[9]

Social workers are dedicated to the welfare and self-realization of human beings; to the development and disciplined use of scientific knowledge regarding human and societal behaviours; to the development of resources to meet individual, group, national and international needs and aspirations; and to the achievement of social justice for all.

Professional Practice Conflicts

If a conflict arises in professional practice, the standards declared in this Code take precedence. Conflicts of interest may occur because of demands from the general public, workplace, organizations or clients. In all cases, if the ethical duties and obligations or ethical responsibilities of this Code would be compromised, the social worker must act in a manner consistent with this Code.

Nature of this Code

The first seven statements in this code establish ethical duties and obligations. These statements provide the basis of a social worker's relationship with a client and are based on the values of social work. A breach of any of these statements forms the basis of a disciplinary action. The remaining three statements are characterized as ethical responsibilities and are to be seen as being different from the ethical duties and obligations. These ethical responsibilities are not likely to form the basis of any disciplinary action if breached. However these sections may form the basis of inquiry. These ethical responsibilities may be used in conjunction with breaches of other sections of this code and may form the basis of necessary background information in any action for discipline. Of equal importance, these ethical responsibilities are desirable goals to be achieved by the social work profession which by its nature is driven by an adherence to the values that form the basis of these desirable ethical behaviours.

Social Work Code of Ethics
Ethical Duties and Obligations

1. A social worker shall maintain the best interest of the client as the primary professional obligation.
2. A social worker shall carry out her or his professional duties and obligations with integrity and objectivity.
3. A social worker shall have and maintain competence in the provision of a social work service to a client.
4. A social worker shall not exploit the relationship with a client for personal benefit, gain or gratification.
5. A social worker shall protect the confidentiality of all information acquired from the client or others regarding the client and the client's family during the professional relationship unless
   (a) the client authorizes in writing the release of specified information,
   (b) the information is released under the authority of a statute or an order of a court of competent jurisdiction, or
   (c) otherwise authorized by this Code.
6. A social worker who engages in another profession, occupation, affiliation or calling shall not allow these outside interests to affect the social work relationship with the client.
7. A social worker in private practice shall not conduct the business of provision of social work services for a fee in a manner that discredits the profession or diminishes the public's trust in the profession.

Ethical Responsibilities

8. A social worker shall advocate for workplace conditions and policies that are consistent with the Code.
9. A social worker shall promote excellence in the social work profession.
10. A social worker shall advocate change
    (a) in the best interest of the client, and
    (b) for the overall benefit of society, the environment and the global community.

Chapter 1: Primary Professional Obligation

1. A social worker shall maintain the best interest of the client as the primary professional obligation.

1.1. The social worker is to be guided primarily by this obligation. Any action which is substantially inconsistent with this obligation is an unethical action.

1.2 A social worker in the practice of social work shall not discriminate against any person on the basis of race, ethnic background, language, religion, marital status, sex, sexual orientation, age, abilities, socio-economic status, political affiliation or national ancestry.[10]

1.3 A social worker shall inform a client of the client's right to consult another professional at any time during the provision of social work services.

1.4 A social worker shall immediately inform the client of any faction, condition[11] or pressure that affects the social worker's ability to perform an acceptable level of service.

1.5 A social worker shall not become involved in a client's personal affairs that are not relevant to the service being provided.

1.6 A social worker shall not state an opinion, judgment or use a clinical diagnosis unless there is a documented assessment, observation or diagnosis to support the opinion, judgment or diagnosis.

1.7 Where possible, a social worker shall provide or secure social work services in the language chosen by the client.

Chapter 2: Integrity and Objectivity

2. A social worker shall carry out his or her professional duties and obligations with integrity and objectivity.[12]

2.1 The social worker shall identify and describe education, training, experience, professional affiliations, competence, and nature of service in an honest and accurate manner.

2.2 The social worker shall explain to the client her or his education, experience, training, competence, nature of service and action at the request of the client.

2.3 A social worker shall cite an educational degree only after it has been received from the institution.

2.4 A social worker shall not claim formal social work education in an area of expertise or training solely by attending a lecture, demonstration, conference, panel discussion, workshop, seminar or other similar teaching presentation.[13]

2.5 The social worker shall not make a false, misleading or exaggerated claim of efficacy regarding past or anticipated achievement with respect to clients.

2.6 The social worker shall distinguish between actions and statements made as a private citizen and statements made as a social worker.[14]

Chapter 3: Competence in the Provision of Social Work Services

3. A social worker shall have and maintain competence in the provision of a social work service to a client.

3.1 The social worker shall not undertake a social work service unless the social worker has the competence to provide the service or the social workers can reasonably acquire the necessary competence without undue delay, risk or expense to the client.

3.2 Where a social worker cannot reasonably acquire the necessary competence in the provision of a service to a client, the social worker shall decline to provide the service to the client, advising the client of the reason and ensuring that the client is referred to another professional person if the client agrees to the referral.

3.3 The social worker, with the agreement of the client, may obtain advice from other professionals in the provision of service to a client.

3.4 A social worker shall maintain an acceptable level of health and wellbeing in order to provide a competent level of service to a client.[15]

3.5 Where a social worker has a physical or mental health problem, disability or illness that affects the ability of the social worker to provide competent service or that would threaten the health or well-being of the client, the social worker shall discontinue the provision of social work service to a client

    (a) advising the client of the reason and,[16]

    (b) ensuring that the client is referred to another professional person if the client agrees to the referral.

3.6 The social worker shall have, maintain and endeavor periodically to update an acceptable level of knowledge and skills to meet the standards of the practice of the profession.

Chapter 4: Limit on Professional Relationship

4. A social worker shall not exploit the relationship with a client for personal benefit, gain or gratification.

4.1 The social worker shall respect the client and act so that the dignity, individuality and rights of the person are protected.

4.2 The social worker shall assess and consider a client's motivation and physical and mental capacity in arranging for the provision of an appropriate service.

4.3 The social worker shall not have a sexual relationship with a client.

4.4 The social worker shall not have a business relationship with a client, borrow money from a client, or loan money to a client.[17]

4.5 The social worker shall not have a sexual relationship with a social work student assigned to the social worker.

4.6 The social worker shall not sexually harass any person.

Chapter 5: Confidential Information

5. A social worker shall protect the confidentiality[18] of all information acquired from the client or others regarding the client and the client's family during the professional relationship[19] unless

    (a) the client authorizes in writing the release of specified information,[20]

    (b) the information is released under the authority of a statute or an order of a court of relevant jurisdiction, or

    (c) otherwise authorized under this Code.

5.1 The requirement of confidentiality also applies to social workers who work as

    (a) supervisors,

    (b) managers,

(c) educators, or

(d) administrators.

5.2 A social worker who works as a supervisor, manager or administrator shall establish policies and practices that protect the confidentiality of client information.

5.3 The social worker may disclose confidential information to other persons in the workplace who, by virtue of their responsibilities, have an identified need to know as determined by the social worker.

5.4 Clients shall be the initial or primary source of information about themselves and their problems unless the client is incapable or unwilling to give information or when corroborative reporting is required.

5.5 The social worker has the obligation to ensure that the client understands what is being asked, why and to what purpose the information will be used, and to understand the confidentiality policies and practices of the workplace setting.

5.6 Where information is required by law, the social workers shall explain to the client the consequences of refusing to provide the requested information.

5.7 Where information is required from other sources, the social worker

(a) shall explain the requirement to the client, and

(b) shall attempt to involve the client in selecting the sources to be used.

5.8 The social worker shall take reasonable care to safeguard the client's personal papers or property if the social worker agrees to keep the property at the request of the client.

Recording Information

5.9 The social worker shall maintain only one master file on each client.[21]

5.10 The social worker shall record all relevant information, and keep all relevant documents in the file.

5.11 The social worker shall not record in a client's file any characterization that is not based on clinical assessment or fact.

Accessibility of Records

5.12 The social worker who contracts for the delivery of social work services with a client is responsible to the client for maintaining the client record.

5.13 The social worker who is employed by a social agency that delivers social work services to clients is responsible

(a) to the client for the maintaining of a client record, and

(b) to the agency to maintain the records to facilitate the objectives of the agency.

5.14 A social worker is obligated to follow the provision of a statute that allows access to records by clients.

5.15 The social worker shall respect the client's right of access to a client record subject to the social worker's right to refuse access for just and reasonable cause.

5.16 Where a social worker refuses a client the right to access a file or part of a file, the social worker shall advise the client of the right to request a review of the decision in accordance with the relevant statute, workplace policy or other relevant procedure.

Disclosure

5.17 The social worker shall not disclose the identity of persons who have sought a social work service or disclose source of information about clients unless compelled legally to do so.[22]

5.18 The obligation to maintain confidentiality continues indefinitely after the social worker has ceased contact with the client.

5.19 The social worker shall avoid unnecessary conversation regarding clients.

5.20 The social worker may divulge confidential information with consent of the client, preferably expressed in writing, where this is essential to a plan of care or treatment.

5.21 The social worker shall transfer information to another agency or individual, only with the informed consent of the client or guardian of the client and then only with the reasonable assurance that the receiving agency provides the same guarantee of confidentiality and respect for the right of privileged communication as provided by the sending agency.

5.22 The social worker shall explain to the client the disclosure of information requirements of the law or of the agency before the commencement of the provision of social work services.

5.23 The social worker in practice with groups and communities shall notify the participants of the likelihood that aspects of their private lives may be revealed in the course of their work together, and therefore require a commitment from each member to respect the privileged and confidential nature of the communication between and among members of the client group.

5.24 Subject to section 5.26, the social worker shall not disclose information acquired from one client to a member of the client's family without the informed consent of the client who provided the information.

5.25 A social worker shall disclose information acquired from one client to a member of the client's family where

(a) the information involves a threat of harm to self or others,[23]

(b) the information was acquired from a child of tender years and the social worker determines that its disclosure is in the best interests of the child.[24]

5.26 A social worker shall disclose information acquired from a client to a person or police officer where the information involves a threat of harm to that person.

5.27 A social worker may release confidential information as part of a discipline hearing of a social worker as directed by the tribunal or disciplinary body.

5.28 When disclosure is required by order of a court, the social worker shall not divulge more information that is reasonably required and shall where possible notify the client of this requirement.

5.29 The social worker shall not use confidential information for the purpose of teaching, public education or research except with the informed consent of the client.

5.30 The social worker may use non-identifying information for the purpose of teaching, public education or research.

Retention and Disposition of Information

5.31 Where the social worker's documentation is stored in a place or computer maintained and operated by an employer, the social worker shall advocate for the responsible retention and disposition of information contained in the file.

Chapter 6: Outside Interest

6. A social worker who engages in another profession, occupation, affiliation or calling shall not allow these outside interests to affect the social work relationship with the client.

6.1 A social worker shall declare to the client any outside interests that would affect the social work relationship with the client.

6.2 A social worker shall not allow an outside interest:

(a) to affect the social worker's ability to practise social work;

(b) to present to the client or to the community that the social worker's ability to practise social work is affected; or

(c) to bring the profession of social work into disrepute.[25]

Chapter 7: Limit on Private Practice

7. A social worker in private practice shall not conduct the business of provision of social work services for a fee in a manner that discredits the profession or diminishes the public's trust in the profession.

7.1 A social worker shall not use the social work relationship within an agency to obtain clients for his or her private practice.

7.2 Subject to section 7.3, a social worker who enters into a contract for service with a client

(a) shall disclose at the outset of the relationship, the fee schedule for the social work services,

(b) shall not charge a fee that is greater than that agreed to and disclosed to the client, and

(c) shall not charge for hours of service other that the reasonable hours of client services, research, consultation and administrative work directly connected to the case.

7.3 A social worker in private practice may charge differential fees for services except where an increased fee is charged based on race, ethnic background, language, religion, marital status, sex, sexual orientation, age, abilities, socio-economic status, political affiliation or national ancestry.

7.4 A social worker in private practice shall maintain adequate malpractice, defamation and liability insurance.

7.5 A social worker in private practice may charge a rate of interest on delinquent accounts as is allowed by law.[26]

7.6 Notwithstanding section 5.17 a social worker in private practice may pursue civil remedies to ensure payment for services to a client where the social worker has advised the client of this possibility at the outset of the social work service.

Chapter 8: Ethical Responsibilities to the Workplace

8. A social worker shall advocate for workplace conditions and policies that are consistent with the Code.

8.1 Where the responsibilities to an employer are in conflict with the social worker's obligations to the client, the social worker shall document the issue in writing and shall bring the situation to the attention of the employer.

8.2 Where a serious ethical conflict continues to exist after the issue has been brought to the attention of the employer, the social worker shall bring the issue to the attention of the Association or regulatory body.[27]

8.3 A social worker shall follow the principles in the Code when dealing with

(a) a social worker under the supervision of the social worker,

(b) an employee under the supervision of the social worker, and

(c) a social work student under the supervision of the social worker.

Chapter 9: Ethical Responsibilities to the Profession

9. A social worker shall promote excellence in the social work profession.

9.1 A social worker shall report to the appropriate association or regulatory body any breach of this Code by another social worker which adversely affects or harms a client or prevents the effective delivery of a social service.

9.2 A social worker shall report to the association or regulatory body any unqualified or unlicensed person who is practising social work.

9.3 A social worker shall not intervene in the professional relationship of a social worker and client unless requested to do so by the client and unless convinced that the best interests and well-being of the client require such intervention.

9.4 Where a conflict arises between a social worker and other professionals, the social worker shall attempt to resolve the professional differences in ways that uphold the principles of this Code and honour of the social work profession.

9.5 A social worker engaged in research shall ensure that the involvement of clients in the research is a result of informed consent.

Chapter 10: Ethical Responsibilities for Social Change

10. A social worker shall advocate change

(a) in the best interest of the client, and

(b) for the overall benefit of society, the environment and the global community.

10.1 A social worker shall identify, document and advocate for the elimination of discrimination.

10.2 A social worker shall advocate for the equal distribution of resources to all persons.

10.3 A social worker shall advocate for the equal access of all persons to resources, services and opportunities.

10.4 A social worker shall advocate for a clean and healthy environment and shall advocate the development of environmental strategies consistent with social work principles.

10.5 A social worker shall provide reasonable professional services in a state of emergency.

10.6 A social worker shall promote social justice.

NOTES

[1] This Social Work Code of Ethics, adopted by the Board of Directors of the Canadian Association of Social Workers (CASW) is effective on January 1, 1994 and replaces The CASW Code of Ethics (1983). The Code is reprinted here with the permission of the CASW. The copyright in the document has been registered with Consumer and Corporate Affairs Canada, registration No. 42737.

[2] A client ceases to be a client 2 years after the termination of a social work service. It is advisable for this termination to be clearly documented on the case file.

[3] This sub-paragraph identifies two situations where a person may be considered a voluntary client. The person who requests a social work service is clearly a voluntary client. A person also may originally be receiving services as a result of a court of other legally mandated entity. This person may receive a service beyond that originally mandated and therefore be able to terminate voluntarily that aspect of the service. A situation where a person is referred by another professional or family member clearly falls into this "voluntary service" relationship when that person agrees with the service to be provided. This type of social work relationship is clearly distinguishable from the relationship in sub-paragraph (ii) where the social worker does not seek or have agreement for the service to be provided.

[4] In this situation, the social worker is providing an assessment, information or a professional opinion to a judge of competent jurisdiction to assist the judge in making a ruling or determination. In this situation, the relationship is with the judge and the person on whom the information, assessment or opinion is provided is not the client. The social worker still has some professional obligations towards that person, for example: competence and dignity.

[5] In reaching a decision in *Re Matthews and Board of Directors of Physiotherapy* (1986) 54 OR (2d) 375, Saunders J. makes three important statements regarding standards of practice and by implication Code of Ethics:

(i) Standards of practice are inherent characteristics of any profession.

(ii) Standards of practice may be written or unwritten.

(iii) Some conduct is clearly regarded as misconduct and need not be written down whereas other conduct may be the subject of dispute within a profession.

6 The importance of the collective opinion of the profession in establishing and ultimately modifying the Code of Ethics was established in a 1884 case involving the medical profession. Lord Esher, M.R., stated:

"If it is shown that a medical man, in the pursuit of his profession, has done something with regard to it which would be reasonably regarded as disgraceful or dishonourable by his professional brethren of good repute and competency," then it is open to the General Medical Council to say that he has been guilty of "infamous conduct in a professional respect."

7 This definition except paragraph (d) has been taken from *An Act to Incorporate the New Brunswick Association of Social Workers*, chapter 78 of the Statutes of New Brunswick, 1988, section 2.

8 The procedure for adding activities under this paragraph will be established as a bylaw by the CASW Board of Directors.

9 Taken from: *Teaching and Learning about Human Rights: A Manual for Schools of Social Work and the Social Work Profession*; UN Centre for Human Rights, Co-operation with International Federation of Social Workers and International Association of Schools of Social Workers, United Nations, New York, 1992.

10 This obligation goes beyond grounds of discrimination stated in most *Human Rights Legislation* and therefore there is a greater professional obligation than that stated in provincial legislation.

11 The term condition means a physical, mental or psychological condition. There is an implied obligation that the social worker shall actively seek diagnosis and treatment for any signs or warnings of a condition. A disclosure under this section may be of a general nature. See also 3.4.

12 The term objectivity is taken from the Québec Code of Professional Conduct: Integrity and Objectivity (6.0 Québec) November 5, 1979 Vo. 2 No. 30. The term objectivity is stated in the following: 3.02.01: A social worker must discharge his professional duties with integrity and objectivity.

13 The provincial associations may regulate the areas of expertise to be stated or advertised by a social worker. This will vary in each province according to its enabling legislation. Where there is not sufficient legislative base for this regulation, the claim of an expertise without sufficient training may form the basis of a determination of unprofessional conduct.

14 Even with a distinction made under this section, a social worker's private actions or statements may be of such a nature that the social worker cannot avoid the responsibilities under this Code. See also 6.2(c).

15 This section should be considered in relation to section 1.4 and involves proper maintenance, prevention and treatment of any type of risk to the health and well-being of the social worker.

16 It is not necessary in all circumstances to explain specifically the nature of the problem.

17 Where a social worker does keep money or assets belonging to a client, the social worker should hold this money or asset in a trust account or hold the money or asset in conjunction with an additional professional person.

18 Confidentiality means that information received or observed about a client by a social worker will be held in confidence and disclosed only when the social worker is properly authorized or obligated legally or professionally to do so. This also means that professionally acquired information may be treated as privileged communication and ordinarily only the client has the right to waive privilege.

Privileged communication means statements made within a protected relationship (i.e. husband-wife, professional-client) which the law protects against disclosure. The extent of the privilege is governed by law and not by this Code.

Maintaining confidentiality of privileged communication means that information about clients does not have to be transmitted in any oral, written or recorded form. Such information, for example, does not have to be disclosed to a supervisor, written into a workplace record, stored in a computer or microfilm data base, held on an audio or videotape or discussed orally. The right of privileged communication is respected by the social worker in the practice of social work notwithstanding that this right is not ordinarily granted in law.

The disclosure of confidential information in social work practice involves the obligation to share information professionally with others in the workplace of the social worker as part of a reasonable service to the client. Social workers recognize the need to obtain permission from clients before releasing information about them to sources outside their workplace and to inform clients at the outset of their relationship that some information acquired may be shared with the officers and personnel of the agency who maintain the case record and who have a reasonable need for the information in the performance of their duties.

[19] The social worker's relationship with a client can be characterized as a fiduciary relationship.

In *Fiduciary Duties in Canada* by Ellis, fiduciary duty is described as follows: ... where one party has placed its "trust and confidence" in another and the latter has accepted—expressly or by operation of the law—to act in a manner consistent with the reposing of such "trust and confidence," a fiduciary relationship has been established.

[20] The "obligation of secrecy" was discussed by the Supreme Court of Canada in *Hollis v. Mitchell* (1928) SCR 125, an action brought by a disabled CNR worker against a company doctor who had disclosed the employee's medical history, to the latter's detriment. Mr Justice Duff reviewed the duty of confidentiality:

We are not required for the purpose of this appeal, to attempt to state with any sort of precision the limits of the obligation of secrecy which rests upon the medical practitioner in relation to the professional secrets acquired by him in the course of his practice. Nobody would dispute that a secret so acquired is the secret of the patient, and, normally, is under his control, and not under that of the doctor. Prima facie, the patient has the right to require that the secret shall not be divulged; and that right is absolute, unless there is some paramount reason which overrides it.

Thus, the right of secrecy/confidentiality rests squarely with the patient: the Court carefully provided that there is an "ownership" extant in the confidentiality of the personal information. Duff J. continued by allowing for "paramount" criteria which vitiates from the right:

Some reasons may arise, no doubt, from the existence of facts which bring into play overpowering considerations connected with public justice; and there may be cases in which reasons connected with the safety of individuals or the public, physical or moral, would be sufficiently cogent to supersede or qualify the obligations prima facie imposed by the confidential relation.

Duff J. continued:

The general duty of medical men to observe secrecy, in relation to information acquired by them confidentially from their patients is subject, no doubt, to some exceptions, which have no operation in the case of solicitors; but the grounds of the legal, social or moral imperatives affecting physicians and surgeons, touching the inviolability of professional confidences, are not, any more than those affecting legal advisers, based exclusively upon the relations between the parties as individuals.

[21] The master file refers to all relevant documents pertaining to the client consisting of such information as demographics, case recordings, court documents, assessments, correspondence, treatment plans, bills, etc. This information is often collected through various means including electronic and computer-driven sources. However the client master file exists as one unit, inclusive of all information pertaining to the client, despite the various sources of the recording process. The description and ownership of the master file is most often defined by workplace standards or policies. The client's master file should be prepared keeping in mind that it may have to be revealed to the client or disclosed in legal proceedings.

[22] A social worker may be compelled to reveal information under the section when directly ordered by the court to do so. Before disclosing the information, the social worker shall advise the court of the professional obligations that exist under this section of the Code and where reasonably possible inform the client.

[23] The case of *Tarasoff v. The Regents of the University of California et al.* (1976) 551 p.2d 334 (Cal. Supreme Court) focused on the obligation of a psychiatrist to maintain the confidentiality

of his patients' statements in their discussions. In that case the patient told the psychiatrist that the patient had an intention to kill a certain woman. When the patient actually did kill this woman, her parents brought suit alleging that the psychiatrist owed a duty to tell the woman of the danger to her.

It was held that the psychiatrist did have a duty to tell the woman of the threat. The court recognized that the psychiatrist owed a duty to the patient to keep in confidence the statements the patient made in therapy sessions, but held there was also a duty to care to anyone whom the psychiatrist knew might be endangered by the patient. At a certain point the obligation of confidentiality would be overridden by the obligation to this third person. The psychiatrist's knowledge itself gave rise to a duty of care. What conduct would be sufficient to fulfil the duty to this person would depend on the circumstances, but it might be necessary to give a warning that would reveal what the patient had said about the third party. The court in this case held that the psychiatrist had a duty to warn the woman about the patient's stated intention to kill her, and having failed to warn her the psychiatrist was liable in negligence. Moreover, the court stated that the principle of this duty of care belonged not just to a psychiatrist but also to a psychologist performing therapy. It would follow that the principle would also apply to social workers performing therapy.

24 For the purpose of this Code, a child of tender years shall usually be determined to be a child under the age of seven years subject to a determination by a social worker considering the child's social, physical, intellectual, emotional or psychological development.

25 This section brings the social worker's outside interest and personal actions in line with the professional duties and obligations as set out in this Code.

26 This rate shall be stated on all invoices or bills sent to the client.

27 In this situation the professional obligations outweigh any obligations to a workplace.

NATIONAL ASSOCIATION OF SOCIAL WORKERS CODE OF ETHICS[1]

Approved by the 1996 NASW Delegate Assembly and revised by the 1999 NASW Delegate Assembly

Preamble

The primary mission of the social work profession is to enhance human well-being and help meet the basic human needs of all people, with particular attention to the needs and empowerment of people who are vulnerable, oppressed, and living in poverty. A historic and defining feature of social work is the profession's focus on individual well-being in a social context and the well-being of society. Fundamental to social work is attention to the environmental forces that create, contribute to, and address problems in living.

Social workers promote social justice and social change with and on behalf of clients. "Clients" is used inclusively to refer to individuals, families, groups, organizations, and communities. Social workers are sensitive to cultural and ethnic diversity and strive to end discrimination, oppression, poverty, and other forms of social injustice. These activities may be in the form of direct practice, community organizing, supervision, consultation, administration, advocacy, social and political action, policy development and implementation, education, and research and evaluation. Social workers seek to enhance the capacity of people to address their own needs. Social workers also seek to promote the responsiveness of organizations, communities, and other social institutions to individuals' needs and social problems.

The mission of the social work profession is rooted in a set of core values. These core values, embraced by social workers throughout the profession's history, are the foundation of social work's unique purpose and perspective:

- service
- social justice
- dignity and worth of the person
- importance of human relationships
- integrity
- competence.

This constellation of core values reflects what is unique to the social work profession. Core values, and the principles that flow from them, must be balanced within the context and complexity of the human experience.

Purpose of the NASW Code of Ethics

Professional ethics are at the core of social work. The profession has an obligation to articulate its basic values, ethical principles, and ethical standards. The *NASW Code of Ethics* sets forth these values, principles, and standards to guide social workers' conduct. The *Code* is relevant to all social workers and social work students, regardless of their professional functions, the settings in which they work, or the populations they serve.

The *NASW Code of Ethics* serves six purposes:

1. The *Code* identifies core values on which social work's mission is based.
2. The *Code* summarizes broad ethical principles that reflect the profession's core values and establishes a set of specific ethical standards that should be used to guide social work practice.
3. The *Code* is designed to help social workers identify relevant considerations when professional obligations conflict or ethical uncertainties arise.
4. The *Code* provides ethical standards to which the general public can hold the social work profession accountable.
5. The *Code* socializes practitioners new to the field to social work's mission, values, ethical principles, and ethical standards.
6. The *Code* articulates standards that the social work profession itself can use to assess whether social workers have engaged in unethical conduct. NASW has formal procedures to adjudicate ethics complaints filed against its members.* In subscribing to this *Code*, social workers are required to cooperate in its implementation,

participate in NASW adjudication proceedings, and abide by any NASW disciplinary rulings or sanctions based on it.

*For information on NASW adjudication procedures, see *NASW Procedures for the Adjudication of Grievances.*

The *Code* offers a set of values, principles, and standards to guide decision making and conduct when ethical issues arise. It does not provide a set of rules that prescribe how social workers should act in all situations. Specific applications of the *Code* must take into account the context in which it is being considered and the possibility of conflicts among the *Code*'s values, principles, and standards. Ethical responsibilities flow from all human relationships, from the personal and familial to the social and professional.

Further, the *NASW Code of Ethics* does not specify which values, principles, and standards are most important and ought to outweigh others in instances when they conflict. Reasonable differences of opinion can and do exist among social workers with respect to the ways in which values, ethical principles, and ethical standards should be rank ordered when they conflict. Ethical decision making in a given situation must apply the informed judgment of the individual social worker and should also consider how the issues would be judged in a peer review process where the ethical standards of the profession would be applied.

Ethical decision making is a process. There are many instances in social work where simple answers are not available to resolve complex ethical issues. Social workers should take into consideration all the values, principles, and standards in this *Code* that are relevant to any situation in which ethical judgment is warranted. Social workers' decisions and actions should be consistent with the spirit as well as the letter of this *Code*.

In addition to this *Code*, there are many other sources of information about ethical thinking that may be useful. Social workers should consider ethical theory and principles generally, social work theory and research, laws, regulations, agency policies, and other relevant codes of ethics, recognizing that among codes of ethics social workers should consider the *NASW Code of Ethics* as their primary source. Social workers also should be aware of the impact on ethical decision making of their clients' and their own personal values and cultural and religious beliefs and practices. They should be aware of any conflicts between personal and professional values and deal with them responsibly. For additional guidance social workers should consult the relevant literature on professional ethics and ethical decision making and seek appropriate consultation when faced with ethical dilemmas. This may involve consultation with an agency-based or social work organization's ethics committee, a regulatory body, knowledgeable colleagues, supervisors, or legal counsel.

Instances may arise when social workers' ethical obligations conflict with agency policies or relevant laws or regulations. When such conflicts occur, social workers must make a responsible effort to resolve the conflict in a manner that is consistent with the values, principles, and standards expressed in this *Code.* If a reasonable resolution of the conflict does not appear possible, social workers should seek proper consultation before making a decision.

The *NASW Code of Ethics* is to be used by NASW and by individuals, agencies, organizations, and bodies (such as licensing and regulatory boards, professional liability insurance providers, courts of law, agency boards of directors, government agencies, and other professional groups) that choose to adopt it or use it as a frame of reference. Violation of standards in this *Code* does not automatically imply legal liability or violation of the law. Such determination can only be made in the context of legal and judicial proceedings. Alleged violations of the *Code* would be subject to a peer review process. Such processes are generally separate from legal or administrative procedures and insulated from legal review or proceedings to allow the profession to counsel and discipline its own members.

A code of ethics cannot guarantee ethical behavior. Moreover, a code of ethics cannot resolve all ethical issues or disputes or capture the richness and complexity involved in striving to make responsible choices within a moral community. Rather, a code of ethics sets forth values, ethical principles, and ethical standards to which professionals aspire and by which their actions can be judged. Social workers' ethical behavior should result from their personal commitment to engage in ethical practice. The *NASW Code of Ethics* reflects the commitment of all social workers to uphold the profession's values and to act ethically. Principles and standards must be applied by individuals of good character who discern moral questions and, in good faith, seek to make reliable ethical judgments.

Ethical Principles

The following broad ethical principles are based on social work's core values of service, social justice, dignity and worth of the person, importance of human relationships, integrity, and competence. These principles set forth ideals to which all social workers should aspire.

Value: *Service*

Ethical Principle: *Social workers' primary goal is to help people in need and to address social problems.*

Social workers elevate service to others above self-interest. Social workers draw on their knowledge, values, and skills to help people in need and to address social problems. Social workers are encouraged to volunteer some portion of their professional skills with no expectation of significant financial return (pro bono service).

Value: *Social Justice*

Ethical Principle: *Social workers challenge social injustice.*

Social workers pursue social change, particularly with and on behalf of vulnerable and oppressed individuals and groups of people. Social workers' social change efforts are focused primarily on issues of poverty, unemployment, discrimination, and other forms of social injustice. These activities seek to promote sensitivity to and knowledge about oppression and cultural and ethnic diversity. Social workers strive to ensure access to needed information, services, and resources; equality of opportunity; and meaningful participation in decision making for all people.

Value: *Dignity and Worth of the Person*

Ethical Principle: *Social workers respect the inherent dignity and worth of the person.*

Social workers treat each person in a caring and respectful fashion, mindful of individual differences and cultural and ethnic diversity. Social workers promote clients' socially responsible self-determination. Social workers seek to enhance clients' capacity and opportunity to change and to address their own needs. Social workers are cognizant of their dual responsibility to clients and to the broader society. They seek to resolve conflicts between clients' interests and the broader society's interests in a socially responsible manner consistent with the values, ethical principles, and ethical standards of the profession.

Value: *Importance of Human Relationships*

Ethical Principle: *Social workers recognize the central importance of human relationships.*

Social workers understand that relationships between and among people are an important vehicle for change. Social workers engage people as partners in the helping process. Social workers seek to strengthen relationships among people in a purposeful effort to promote, restore, maintain, and enhance the well-being of individuals, families, social groups, organizations, and communities.

Value: *Integrity*

Ethical Principle: *Social workers behave in a trustworthy manner.*

Social workers are continually aware of the profession's mission, values, ethical principles, and ethical standards and practice in a manner consistent with them. Social workers act honestly and responsibly and promote ethical practices on the part of the organizations with which they are affiliated.

Value: *Competence*

Ethical Principle: *Social workers practice within their areas of competence and develop and enhance their professional expertise.*

Social workers continually strive to increase their professional knowledge and skills and to apply them in practice. Social workers should aspire to contribute to the knowledge base of the profession.

Ethical Standards

The following ethical standards are relevant to the professional activities of all social workers. These standards concern (1) social workers' ethical responsibilities to clients, (2) social workers' ethical responsibilities to colleagues, (3) social workers' ethical responsibilities in practice settings, (4) social workers' ethical responsibilities as professionals, (5) social workers' ethical responsibilities to the social work profession, and (6) social workers' ethical responsibilities to the broader society.

Some of the standards that follow are enforceable guidelines for professional conduct, and some are aspirational. The extent to which each standard is enforceable is a matter of professional judgment to be exercised by those responsible for reviewing alleged violations of ethical standards.

1. Social Workers' Ethical Responsibilities to Clients

1.01 Commitment to Clients

Social workers' primary responsibility is to promote the well-being of clients. In general, clients' interests are primary. However, social workers' responsibility to the larger society or specific legal obligations may on limited occasions supersede the loyalty owed clients, and clients should be so advised. (Examples include when a social worker is required by law to report that a client has abused a child or has threatened to harm self or others.)

1.02 Self-Determination

Social workers respect and promote the right of clients to self-determination and assist clients in their efforts to identify and clarify their goals. Social workers may limit clients' right to self-determination when, in the social workers' professional judgment, clients' actions or potential actions pose a serious, foreseeable, and imminent risk to themselves or others.

1.03 Informed Consent

(a) Social workers should provide services to clients only in the context of a professional relationship based, when appropriate, on valid informed consent. Social workers should use clear and understandable language to inform clients of the purpose of the services, risks related to the services, limits to services because of the requirements of a third-party payer, relevant costs, reasonable alternatives, clients' right to refuse or withdraw consent, and the time frame covered by the consent. Social workers should provide clients with an opportunity to ask questions.

(b) In instances when clients are not literate or have difficulty understanding the primary language used in the practice setting, social workers should take steps to ensure clients' comprehension. This may include providing clients with a detailed verbal explanation or arranging for a qualified interpreter or translator whenever possible.

(c) In instances when clients lack the capacity to provide informed consent, social workers should protect clients' interests by seeking permission from an appropriate third party, informing clients consistent with the clients' level of understanding. In such instances social workers should seek to ensure that the third party acts in a manner consistent with clients' wishes and interests. Social workers should take reasonable steps to enhance such clients' ability to give informed consent.

(d) In instances when clients are receiving services involuntarily, social workers should provide information about the nature and extent of services and about the extent of clients' right to refuse service.

(e) Social workers who provide services via electronic media (such as computer, telephone, radio, and television) should inform recipients of the limitations and risks associated with such services.

(f) Social workers should obtain clients' informed consent before audio-taping or videotaping clients or permitting observation of services to clients by a third party.

1.04 Competence

(a) Social workers should provide services and represent themselves as competent only within the boundaries of their education, training, license, certification, consultation received, supervised experience, or other relevant professional experience.

(b) Social workers should provide services in substantive areas or use intervention techniques or approaches that are new to them only after engaging in appropriate study, training, consultation, and supervision from people who are competent in those interventions or techniques.

(c) When generally recognized standards do not exist with respect to an emerging area of practice, social workers should exercise careful judgment and take responsible steps (including appropriate education, research, training, consultation, and supervision) to ensure the competence of their work and to protect clients from harm.

1.05 Cultural Competence and Social Diversity

(a) Social workers should understand culture and its function in human behavior and society, recognizing the strengths that exist in all cultures.

(b) Social workers should have a knowledge base of their clients' cultures and be able to demonstrate competence in the provision of services that are sensitive to clients' cultures and to differences among people and cultural groups.

(c) Social workers should obtain education about and seek to understand the nature of social diversity and oppression with respect to race, ethnicity, national origin, color, sex, sexual orientation, age, marital status, political belief, religion, and mental or physical disability.

1.06 Conflicts of Interest

(a) Social workers should be alert to and avoid conflicts of interest that interfere with the exercise of professional discretion and impartial judgment. Social workers should inform clients when a real or potential conflict of interest arises and take reasonable steps to resolve the issue in a manner that makes the clients' interests primary and protects clients' interests to the greatest extent possible. In some cases, protecting clients' interests may require termination of the professional relationship with proper referral of the client.

(b) Social workers should not take unfair advantage of any professional relationship or exploit others to further their personal, religious, political, or business interests.

(c) Social workers should not engage in dual or multiple relationships with clients or former clients in which there is a risk of exploitation or potential harm to the client. In instances when dual or multiple relationships are unavoidable, social workers should take steps to protect clients and are responsible for setting clear, appropriate, and culturally sensitive boundaries. (Dual or multiple relationships occur when social workers relate to clients in more than one relationship, whether professional, social, or business. Dual or multiple relationships can occur simultaneously or consecutively.)

(d) When social workers provide services to two or more people who have a relationship with each other (for example, couples, family members), social workers should clarify with all parties which individuals will be considered clients and the nature of social workers' professional obligations to the various individuals who are receiving services. Social workers who anticipate a conflict of interest among the individuals receiving services or who anticipate having to perform in potentially conflicting roles (for example, when a social worker is asked to testify in a child custody dispute or divorce proceedings involving clients) should clarify their role with the parties involved and take appropriate action to minimize any conflict of interest.

1.07 Privacy and Confidentiality

(a) Social workers should respect clients' right to privacy. Social workers should not solicit private information from clients unless it is essential to providing services or conducting social work evaluation or research. Once private information is shared, standards of confidentiality apply.

(b) Social workers may disclose confidential information when appropriate with valid consent from a client or a person legally authorized to consent on behalf of a client.

(c) Social workers should protect the confidentiality of all information obtained in the course of professional service, except for compelling professional reasons. The general expectation that social workers will keep information confidential does not apply when disclosure is necessary to prevent serious, foreseeable, and imminent harm to a client or other identifiable person. In all instances, social workers should disclose the least amount of confidential information necessary to achieve the desired purpose; only information that is directly relevant to the purpose for which the disclosure is made should be revealed.

(d) Social workers should inform clients, to the extent possible, about the disclosure of confidential information and the potential consequences, when feasible before the disclosure is made. This applies whether social workers disclose confidential information on the basis of a legal requirement or client consent.

(e) Social workers should discuss with clients and other interested parties the nature of confidentiality and limitations of clients' right to confidentiality. Social workers should review with clients circumstances where confidential information may be requested and where disclosure of confidential information may be legally required. This discussion should occur as soon as possible in the social worker-client relationship and as needed throughout the course of the relationship.

(f) When social workers provide counseling services to families, couples, or groups, social workers should seek agreement among the parties involved concerning each individual's right to confidentiality and obligation to preserve the confidentiality of information shared by others. Social workers should inform participants in family, couples, or group counseling that social workers cannot guarantee that all participants will honor such agreements.

(g) Social workers should inform clients involved in family, couples, marital, or group counseling of the social worker's, employer's, and agency's policy concerning the social worker's disclosure of confidential information among the parties involved in the counseling.

(h) Social workers should not disclose confidential information to third-party payers unless clients have authorized such disclosure.

(i) Social workers should not discuss confidential information in any setting unless privacy can be ensured. Social workers should not discuss confidential information in public or semipublic areas such as hallways, waiting rooms, elevators, and restaurants.

(j) Social workers should protect the confidentiality of clients during legal proceedings to the extent permitted by law. When a court of law or other legally authorized body orders social workers to disclose confidential or privileged information without a client's consent and such disclosure could cause harm to the client, social workers should request that the court withdraw the order or limit the order as narrowly as possible or maintain the records under seal, unavailable for public inspection.

(k) Social workers should protect the confidentiality of clients when responding to requests from members of the media.

(l) Social workers should protect the confidentiality of clients' written and electronic records and other sensitive information. Social workers should take reasonable steps to ensure that clients' records are stored in a secure location and that clients' records are not available to others who are not authorized to have access.

(m) Social workers should take precautions to ensure and maintain the confidentiality of information transmitted to other parties through the use of computers, electronic mail, facsimile machines, telephones and telephone answering machines, and other electronic or computer technology. Disclosure of identifying information should be avoided whenever possible.

(n) Social workers should transfer or dispose of clients' records in a manner that protects clients' confidentiality and is consistent with state statutes governing records and social work licensure.

(o) Social workers should take reasonable precautions to protect client confidentiality in the event of the social worker's termination of practice, incapacitation, or death.

(p) Social workers should not disclose identifying information when discussing clients for teaching or training purposes unless the client has consented to disclosure of confidential information.

(q) Social workers should not disclose identifying information when discussing clients with consultants unless the client has consented to disclosure of confidential information or there is a compelling need for such disclosure.

(r) Social workers should protect the confidentiality of deceased clients consistent with the preceding standards.

1.08 Access to Records

(a) Social workers should provide clients with reasonable access to records concerning the clients. Social workers who are concerned that clients' access to their records could cause serious misunderstanding or harm to the client should provide assistance in interpreting the records and consultation with the client regarding the records. Social workers should limit clients' access to their records, or portions of their records, only in exceptional circumstances when there is compelling evidence that such access would cause serious harm to the client. Both clients' requests and the rationale for withholding some or all of the record should be documented in clients' files.

(b) When providing clients with access to their records, social workers should take steps to protect the confidentiality of other individuals identified or discussed in such records.

1.09 Sexual Relationships

(a) Social workers should under no circumstances engage in sexual activities or sexual contact with current clients, whether such contact is consensual or forced.

(b) Social workers should not engage in sexual activities or sexual contact with clients' relatives or other individuals with whom clients maintain a close personal relationship when there is a risk of exploitation or potential harm to the client. Sexual activity or sexual contact with clients' relatives or other individuals with whom clients maintain a personal relationship has the potential to be harmful to the client and may make it difficult for the social worker and client to maintain appropriate professional boundaries. Social workers—not their clients, their clients' relatives, or other individuals with whom the client maintains a personal relationship—assume the full burden for setting clear, appropriate, and culturally sensitive boundaries.

(c) Social workers should not engage in sexual activities or sexual contact with former clients because of the potential for harm to the client. If social workers engage in conduct contrary to this prohibition or claim that an exception to this prohibition is warranted because of extraordinary circumstances, it is social workers—not their clients—who assume the full burden of demonstrating that the former client has not been exploited, coerced, or manipulated, intentionally or unintentionally.

(d) Social workers should not provide clinical services to individuals with whom they have had a prior sexual relationship. Providing clinical services to a former sexual partner has the potential to be harmful to the individual and is likely to make it difficult for the social worker and individual to maintain appropriate professional boundaries.

1.10 Physical Contact

Social workers should not engage in physical contact with clients when there is a possibility of psychological harm to the client as a result of the contact (such as cradling or caressing clients). Social workers who engage in appropriate physical contact with clients are responsible for setting clear, appropriate, and culturally sensitive boundaries that govern such physical contact.

1.11 Sexual Harassment

Social workers should not sexually harass clients. Sexual harassment includes sexual advances, sexual solicitation, requests for sexual favors, and other verbal or physical conduct of a sexual nature.

1.12 Derogatory Language

Social workers should not use derogatory language in their written or verbal communications to or about clients. Social workers should use accurate and respectful language in all communications to and about clients.

1.13 Payment for Services

(a) When setting fees, social workers should ensure that the fees are fair, reasonable, and commensurate with the services performed. Consideration should be given to clients' ability to pay.

(b) Social workers should avoid accepting goods or services from clients as payment for professional services. Bartering arrangements, particularly involving services, create the potential for conflicts of interest, exploitation, and inappropriate boundaries in social workers' relationships with clients. Social workers should explore and may participate in bartering only in very limited circumstances when it can be demonstrated that such arrangements are an accepted practice among professionals in the local community, considered to be essential for the provision of services, negotiated without coercion, and entered into at the client's initiative and with the client's informed consent. Social workers who accept goods or services from clients as payment for professional services assume the full burden of demonstrating that this arrangement will not be detrimental to the client or the professional relationship.

(c) Social workers should not solicit a private fee or other remuneration for providing services to clients who are entitled to such available services through the social workers' employer or agency.

1.14 Clients Who Lack Decision-Making Capacity

When social workers act on behalf of clients who lack the capacity to make informed decisions, social workers should take reasonable steps to safeguard the interests and rights of those clients.

1.15 Interruption of Services

Social workers should make reasonable efforts to ensure continuity of services in the event that services are interrupted by factors such as unavailability, relocation, illness, disability, or death.

1.16 Termination of Services

(a) Social workers should terminate services to clients and professional relationships with them when such services and relationships are no longer required or no longer serve the clients' needs or interests.

(b) Social workers should take reasonable steps to avoid abandoning clients who are still in need of services. Social workers should withdraw services precipitously only under unusual circumstances, giving careful consideration to all factors in the situation and taking care to minimize possible adverse effects. Social workers should assist in making appropriate arrangements for continuation of services when necessary.

(c) Social workers in fee-for-service settings may terminate services to clients who are not paying an overdue balance if the financial contractual arrangements have been made clear to the client, if the client does not pose an imminent danger to self or others, and if the clinical and other consequences of the current nonpayment have been addressed and discussed with the client.

(d) Social workers should not terminate services to pursue a social, financial, or sexual relationship with a client.

(e) Social workers who anticipate the termination or interruption of services to clients should notify clients promptly and seek the transfer, referral, or continuation of services in relation to the clients' needs and preferences.

(f) Social workers who are leaving an employment setting should inform clients of appropriate options for the continuation of services and of the benefits and risks of the options.

2. Social Workers' Ethical Responsibilities to Colleagues

2.01 Respect

(a) Social workers should treat colleagues with respect and should represent accurately and fairly the qualifications, views, and obligations of colleagues.

(b) Social workers should avoid unwarranted negative criticism of colleagues in communications with clients or with other professionals. Unwarranted negative criticism may include demeaning comments that refer to colleagues' level of competence or to individuals' attributes such as race, ethnicity, national origin, color, sex, sexual orientation, age, marital status, political belief, religion, and mental or physical disability.

(c) Social workers should cooperate with social work colleagues and with colleagues of other professions when such cooperation serves the well-being of clients.

2.02 Confidentiality

Social workers should respect confidential information shared by colleagues in the course of their professional relationships and transactions. Social workers should ensure that such colleagues understand social workers' obligation to respect confidentiality and any exceptions related to it.

2.03 Interdisciplinary Collaboration

(a) Social workers who are members of an interdisciplinary team should participate in and contribute to decisions that affect the well-being of clients by drawing on the perspectives, values, and experiences of the social work profession. Professional and ethical obligations of the interdisciplinary team as a whole and of its individual members should be clearly established.

(b) Social workers for whom a team decision raises ethical concerns should attempt to resolve the disagreement through appropriate channels. If the disagreement cannot be resolved, social workers should pursue other avenues to address their concerns consistent with client well-being.

2.04 Disputes Involving Colleagues

(a) Social workers should not take advantage of a dispute between a colleague and an employer to obtain a position or otherwise advance the social workers' own interests.

(b) Social workers should not exploit clients in disputes with colleagues or engage clients in any inappropriate discussion of conflicts between social workers and their colleagues.

2.05 Consultation

(a) Social workers should seek the advice and counsel of colleagues whenever such consultation is in the best interests of clients.

(b) Social workers should keep themselves informed about colleagues' areas of expertise and competencies. Social workers should seek consultation only from colleagues who have demonstrated knowledge, expertise, and competence related to the subject of the consultation.

(c) When consulting with colleagues about clients, social workers should disclose the least amount of information necessary to achieve the purposes of the consultation.

2.06 Referral for Services

(a) Social workers should refer clients to other professionals when the other professionals' specialized knowledge or expertise is needed to serve clients fully or when social workers believe that they are not being effective or making reasonable progress with clients and that additional service is required.

(b) Social workers who refer clients to other professionals should take appropriate steps to facilitate an orderly transfer of responsibility. Social workers who refer clients to other professionals should disclose, with clients' consent, all pertinent information to the new service providers.

(c) Social workers are prohibited from giving or receiving payment for a referral when no professional service is provided by the referring social worker.

2.07 Sexual Relationships

(a) Social workers who function as supervisors or educators should not engage in sexual activities or contact with supervisees, students, trainees, or other colleagues over whom they exercise professional authority.

(b) Social workers should avoid engaging in sexual relationships with colleagues when there is potential for a conflict of interest. Social workers who become involved in, or anticipate becoming involved in, a sexual relationship with a colleague have a duty to transfer professional responsibilities, when necessary, to avoid a conflict of interest.

2.08 Sexual Harassment

Social workers should not sexually harass supervisees, students, trainees, or colleagues. Sexual harassment includes sexual advances, sexual solicitation, requests for sexual favors, and other verbal or physical conduct of a sexual nature.

2.09 Impairment of Colleagues

(a) Social workers who have direct knowledge of a social work colleague's impairment that is due to personal problems, psychosocial distress, substance abuse, or mental health difficulties and that interferes with practice effectiveness should consult with that colleague when feasible and assist the colleague in taking remedial action.

(b) Social workers who believe that a social work colleague's impairment interferes with practice effectiveness and that the colleague has not taken adequate steps to address the impairment should take action through appropriate channels established by employers, agencies, NASW, licensing and regulatory bodies, and other professional organizations.

2.10 Incompetence of Colleagues

(a) Social workers who have direct knowledge of a social work colleague's incompetence should consult with that colleague when feasible and assist the colleague in taking remedial action.

(b) Social workers who believe that a social work colleague is incompetent and has not taken adequate steps to address the incompetence should take action through appropriate channels established by employers, agencies, NASW, licensing and regulatory bodies, and other professional organizations.

2.11 Unethical Conduct of Colleagues

(a) Social workers should take adequate measures to discourage, prevent, expose, and correct the unethical conduct of colleagues.

(b) Social workers should be knowledgeable about established policies and procedures for handling concerns about colleagues' unethical behavior. Social workers should be familiar with national, state, and local procedures for handling ethics complaints. These include policies and procedures created by NASW, licensing and regulatory bodies, employers, agencies, and other professional organizations.

(c) Social workers who believe that a colleague has acted unethically should seek resolution by discussing their concerns with the colleague when feasible and when such discussion is likely to be productive.

(d) When necessary, social workers who believe that a colleague has acted unethically should take action through appropriate formal channels (such as contacting a state licensing board or regulatory body, an NASW committee on inquiry, or other professional ethics committees).

(e) Social workers should defend and assist colleagues who are unjustly charged with unethical conduct.

3. Social Workers' Ethical Responsibilities in Practice Settings

3.01 Supervision and Consultation

(a) Social workers who provide supervision or consultation should have the necessary knowledge and skill to supervise or consult appropriately and should do so only within their areas of knowledge and competence.

(b) Social workers who provide supervision or consultation are responsible for setting clear, appropriate, and culturally sensitive boundaries.

(c) Social workers should not engage in any dual or multiple relationships with supervisees in which there is a risk of exploitation of or potential harm to the supervisee.

(d) Social workers who provide supervision should evaluate supervisees' performance in a manner that is fair and respectful.

3.02 Education and Training

(a) Social workers who function as educators, field instructors for students, or trainers should provide instruction only within their areas of knowledge and competence and should provide instruction based on the most current information and knowledge available in the profession.

(b) Social workers who function as educators or field instructors for students should evaluate students' performance in a manner that is fair and respectful.

(c) Social workers who function as educators or field instructors for students should take reasonable steps to ensure that clients are routinely informed when services are being provided by students.

(d) Social workers who function as educators or field instructors for students should not engage in any dual or multiple relationships with students in which there is a risk of exploitation or potential harm to the student. Social work educators and field instructors are responsible for setting clear, appropriate, and culturally sensitive boundaries.

3.03 Performance Evaluation

Social workers who have responsibility for evaluating the performance of others should fulfill such responsibility in a fair and considerate manner and on the basis of clearly stated criteria.

3.04 Client Records

(a) Social workers should take reasonable steps to ensure that documentation in records is accurate and reflects the services provided.

(b) Social workers should include sufficient and timely documentation in records to facilitate the delivery of services and to ensure continuity of services provided to clients in the future.

(c) Social workers' documentation should protect clients' privacy to the extent that is possible and appropriate and should include only information that is directly relevant to the delivery of services.

(d) Social workers should store records following the termination of services to ensure reasonable future access. Records should be maintained for the number of years required by state statutes or relevant contracts.

3.05 Billing

Social workers should establish and maintain billing practices that accurately reflect the nature and extent of services provided and that identify who provided the service in the practice setting.

3.06 Client Transfer

(a) When an individual who is receiving services from another agency or colleague contacts a social worker for services, the social worker should carefully consider the client's needs before agreeing to provide services. To minimize possible confusion and conflict, social workers should discuss with potential clients the nature of the clients' current relationship with other service providers and the implications, including possible benefits or risks, of entering into a relationship with a new service provider.

(b) If a new client has been served by another agency or colleague, social workers should discuss with the client whether consultation with the previous service provider is in the client's best interest.

3.07 Administration

(a) Social work administrators should advocate within and outside their agencies for adequate resources to meet clients' needs.

(b) Social workers should advocate for resource allocation procedures that are open and fair. When not all clients' needs can be met, an allocation procedure should be developed that is nondiscriminatory and based on appropriate and consistently applied principles.

(c) Social workers who are administrators should take reasonable steps to ensure that adequate agency or organizational resources are available to provide appropriate staff supervision.

(d) Social work administrators should take reasonable steps to ensure that the working environment for which they are responsible is consistent with and encourages compliance with the NASW Code of Ethics. Social work administrators should take reasonable steps to eliminate any conditions in their organizations that violate, interfere with, or discourage compliance with the Code.

3.08 Continuing Education and Staff Development

Social work administrators and supervisors should take reasonable steps to provide or arrange for continuing education and staff development for all staff for whom they are responsible. Continuing education and staff development should address current knowledge and emerging developments related to social work practice and ethics.

3.09 Commitments to Employers

(a) Social workers generally should adhere to commitments made to employers and employing organizations.

(b) Social workers should work to improve employing agencies' policies and procedures and the efficiency and effectiveness of their services.

(c) Social workers should take reasonable steps to ensure that employers are aware of social workers' ethical obligations as set forth in the NASW Code of Ethics and of the implications of those obligations for social work practice.

(d) Social workers should not allow an employing organization's policies, procedures, regulations, or administrative orders to interfere with their ethical practice of social work. Social workers should take reasonable steps to ensure that their employing organizations' practices are consistent with the NASW Code of Ethics.

(e) Social workers should act to prevent and eliminate discrimination in the employing organization's work assignments and in its employment policies and practices.

(f) Social workers should accept employment or arrange student field placements only in organizations that exercise fair personnel practices.

(g) Social workers should be diligent stewards of the resources of their employing organizations, wisely conserving funds where appropriate and never misappropriating funds or using them for unintended purposes.

3.10 Labor-Management Disputes

(a) Social workers may engage in organized action, including the formation of and participation in labor unions, to improve services to clients and working conditions.

(b) The actions of social workers who are involved in labor-management disputes, job actions, or labor strikes should be guided by the profession's values, ethical principles, and ethical standards. Reasonable differences of opinion exist among social workers concerning their primary obligation as professionals during an actual or threatened labor strike or job action. Social workers should carefully examine relevant issues and their possible impact on clients before deciding on a course of action.

4. Social Workers' Ethical Responsibilities as Professionals

4.01 Competence

(a) Social workers should accept responsibility or employment only on the basis of existing competence or the intention to acquire the necessary competence.

(b) Social workers should strive to become and remain proficient in professional practice and the performance of professional functions. Social workers should critically examine and keep current with emerging knowledge relevant to social work. Social workers should routinely review the professional literature and participate in continuing education relevant to social work practice and social work ethics.

(c) Social workers should base practice on recognized knowledge, including empirically based knowledge, relevant to social work and social work ethics.

4.02 Discrimination

Social workers should not practice, condone, facilitate, or collaborate with any form of discrimination on the basis of race, ethnicity, national origin, color, sex, sexual orientation, age, marital status, political belief, religion, or mental or physical disability.

4.03 Private Conduct

Social workers should not permit their private conduct to interfere with their ability to fulfill their professional responsibilities.

4.04 Dishonesty, Fraud, and Deception

Social workers should not participate in, condone, or be associated with dishonesty, fraud, or deception.

4.05 Impairment

(a) Social workers should not allow their own personal problems, psychosocial distress, legal problems, substance abuse, or mental health difficulties to interfere with their professional judgment and performance or to jeopardize the best interests of people for whom they have a professional responsibility.

(b) Social workers whose personal problems, psychosocial distress, legal problems, substance abuse, or mental health difficulties interfere with their professional judgment and performance should immediately seek consultation and take appropriate remedial action by seeking professional help, making adjustments in workload, terminating practice, or taking any other steps necessary to protect clients and others.

4.06 Misrepresentation

(a) Social workers should make clear distinctions between statements made and actions engaged in as a private individual and as a representative of the social work profession, a professional social work organization, or the social worker's employing agency.

(b) Social workers who speak on behalf of professional social work organizations should accurately represent the official and authorized positions of the organizations.

(c) Social workers should ensure that their representations to clients, agencies, and the public of professional qualifications, credentials, education, competence, affiliations, services provided, or results to be achieved are accurate. Social workers should claim only those relevant professional credentials they actually possess and take steps to correct any inaccuracies or misrepresentations of their credentials by others.

4.07 Solicitations

(a) Social workers should not engage in uninvited solicitation of potential clients who, because of their circumstances, are vulnerable to undue influence, manipulation, or coercion.

(b) Social workers should not engage in solicitation of testimonial endorsements (including solicitation of consent to use a client's prior statement as a testimonial endorsement) from current clients or from other people who, because of their particular circumstances, are vulnerable to undue influence.

4.08 Acknowledging Credit

(a) Social workers should take responsibility and credit, including authorship credit, only for work they have actually performed and to which they have contributed.

(b) Social workers should honestly acknowledge the work of and the contributions made by others.

5. Social Workers' Ethical Responsibilities to the Social Work Profession

5.01 Integrity of the Profession

(a) Social workers should work toward the maintenance and promotion of high standards of practice.

(b) Social workers should uphold and advance the values, ethics, knowledge, and mission of the profession. Social workers should protect, enhance, and improve the integrity of the profession through appropriate study and research, active discussion, and responsible criticism of the profession.

(c) Social workers should contribute time and professional expertise to activities that promote respect for the value, integrity, and competence of the social work profession. These activities may include teaching, research, consultation, service, legislative testimony, presentations in the community, and participation in their professional organizations.

(d) Social workers should contribute to the knowledge base of social work and share with colleagues their knowledge related to practice, research, and ethics. Social workers should seek to contribute to the profession's literature and to share their knowledge at professional meetings and conferences.

(e) Social workers should act to prevent the unauthorized and unqualified practice of social work.

5.02 Evaluation and Research

(a) Social workers should monitor and evaluate policies, the implementation of programs, and practice interventions.

(b) Social workers should promote and facilitate evaluation and research to contribute to the development of knowledge.

(c) Social workers should critically examine and keep current with emerging knowledge relevant to social work and fully use evaluation and research evidence in their professional practice.

(d) Social workers engaged in evaluation or research should carefully consider possible consequences and should follow guidelines developed for the protection of evaluation and research participants. Appropriate institutional review boards should be consulted.

(e) Social workers engaged in evaluation or research should obtain voluntary and written informed consent from participants, when appropriate, without any implied or actual deprivation or penalty for refusal to participate; without undue inducement to participate; and with due regard for participants' well-being, privacy, and dignity. Informed consent should include information about the nature, extent, and duration of the participation requested and disclosure of the risks and benefits of participation in the research.

(f) When evaluation or research participants are incapable of giving informed consent, social workers should provide an appropriate explanation to the participants, obtain the participants' assent to the extent they are able, and obtain written consent from an appropriate proxy.

(g) Social workers should never design or conduct evaluation or research that does not use consent procedures, such as certain forms of naturalistic observation and archival research, unless rigorous and responsible review of the research has found it to be justified because of its prospective scientific, educational, or applied value and unless equally effective alternative procedures that do not involve waiver of consent are not feasible.

(h) Social workers should inform participants of their right to withdraw from evaluation and research at any time without penalty.

(i) Social workers should take appropriate steps to ensure that participants in evaluation and research have access to appropriate supportive services.

(j) Social workers engaged in evaluation or research should protect participants from unwarranted physical or mental distress, harm, danger, or deprivation.

(k) Social workers engaged in the evaluation of services should discuss collected information only for professional purposes and only with people professionally concerned with this information.

(l) Social workers engaged in evaluation or research should ensure the anonymity or confidentiality of participants and of the data obtained from them. Social workers should inform participants of any limits of confidentiality, the measures that will be taken to ensure confidentiality, and when any records containing research data will be destroyed.

(m) Social workers who report evaluation and research results should protect participants' confidentiality by omitting identifying information unless proper consent has been obtained authorizing disclosure.

(n) Social workers should report evaluation and research findings accurately. They should not fabricate or falsify results and should take steps to correct any errors later found in published data using standard publication methods.

(o) Social workers engaged in evaluation or research should be alert to and avoid conflicts of interest and dual relationships with participants, should inform participants when a real or potential conflict of interest arises, and should take steps to resolve the issue in a manner that makes participants' interests primary.

(p) Social workers should educate themselves, their students, and their colleagues about responsible research practices.

6. Social Workers' Ethical Responsibilities to the Broader Society

6.01 Social Welfare

Social workers should promote the general welfare of society, from local to global levels, and the development of people, their communities, and their environments. Social workers should advocate for living conditions conducive to the fulfillment of basic human needs and should promote social, economic, political, and cultural values and institutions that are compatible with the realization of social justice.

6.02 Public Participation

Social workers should facilitate informed participation by the public in shaping social policies and institutions.

6.03 Public Emergencies

Social workers should provide appropriate professional services in public emergencies to the greatest extent possible.

6.04 Social and Political Action

(a) Social workers should engage in social and political action that seeks to ensure that all people have equal access to the resources, employment, services, and opportunities they require to meet their basic human needs and to develop fully. Social workers should be aware of the impact of the political arena on practice and should advocate for changes in policy and legislation to improve social conditions in order to meet basic human needs and promote social justice.

(b) Social workers should act to expand choice and opportunity for all people, with special regard for vulnerable, disadvantaged, oppressed, and exploited people and groups.

(c) Social workers should promote conditions that encourage respect for cultural and social diversity within the United States and globally. Social workers should promote policies and practices that demonstrate respect for difference, support the expansion of cultural knowledge and resources, advocate for programs and institutions that demonstrate cultural competence, and promote policies that safeguard the rights of and confirm equity and social justice for all people.

(d) Social workers should act to prevent and eliminate domination of, exploitation of, and discrimination against any person, group, or class on the basis of race, ethnicity, national origin, color, sex, sexual orientation, age, marital status, political belief, religion, or mental or physical disability.

NOTE

1 Copyright 1996, National Association of Social Workers, Inc., NASW Code of Ethics. Reprinted with permission.

REFLECTING ON
YOUR FAMILY

W e all have intimate knowledge of at least one family—the family or families in which we have lived or are currently living. One of the best ways to begin to understand family structure and family functioning in light of the social, political, and economic conditions is to spend some time reflecting on your own family or a family grouping with which you are intimately acquainted. This process of examining your own family can prepare you to understand families who will come for help.[1]

In the process of reflecting on your family ask yourself the questions you might ask a client family should you wish to work with them within a structural perspective. The best way to proceed is to select a particular time period when you were growing up and respond to the following family assessment questions.

1. Family Composition and History

- Who are the members of your family?
- Did they change over time—i.e., separation of parents, new partnerships, death, extended family entering or leaving?
- What were the circumstances in which your family immigrated to Canada?
- Were family members separated during immigration to another country?
- In the case of Aboriginal heritage, what was the impact of colonization on your family?

- What is the history of your family and your culture?
- Construct a genogram of your family.

2. Problem Identification

In all families there are usually certain conflicts and tensions among members that develop over time—tensions in regards to ideas, behaviours or feelings, health, financial difficulties, losses, and/or discrimination from outside the family.

- In your family, which family members, if any, identified concerns/problems? To whom was this communicated? If the problem was not identified or communicated to all members of the family, how was it kept from the others?
- Did someone outside of the family (i.e., teachers, neighbours, social agency representatives, important relatives) label anything/anyone a problem?
- To what extent was what was labelled a problem in the family related to: who the family was within the community (e.g., an immigrant family, an Aboriginal family, a family headed by a same-sex couple or a single parent); experiences of racism, heterosexism, sexism, discrimination based on religion or physical and or mental ability; who the person was with the problem and how much power they had in the family; or the family's social class, income, debts, and access to resources.

3. Strengths and Solution Patterns

- Identify the strengths of your family.
- Who in the family usually took the initiative and acted on problem situations? What solutions were proposed by whom?
- How was the situation dealt with when a family member had a problem? Did family members usually turn to people outside the family for help or was the rule to keep family problems inside the family? To what extent was the way a problem was to be solved in the family related to the dominant ideas regarding men, women, and children's problem solving capacities and/or cultural factors within the family?

4. Material Conditions of the Family

- How did the family's material conditions influence how members related to each other and participated in the community?
- Neighbourhood resources: Did needed resources exist in your neighbourhood—e.g., day care, homemaker service, health care, etc.—and if so were they accessible, affordable, and appropriate?
- Personal resources: Could neighbours be counted on for help? In what situations? What kind? If not, why not? What friends and/or relatives could be counted on to help?
- Home: What was the quality and quantity of housing space and furnishings? Did your family own their home or rent?
- Work: Who in the family does the domestic and/or wage labour? What was the nature of wage labour (monotonous, fast-paced, dangerous, shift work, week-end work)? What were the positions held? Were the jobs permanent or contract? Were they unionized? What were the salaries/benefits?

5. Power and Authority Within the Family

- Who made the rules inside the family and who enforced them?
- How did the cultural background of the family contribute to the rules?
- Did gender, age, or ability play a part in differences in the family regarding these messages?
- Who brought in the money and how was it distributed and managed?
- Who pushed their weight around and who didn't?
- Who allied with whom?

6. Communication Patterns Within in the Family

What messages were given or rules transmitted regarding:
- How close family members should get to one and another and how this closeness should be expressed?
- Asking directly for what you needed or refusing or rejecting what you did not need or want?
- How were family rules communicated, and what happened when they were not followed? How were differences/disagreements discussed?

7. Parental Models

Think about the relationship between the experiences your mother and father had in their own families of origin (what happened to them, what they saw happen, what they heard was right and wrong as they grew up) and their expectations vis-à-vis themselves, you, and your siblings; each other as mates; and themselves as parents. If you are a parent, how similar or different are you from your parents?

NOTE

1 This exercise is adapted from one that is thought to have been developed by Mike Brake while he was a professor in the School of Social Work, Carleton University.

SELECTED REFERENCES

Abella, Irving, and Harold Troper. *None is Too Many: Canada and the Jews of Europe 1933-1948*. Toronto, ON: Lester and Orpen Dennys, 1983.

Abramovitz, Mimi. *Under Attack, Fighting Back: Women and Welfare in the United States*. New York: Monthly Review Press, 2000.

Adams, Brian R., and Joan MacKenzie Davies. "Social Work Profession Speaks Out About Press Coverage of Heikamp Inquest." Press Release, 26 March 2001: 2.

Addams, Jane. "Charity and Social Justice." *Proceedings*, National Conference of Charities and Corrections. St. Louis, MO: The Archer Printing Co., 1910:1–14.

Addams, Jane. *Peace and Bread in Time of War*. New York, NY: Macmillan, 1922.

Akamatsu, Norma. "The Talking Oppression Blues." McGoldrick 129–43.

Alexander, Bruce K. "The Empirical and Theoretical Bases for an Adaptive Model of Addiction." *The Journal of Drug Issues* 20.1 (1990): 37–65.

Alexander, Leslie, Philip Lichtenberg, and Dennis Brunn. "Social Workers in Unions: A Survey." *Social Work* (May 1980): 216–23.

Allahar, Anton L., and James E. Côté. *Richer and Poorer*. Toronto, ON: Lorimer, 1998.

American Association of Social Workers. *Social Case Work: Generic and Specific: An Outline, A Report of the Milford Conference*. New York, NY: American Association of Social Workers, 1929.

Applewhite Larry W., and M. Vincentia Joseph. "Confidentiality: Issues in Working with Self-harming Adolescents." *Child and Adolescent Social Work Journal* 11.4 (August 1994): 279–94.

Arches, Joan L. "Burnout and Social Action." *Journal of Progressive Human Services* 8.2 (1997): 51–62.

Aronson, Jane. "Lesbians in Social Work Education: Processes and Puzzles in Claiming Visibility." *Journal of Progressive Human Services* 6.1 (1995): 5–26.

Atherton, Charles R., and Kathleen A. Bollard. "Postmodernism: A Dangerous Illusion for Social Work." *International Social Work*, 45.4 (2002): 421–33.

Backhouse, Constance. *Colour-Coded: A Legal History of Racism in Canada 1900-1950*. Toronto, ON: University of Toronto Press, 1999.

Bailey, Roy, and Mike Brake (Eds.). *Radical Social Work*. New York, NY: Pantheon Books, 1975.

Baines, Donna. "Feminist Social Work in the Inner City: The Challenges of Race, Class, and Gender." *Affilia* 12.3 (1997): 297–317.

Ball, Brenda, John Gaventa, John Peters, Myles Horton, and Paulo Freire. *We Make the Road by Walking: Conversation on Education and Social Change*. Philadelphia, PA: Temple University Press, 1990.

Barlow, Maude. "The Fourth Ministerial Meeting of the World Trade Organization—An Analysis." October 16, 2001. Available at http://www.canadians.org/campaigns/campaigns-tradepub-4minmtg.html.

————. *The Free Trade Areas of the Americas and the Threat to Social Programs, Environmental Sustainability and Social Justice in Canada and the Americas.* Ottawa, ON: Council of Canadians, 19 January 2001.

Barter, Ken. "Reclaiming Community: Shaping the Social Work Agenda." *Canadian Social Work* 2.2 (Fall 2000): 6–18.

Bellamy, Donald, and Allan Irving. "Pioneers." *Canadian Social Welfare.* 3rd ed. Ed. Joanne C. Turner and Francis J. Turner. Scarborough, ON: Allyn and Bacon, 1995. 89–117.

Berg, Insoo. *Family-Based Services: A Solution-Focused Approach.* New York, NY: Norton, 1994.

Best, Katherine, "Another Point of View on Staff Associations." *The Social Worker* 12.2 (November 1943).

Bishop, Anne. *Becoming an Ally: Breaking the Cycle of Oppression.* Halifax, NS: Fernwood Publishing, 1994.

Bisno, Herbert. "How Social Will Social Work Be?" *Social Work* 1.2 (April 1956): 12–18.

Bitensky, Reuben. "The Influence of Political Power in Determining the Theoretical Developments of Social Work." *Journal of Social Policy* 2, Pt. 2 (April 1973): 119–30.

Blakeney, Jill, Fadumo Jama Dirie, and Mary Ann MacRae. "Empowering Traumatized Somali Women: A Support Group Model for Helping Survivors to Cope." Ed. Karen Price, *Community Support for Survivors of Torture.* Toronto, ON: Canadian Centre for Victims of Torture, n.d. 50–58.

Bock, Scott. "Conscientization: Paulo Freire and Class-based Practice." *Catalyst* 6 (1980): 5–25.

Boggs, James. *Racism and the Class Struggle: Further Pages From a Black Worker's Notebook.* New York, NY: Monthly Review Press, 1970.

Bolt, Clarence. "Our Destiny to be Decided More by TNCs than by MPs." *The CCPA Monitor* 6.6 (1999).

Bourgeon, Michèle, and Nancy Guberman. "How Feminism Can Take the Crazy out of Your Head and Put it Back into Society: The Example of Social Work Practice." *Limited Edition: Voices of Women, Voices of Feminism.* Ed. Geraldine Finn. Halifax, NS: Fernwood Publishing, 1993. 301–21.

Brager, George, and Harry Specht. *Community Organizing.* New York, NY: Columbia University Press, 1973.

Brenner, Johanna. *Women and the Politics of Class.* New York, NY: Monthly Review Pres, 2000.

Bricker-Jenkins, Mary. "Hidden Treasures: Unlocking Strengths in the Public Social Services." *The Strengths Perspective in Social Work Practice.* 2nd ed. Ed. Dennis Saleeby. New York, NY: Longman, 1997. 133–50.

Brookfield, Stephen D. *Developing Critical Thinkers: Challenging Adults to Explore Alternate Ways of Thinking and Acting.* London: Jossey-Bass Publishers, 1987.

Brotman, Shari, and Shoshana Pollock. "Loss of Context: The Problem of Merging Postmodernism with Feminist Social Work." *Canadian Social Work Review* 14.1 (Winter 1997): 9–21.

Brown, Allan, and Tara Mistry. "Group Work with Mixed Membership Groups: Issues of Race and Gender." *Social Work with Groups* 17.3 (1994): 5–21.

Brown, Pam A., and Claire E. Dickey. "Facilitating Critical Thinking in an Abused Women's Group." *Proceedings of the Eleventh Annual Symposium of the Association for the Advancement of Social Work with Groups.* Montreal, 26–29 October 1989. 438–54.

Bunch, Charlotte. "Transforming Human Rights From a Feminist Perspective." *Women's Rights: Human Rights.* Ed. Julie Peters and Andrea Wolpe. New York, NY: Routledge, 1995. 11–17.

Burrell, Gibson, and Gareth Morgan. *Sociological Paradigms and Organizational Analysis.* London: Heinemann Educational Books, 1979.

Burstow, Bonnie. "Freirian Codifications and Social Work Education." *Journal of Social Work Education* 272 (1991): 196–207.

Butler, Sandra, and Claire Wintram. *Feminist Groupwork.* Newbury Park, CA: Sage, 1992.

Callahan, Marilyn. "Feminist Community Organizing in Canada." *Community Organizing.* Ed. Brian Wharf and Michael Clague. Don Mills, ON: Oxford University Press, 1997. 181–204.

Canadian Association of Social Workers. *Social Work Code of Ethics.* Ottawa, ON: CASW, 1994.

Canadian Panel on Violence Against Women. *Changing the Landscape; Ending Violence— Achieving Equality.* Ottawa: Minister of Supply and Services Canada, 1993.Chapter 15: Aboriginal Women.

Canadian Union of Public Employees. *Overloaded and Under Fire.* Report of the Ontario Social Services Work Environment Survey. Ottawa: CUPE, 1999. http://www.cupe.ca/overloaded.html.

Carniol, Ben. *Case Critical: Challenging Social Work in Canada.* 2nd ed. Toronto, ON: Between the Lines, 1990.

———. "Clash of Ideologies in Social Work Education." *Canadian Social Work Review* (1984): 184–99.

———. "Social Work and the Labour Movement." Wharf 114–43.

Carniol, Ben, and Brigitte Kitchen. "OAPSW Proposal is a Disaster and Must be Defeated." *Canadian Review of Social Policy* 25 (May 1990): 62–63.

Castro, Fidel. "Third World Must Unite or Die: Opening of the South Summit, Havana." *Capitalism in Crisis: Globalization and World Politics Today.* Ed. David Deutschman. New York: Ocean Press, 2000. 279–87.

Cattell-Gordon, David. "The Appalachian Inheritance: A Culturally Transmitted Traumatic Stress Syndrome?" *Journal of Progressive Human Services* 1.1 (1990): 41–57.

Chambers, Clarke A. "Women in the Creation of the Profession of Social Work." *Social Service Review* (March 1986): 1–33.

Chambon, Adrienne S., and Allan Irving (Eds.). *Essays on Postmodernism and Social Work.* Toronto, ON: Canadian Scholar's Press, 1994.

Chossudovsky, Michel. *The Globalization of Poverty: Impacts of IMF and the World Bank Reforms.* London: Zed Books, 1997.

Clarke, Tony. "Transnational Corporate Agenda Behind the Harris Regime." *Mike Harris's Ontario: Open for Business: Closed to People.* Ed. Diana Ralph, André Regimbald, and Nerée St-Amand. Halifax, NS: Fernwood Publishing, 1990. 28–36.

Clement, Wallace. "Canada's Social Structure: Capital, Labour, and the State, 1930–1980." *Modern Canada 1930 -1980's.* Ed. Michael S. Cross and Gregory S. Kealey. Toronto, ON: McClelland and Stewart, 1984. 81–101.

———. *The Challenge of Class Analysis.* Ottawa, ON: Carleton University Press, 1988.

Clement, Wallace, and John Myles. *Relations of Ruling: Class and Gender in Postindustrial Societies.* Montreal, QC: McGill-Queen's University Press, 1994.

Cloward, Richard A., and Francis Fox Piven. "The Acquiesence of Social Work." *Strategic Perspectives on Social Policy.* Ed. J. Tropman, M. Duluhy, and R. Lind. New York, NY: Pergamon Press, 1981.

———. "Disruptive Dissensus: People and Power in the Industrial Age." *Reflections on Community Organization: Enduring Themes and Critical Issues.* Ed. Jack Rothman. Itasca, IL: F.E. Peacock Publishers, 1999. 165–93.

Coates, John. "Ideology and Education for Social Work Practice." *Journal of Progressive Human Services* 3.2 (1992): 15–30.

Cohen, Marcia, and Audrey Mullender. "The Personal is Political: Exploring the Group Work Continuum from Individual to Social Change Goals." *Social Work with Groups* 22.1 (1999): 13–31.

Colton, Matthew. "Editorial." *British Journal of Social Work* 32 (2002): 659–667.

Coombs, Mary. "Transgenderism and Sexual Orientation: More Than a Marriage of Convenience?" *Queer Families: Queer Politics.* Ed. Mary Bernstein and Renate Reimann. New York, NY: Columbia University Press, 2001. 397–419.

Cooper, Marlene. "Life-Threatening Disability in Adolescence: Adjusting to a Limited Future." *Clinical Social Work Journal* 22.4 (1994): 435–48.

Corey, Gerald, Marianne Schneider Corey, Patrick Callanan, and J. Michael Russell. *Group Techniques.* 2nd ed. Pacific Grove, CA: Brooks/Cole Publishing, 1992.

Corey, Marianne Schneider, and Gerald Corey. *Group Process and Practice.* 4th ed. Belmont, CA: Brooks/Cole, 1992.

Corrigan, Paul, and Peter Leonard. *Social Work Practice Under Capitalism: A Marxist Approach.* London: Macmillan, 1978.

Coyle, Grace Longwell. *Social Process in Organized Groups.* New York, NY: R.R. Smith, 1930.

Craig, Gary. "Poverty, Social Work and Social Justice." *British Journal of Social Work* 32 (2002): 669–82.

Creese, Gillian, and Brenda Beagan. "Gender at Work: Seeking Solutions for Women's Equality." Curtis et al. 199–211.

Curtis, James, Edward Grabb, and Neil Guppy (Eds.). *Social Inequality in Canada: Patterns, Problems and Policies.* Scarborough, ON: Prentice-Hall, 1999.

Dance Network News 9.35 (Winter-Spring 2002): 3–4.

de Shazer, Steven, *Keys to Solution in Brief Therapy.* New York, NY: Norton, 1985.

de Shazer, Steven, et al. "Brief Therapy: Focussed Solution Development." *Family Process* 25.2 (1986): 207–21.

Degado, Melvin. *Community Social Work Practice in an Urban Context: The Potential of a Capacity-Enhancement Perspective.* New York, NY: Oxford University Press, 2000.

Derman-Sparks Louise, and Carol Brunson Phillips. *Teaching/Learning Anti-Racism: A Developmental Approach.* New York, NY: Teachers College Press, 1997.

DiAngelo, Robin. "Heterosexism: Addressing Internalized Dominance" *Journal of Progressive Human Services* 8.1 (1997): 5–21.

Dominelli, Lena. *Anti-Racist Social Work.* London: Macmillan, 1988.

Dore, Martha M. "Functional Theory: Its History and Influence on Contemporary Social Work Practice." *Social Service Review* 64.3 (1990): 358–74.

Doyal, Len, and Ian Gough. *A Theory of Human Need.* New York, NY: Guilford Press, 1991.

DuBois, W.E.B. *The Soul of Black Folks.* 1903; New York, NY: Bantam Books, 1989.

Editorial. "Structurally Maladjusted." *The CCPA Monitor* 9.2 (June 2002): 2.

Editors. "The 'New Economy' and the Speculative Bubble: an Interview with Doug Henwood. *Monthly Review* 52.11 (April 2000): 72–80.

Elliott, Catherine Canfield. "A Board Member Speaks Out." *The Social Worker* 12.2 (November 1943).

Ephross, Paul H., and Michael Reisch. "The Ideology of Some Social Work Texts." *Social Service Review* (June 1982): 273–91.

Etherden, Laura. "Criminalization of the Poor: Government Complicity in the Death of Kim Rogers." *NAPO News* 81 (December 2001): 8–9

Ferguson, Iain. "Identity Politics or Class Struggle? The Case of the Mental Health Users' Movement." *Class Struggle and Social Welfare.* Ed. Michael Lavalette and Gerry Mooney. London: Routledge, 2000. 228–49.

Fisher, Dena. "Problems for Social Work in a Strike Situation: Professional, Ethical, and Value Considerations," *Social Work* 32.3 (1987).

Fisher, Jacob. "The Rank and File Movement 1930–1936." *Social Work Today* 3.5–6, (February 1936); reprinted in *Journal of Progressive Human Service* 1.1 (1990): 95–99.

———. *The Response of Social Work to the Depression.* Cambridge, MA: Schenkman, 1980.

Flexner, Abraham. "Is Social Work a Profession." *Proceedings,* National Conference of Charities and Corrections. Baltimore, MD: Hildmann Printing Co., 1915: 576–90.

Foley, Duncan K. *Understanding Capital: Marx Economic Theory.* Cambridge, MA: Harvard University Press, 1986.

Foley, Juliet. "Professional Associations in Canada." Turner, F.J. 477–91.

Fook, Janis. *Radical Casework: A Theory of Practice.* St. Leonards, NSW: Allen and Unwin, 1993.

Fook, Jan, Martin Ryan, and Linette Hawkins. "Toward a Theory of Social Work Expertise." *British Journal of Social Work* 27 (1997): 399–417.

Franklin, Donna L. "Mary Richmond and Jane Addams: From Moral Certainty to Rational Inquiry in Social Work Practice." *Social Service Review* (December, 1986): 504–25.

Freire, Paulo. "A Critical Understanding of Social Work." *Journal of Progressive Human Services* 1.1 (1990): 3–9.

———. *Pedagogy of the Oppressed.* 30th anniversary ed. New York, NY: Continuum, 2001.

Freire, Paulo, and Donaldo Macedo. *Ideology Matters.* Boulder CO: Rowman and Littlefield, forthcoming.

Freud, Sophie, and Stefan Krug. "Beyond the Code of Ethics, Part 1: Complexities of Ethical Decision-Making in Social Work Practice." *Families in Society: The Journal of Contemporary Human Services* 83.5/6 (2002): 474–82.

Galper, Jeffry H. *The Politics of Social Services.* Englewood Cliffs, NJ: Prentice-Hall, 1975.

———. *Social Work Practice: A Radical Perspective.* Englewood Cliffs, NJ: Prentice-Hall, 1980.

Germain, Carel B., and Alex Gitterman. *The Life Model of Social Work Practice.* New York, NY: Columbia University Press, 1996.

Gil, David G. *Confronting Injustice and Oppression: Concepts and Strategies for Social Workers.* New York, NY: Columbia University Press, 1999.

Gilbert, Neil. "The Search for Professional Identity." *Social Work* 22.5 (1977): 401–06.

Gilligan, Carol. *In a Different Voice: Psychological Theory and Women's Development.* Cambridge, MA: Harvard University Press, 1982.

Gindin, Sam. "Social Justice and Globalization: Are They Compatible?" *Monthly Review* 54.2 (June 2002): 1–11.

Ginsburg, Norman. *Class, Capital and Social Policy.* London: Macmillan, 1979.

Gitterman, Alex. "Developing a New Group Service: Strategies and Skills." *Mutual Aid and the Life Cycle.* Ed. Alex Gitterman and Lawrence Shulman. Itasca, IL: F.E. Peacock Publishers, 1986. 53–71.

Globerman, Judith. "Regulating Social Work: Illuminating Motives." *Canadian Social Work Review* 9.2 (Summer 1992): 229–43.

Gold, Nora. "Putting Anti-Semitism on the Anti-Racism Agenda in North American Schools of Social Work." *Journal of Social Work Education* 32.1 (Winter 1996): 77–89.

Goldberg, Gale. "Structural Approach to Practice: A New Model." *Social Work* (March 1974): 150–55.

Goldberg Wood, Gale, and Ruth R. Middleman. *The Structural Approach to Direct Practice in Social Work.* New York, NY: Columbia University Press, 1989.

Goldstein, Howard. *Social Work Practice: A Unitary Approach.* Columbia, SC: University of South Carolina Press, 1979.

Gottlieb, M.C. "Avoiding Dual Relationships: A Decision-making Model." *Psychotherapy* 30.1 (1993): 41–48. http://kspope.com/gottlieb.html.

Gough, Ian. *The Political Economy of the Welfare State*. London: Macmillan, 1979.

Greene, Gilbert. "Using the Written Contract for Evaluating and Enhancing Practice Effectiveness." *Journal of Independent Social Work* 4.2 (1990): 135–55.

Greenspan, Miriam. "Out of Bounds." Lazarus and Zur 425–31.

———. *A New Approach to Women and Therapy*. 2nd ed. Bradenton FL.: Human Services Institute, 1993.

Greenwood, E. "Attributes of a Profession." *Social Work* 2 (1957): 45–55.

Guevara, Che. *To His Children: Che's Letters of Farewell*. Trans. Carmen González. Havana: Editorial José Marti/Artex, 1995.

Gutierrez, Lorraine M., Ruth J. Parsons, and Enid Opal Cox. *Empowerment in Social Work Practice: A Sourcebook*. Pacific Grove, CA: Brooks/Cole Publishing, 1998.

Hanmer, Jalna, and Daphne Statham. *Women and Social Work: Towards a Woman-Centered Practice*. London: Macmillan, 1989.

Harding, A.K., L.A. Gray, and M. Neal. "Confidentiality Limits with Clients Who Have HIV: A Review of Ethical and Legal Guidelines and Professional Policies." *Journal of Counseling and Development* 71.3 (1993): 297–305.

Hardy, Kenneth V., and Tracy A. Laszloffy. "The Dynamics of a Pro-Racist Ideology: Implications for Family Therapists." McGoldrick 118–28.

Harney, Stefano. "Anti-racism, Ontario Style." *Race and Class* 37.3 (1996): 35–45.

Hartman, Ann. "Diagrammatic Assessment of Family Relations." *Social Casework* (October 1978): 465–76.

Hartman, Ann, and Joan Laird. *Family-Centered Social Work Practice*. New York, NY: The Free Press, 1983.

Healy, Karen. "Power and Activist Social Work." Pease and Fook 115–34.

Henwood, Doug. *Wall Street: How it Works and for Whom*. New York, NY: Verso, 1999.

Hill-Collins, Patricia. *Black Feminist Thought: Knowledge, Consciousness, and the Politics of Empowerment*. London: Unwin Hyman, 1990.

Hoekman, Bernard M., and Michel M. Kostecki. *The Political Economy of the World Trading System*. New York, NY: Oxford Press, 2001.

Hollis, Ernest V., and Alice L. Taylor. *Social Work Education in the United States*. New York, NY: Columbia University Press, 1951.

Hollis, Florence. *Casework: A Psycho Social Therapy*. New York, NY: Random House, 1964.

———. "The Psycho Social Approach to Casework." *Theories of Social Casework*. Ed. Robert W. Roberts and Robert H. Nee. Chicago, IL: University of Chicago Press, 1970. 33–78.

Horn, Kahn-Tineta. "Interview: Oka and Mohawk Sovereignty." *Studies in Political Economy* 35 (Summer 1991): 29–41.

Horn, Michael. *The League for Social Reconstruction: Intellectual Origins of the Democratic Left in Canada 1930-1942*. Toronto, ON: University of Toronto Press, 1980.

Horton, John. "Order and Conflict Theories of Social Problems as Competing Ideologies." *The American Journal of Sociology* LXXI.6 (May 1966): 701–13.

Howe, David. *An Introduction to Social Work Theory*. Aldershot: Wildwood House, 1987.

Hurtado, Aida. *The Colour of Privilege: Three Blasphemies on Race and Feminism*. Ann Arbor, MI: The University of Michigan Press, 1996.

In Unison 2000: Persons with Disabilities in Canada. http://www.socialunion2000

Inter Parliamentary Union. "Women in National Parliaments" (1 March 2002).

Irving, Allan. "From Image to Simulacra: The Modern/Postmodern Divide and Social Work."

Essays on Postmodernism and Social Work. Ed. A.S. Chambron and A. Irving. Toronto, ON: Canadian Scholar's Press, 1994. 19–32.

Irving, Allan, Harriet Parsons, and Donald Bellamy. *Neighbours: Three Social Settlements in Downtown Toronto.* Toronto, ON: Canadian Scholar's Press, 1995.

Isajiw, Wsevolod W. *Understanding Diversity: Ethnicity and Race in the Canadian Context.* Toronto, ON: Thompson Educational Publishing, 1999.

James, Carl E. *Perspectives on Racism and the Human Services Sector: A Case for Change.* Toronto: University of Toronto Press, 1996.

Jessel, Ethel. "Staff Associations." *The Social Worker* 11.4 (May 1943).

Johnson, Holly. *Dangerous Domains: Violence Against Women in Canada.* Scarborough, ON: Nelson, 1996.

Kadushin, Alfred, and Goldie Kadushin. *The Social Work Interview: A Guide for Human Service Professionals.* 4th ed. New York, NY: Columbia, 1997.

Kagle, Jill Donner. "Record Keeping in the 1990s." *Social Work* 38.2 (March 1993): 190–96.

Kagle, Jill Donner, and Sandra Kopels. "Confidentiality After Tarasoff." *Health and Social Work* 193 (1994): 217–22.

Kahn, Si. "Leadership: Realizing Concepts Through Creative Process." *Community Practice: Models in Action.* Ed. Marie Weil. Binghamton, NY: The Haworth Press, 1997. 109–136.

Kain, C.D. "To Breach or Not To Breach: Is That the Question? A Response to Gray and Harding." *Journal of Counseling and Development* 66.5 (1988): 224–25.

Kardon, Sidney. "Confidentiality: A Different Perspective." *Social Work in Education* 15.4 (October 1993). 247–50.

Karger, Howard Jacob. *Social Work and Labor Unions.* New York, NY: Greenwood Press, 1988.

Kazemipur, A., and S.S. Halli. *The New Poverty in Canada: Ethnic Groups and Ghetto Neighbourhoods.* Toronto, ON: Thompson Educational Publishing, 2000.

Keefe, Thomas. "Empathy and Critical Consciousness." *Social Casework* 61.7 (1980): 387–93.

Keefe, Thomas. "Empathy: The Critical Skill." *Social Work* 21.1 (1976): 10–14.

Kerstetter, Steve. *Rags and Riches: Wealth Inequality in Canada.* Ottawa, ON: Canadian Centre for Policy Alternatives, December 2002.

Khayatt, Didi. "The Boundaries of Identity at the Intersection of Race, Class and Gender." *Canadian Women's Studies* 14.2 (1994): 6–12.

Kopels, Sandra. "Confidentiality and the School Social Worker." *Social Work in Education* 14.4 (October 1992): 203–04.

Kuyek, Joan Newman. *Fighting for Hope: Organizing to Realize Our Dreams.* Montreal, QC: Black Rose Books, 1990.

Laird, Joan. "Changing Women's Narratives: Taking Back the Discourse." Peterson and Lieberman 271–301.

Laird, Joan (Ed.). *Revisioning Social Work Education: A Social Constructionist Approach.* New York, NY: The Haworth Press, 1993.

Lamoureux, Henri, Robert Mayer, and Jean Panet-Raymond. *Community Action.* Montreal, QC: Black Rose Books, 1989.

Larson, Magali Sarfatti. *The Rise of Professionalism: A Sociological Analysis.* Berkeley, CA: University of California Press, 1977.

Lazarus, Arnold, and Ofer Zur (Eds.). *Dual Relationships and Psychotherapy.* New York, NY: Springer, 2002.

Lecomte, Roland. "Connecting Private Troubles and Public Issues in Social Work Education." Wharf 31–51.

Leighninger, Leslie. *Creating a New Profession: The Beginnings of Social Work Education in the United States.* Alexandria, VA: Council on Social Work Education, 2000.

———. "The Generalist-Specialist Debate in Social Work." *Social Service Review* (March 1980): 1–12.

Leighninger, Leslie, and Robert Knickmeyer. "The Rank and File Movement: The Relevance of Radical Social Work Traditions to Modern Social Work Practice," *Journal of Sociology and Social Welfare* 4.2 (1976): 166–77.

Leonard, Peter. "Knowledge/Power and Postmodernism: Implications for the Practice of a Critical Social Work Education." *Canadian Social Work Review* 11.1 (Winter 1994): 11–24.

———. *Personality and Ideology: Towards a Materialist Understanding of the Individual.* London: Macmillan, 1984.

———. *Postmodern Welfare: Reconstructing an Emancipatory Project.* London: Sage, 1997.

———. "Postmodernism, Socialism and Social Welfare." *Journal of Progressive Human Services* 6.2 (1995): 3–19.

———. "Three Discourses on Practice: A Postmodern Re-appraisal." *Journal of Sociology and Social Welfare* 23.2 (June 1996): 7–26.

Levine, Helen. "The Personal is Political: Feminism and the Helping Professions." *Feminism in Canada.* Ed. Angela Miles and Geraldine Finn. Montreal, QC: Black Rose Books, 1982. 175–210.

Lewin, Kurt. "Problems of Research in Social Psychology (1943–1944)." *Field Theory in Social Psychology: Selected Theoretical Papers.* Ed. D. Cartwright. Chicago, IL: University of Chicago Press, 1976. 155–69.

Li, Peter. *Race and Ethnic Relations in Canada.* Toronto, ON: Oxford Press, 1990.

Lightman, Ernie. *Social Policy in Canada.* Don Mills, ON: Oxford University Press, 2003.

———. "Social Workers, Strikes, and Service to Clients." *Social Work* 28.2 (March-April 1983): 142–47.

London Edinburgh Weekend Return Group. *In and Against the State.* London: Pluto Press, 1979.

Longres, John F. "Marxian Theory and Social Work Practice." *Catalyst* 20 (1986):13–34.

———. "Reactions to Working Statement on Purpose." *Social Work* 26.1 (1981): 85–87.

Lubove, Roy. *The Professional Altruist: The Emergence of Social Work as a Career 1880-1930.* Cambridge, MA: Harvard University Press, 1965.

Lundblad, Karen. "Jane Addams and Social Reform: A Role Model for the 1990s." *Social Work* 40.5 (1995): 661–69.

Lundy, Colleen, and Larry Gauthier. "Social Work Practice and the Master-Servant Relationship." *Le Travailleur / The Social Worker* 57.4 (1989): 90–94.

Lundy, Colleen, and Mark Totten. "Youth on the Fault Line." *The Social Worker* 65.3 (1997): 98–106.

Maglin, Arthur. "Alienation and Therapeutic Intervention," *Catalyst* 2 (1978): 70–73.

Mahtani, Minelle K. "Polarity Versus Plurality" *Canadian Woman Studies* 14.2 (1994): 14–18.

Maines, Joy. "Through the Years in CASW." NAC, FA 1713, MG 28I441.

Malik, Kenan. "Universalism and Difference: Race and the Postmodernists." *Race and Class* 37.3 (1996): 1–17.

Marable, Manning. "Beyond Racial Identity Politics: Towards a Liberation Theory For Multicultural Democracy." *Race and Class: A Journal for Black and Third World Liberation* 35.1 (July-September 1993): 113–30.

———. "History and Black Consciousness: The Political Culture of Black America." *Monthly Review* (July-August, 1995): 71–88.

Marchant, Helen, and Betsy Wearing (Eds.). *Gender Reclaimed: Women in Social Work.* Sydney, NSW: Hale and Iremonger, 1986.

Marx, Karl, and Friedrich Engels. *The Communist Manifesto* (1848). *The Communist Manifesto Now: Socialist Register.* Ed. Leo Panitch and Colin Leys. Halifax, NS: Fernwood Publishing, 1998. 240–68.

Maslow, A. *Toward a Psychology of Being.* New York, NY: Van Nostrand, 1962.

McClung, Nellie. *In Times Like These.* Social History of Canada Series. Toronto, ON: University of Toronto Press, 1972.

McCorquodale, Shannon. "The Role of Regulators in Practice." Turner, F.J. 462–76.

McGee, David. "To Be on Welfare is to..." Eastern Branch Ontario Association of Social Workers *Bulletin* 27.3 (Fall 1998): 4.

McGoldrick, Monica (Ed.). *Re-visioning Family Therapy: Race, Culture, and Gender in Clinical Practice.* New York, NY: The Guilford Press, 1998.

McGoldrick, Monica, and Joe Giordano. "Overview: Ethnicity and Family Therapy." *Ethnicity and Family Therapy.* 2nd. ed. Ed. Monica McGoldrick, Joe Giordano, and John K. Pearce. New York, NY: The Guilford Press, 1996.

McGowan, Kelly, and Nancy McKenzie. "A Community Response to the Needs of Drug Users, Stand Up Harlem." *Health/PAC Bulletin* (Winter 1993): 4–13.

McIntyre, Deborah. "Domestic Violence: A Case of the Disappearing Victim." *Australian Journal of Family Therapy* 5.4 (1984): 249–58.

McQuillan, Kevin, and Marilyn Belle. "Who Does What? Gender and the Division of Labour in Canadian Households," Curtis et al. 186–98.

Mederos, Fernando. " Batterer Intervention Programs: Past and Future Prospects." *Coordinated Community Response to Domestic Violence: Lessons from the Duluth Model.* Ed. Melanie F. Shepherd and Ellen L. Pence. Newbury Park, CA: Sage, 1998. 127–50.

Meister, Joan. "Keynote Address: The More We Get Together," *The More We Get Together.* Ed. Houston Stewart, Beth Percival, and Elizabeth R. Epperley. Charlottetown, PEI: CRIAW and Gynergy Books, 1992. 11–18.

Middleman, Ruth R., and Gale Goldberg Wood. "So Much for the Bell Curve: Constructionism, Power/Conflict, and the Structural Approach to Direct Practice in Social Work." Laird 129–46.

Middleman, Ruth R., and Gale Goldberg. *Social Service Delivery: A Structural Approach to Social Work Practice.* New York, NY: Columbia University Press, 1974.

Miller, Dorothy C. "What is Needed for True Equality: An Overview of Policy Issues for Women." Peterson and Lieberman 45–65.

Mills, C. Wright. *Power, Politics and People.* New York, NY: Oxford University Press, 1963.

Minahan, Anne, and Allan Pincus. "Conceptual Framework for Social Work Practice." *Social Work* 22.5 (1977): 347–52.

Minahan, Anne. "Introduction to Special Issue." *Social Work* 26.1 (1981): 5–6.

Moreau, Maurice. *Empowerment Through a Structural Approach to Social Work: A Report From Practice.* Ottawa, ON: Carleton University, 1989.

———. "Empowerment Through Advocacy and Consciousness-Raising: Implications of a Structural Approach to Social Work." *Journal of Sociology and Social Welfare* 17.2 (June 1990): 53–67.

———. "A Structural Approach to Social Work Practice." *Canadian Journal of Social Work Education* 5.1 (1979): 78–94.

Moreau, Maurice, and Sandra Frosst. *Empowerment II: Snapshots of the Structural Approach in Action.* Ottawa, ON: Carleton University Press, 1993.

Mullaly, Bob. *Challenging Oppression: A Critical Social Work Approach.* Don Mills, ON: Oxford University Press, 2002.

Mullaly, Bob. *Structural Social Work: Ideology, Theory, and Practice.* Don Mills, ON: Oxford University Press, 1997.

Myer, Carol H. "Social Work Purpose: Status by Choice or Coercion?" *Social Work* 26.6 (1981): 69–75.

———. "The Search for Coherence." *Clinical Social Work in an Eco-Systems Perspective.* Ed. Carol H. Myer. New York, NY: Columbia University Press, 1983.

Naiman, Joanne. *How Societies Work: Class, Power and Change in a Canadian Society.* Concord, ON: Irwin Publishing, 1997.

Naiman, Joanne. *How Societies Work: Class, Power and Change in a Canadian Context.* 2nd ed. Toronto, ON: Irwin Publishing, 2000.

National Archives of Canada. "Through the Years." FA 1713, MG 28 I441.

National Association of Social Workers. "International Policy on Human Rights." *Social Work Speaks: NASW Policy Statements* (Washington, DC: NASW Press, 2002) 178–86. Also found at http://www.naswdc.org/.

National Association of Social Workers. "Peace and Social Justice." *Social Work Speaks: National Association of Social Workers Policy Statements 2000-2003.* Washington, DC: NASW Press, 2000. 238–243.

National Council of Welfare Reports. *Poverty Profile 1998.* Ottawa, ON: Minister of Public Works and Government Services Canada, 2000.

Neville, Robert. "Commentary." *CBC Morning.* January 2000.

Newdom, Fred. "Progressive and Professional: A Contradiction in Terms?" *BCR Reports* 8.1 (1996).

North York Health Network. *Inequality is Bad for Our Hearts: Why Low Income and Social Exclusion are Major Causes of Heart Disease in Canada.* Toronto, ON: North York Health Network, 2001. http://www.yorku.ca/wellness/heart.

OAPSW. Strategic Planning Committee. *Interim Report.* Toronto, ON: Ontario Association of Professional Social Workers, September 1987.

OASW Eastern Branch Survey. "Observations of Social Workers In Eastern Ontario on Effects on Clients/Families of Recent Funding and Policy Changes and Strategies Clients/Families are Using to Cope." January-February 1996.

O'Connor, James. *The Fiscal Crisis of the State.* New York, NY: St. Martin's Press, 1973.

Oliver, Michael. *Social Work With Disabled People.* London: Macmillan, 1983.

———. *Understanding Disability: From Theory to Practice.* New York, NY: St. Martin's Press, 1996.

Ontario. Ministry of the Solicitor General and Correctional Services. "Implementation of the 'Interim Accountability and Accessibility Requirements for Male Batterer Programs.'" Toronto: Ontario Ministry of the Solicitor General and Correctional Services, March 1994.

Palazzoli, Mara Selvini. "An Interview with Mara Selvini Palazzoli." *Networker* (September-October 1987): 26–33.

Pantoja, Antonia, and Wilhelmina Perry. "Community Development and Restoration: A Perspective and Case Study." *Community Organizing in a Diverse Society.* Ed. Felix G. Rivera and John L. Erlich. Toronto ON: Allyn and Bacon, 1998. 220–42.

Parry, Alan, and Robert E. Doan. *Story Re-visions: Narrative Therapy in a Postmodern World.* New York, NY: The Guilford Press, 1994.

Parsons, Ruth J., Lorraine M. Gutierrez, and Enid Opal Cox. "A Model for Empowerment Practice." *Empowerment in Social Work Practice: A Sourcebook.* Ed. Ruth J. Parsons, Lorraine M. Gutierrez, and Enid Opal Cox. Pacific Grove, CA.: Brooks/Cole Publishing Company, 1998. 3–51.

Paterson, Rosemary, and Salli Trathen. "Feminist In (ter)ventions in Family Therapy." *ANZ Journal of Family Therapy* 15.2 (1994): 91–98.

Patricia, Hannah. "Preparing Members for the Expectations of Social Work with Groups: An Approach to the Prepatory Interview." *Social Work With Groups* 22.4 (2000): 51–66.

Payne, Malcolm, "The Code of Ethics, the Social Work Manager and the Organization." *A Code of Ethics for Social Work: The Second Step.* Ed. David Watson. London: Routledge and Kegan Paul, 1985. 104–22.

Payne, Malcolm. *Modern Social Work Theory: A Critical Introduction.* Chicago, IL: Lyceum Books, 1991.

Pease, Bob, and Jan Fook (Eds.). *Transforming Social Work Practice: Postmodern Critical Perspectives.* London: Routledge, 1999.

Pence, Ellen, and Michael Paymar. *Education Groups for Men Who Batter: The Duluth Model.* New York, NY: Springer, 1993.

Pennell, Joan. "Consensual Bargaining: Labor Negotiations in Battered Women's Programs." *Journal of Progressive Human Services* 1.1 (1990): 59–74.

———. "Feminism and Labor Unions: Transforming State Regulation of Women's Programs," *Journal of Progressive Human Services* 6.1 (1995): 45–72.

Perlman, Helen Harris. *Relationship: The Heart of Helping People.* Chicago, IL: University of Chicago Press, 1979.

———. *Social Casework: A Problem Solving Process.* Chicago, IL: University of Chicago Press, 1957.

Peterson, K. Jean, and Alice A. Lieberman. (Eds.). *Building on Women's Strengths: A Social Work Agenda for the Twenty-First Century.* New York, NY: The Haworth Social Work Practice Press, 2001.

Pharr, Suzanne. *Homophobia: A Weapon of Sexism.* Little Rock, AR: Chardon Press, 1988.

Pincus, Allen, and Anne Minahan. *Social Work Practice: Model and Method.* Itasca, IL: F.E. Peacock Publishers, 1973.

Pinderhughes, Elaine B. "Empowerment for Our Clients and for Ourselves." *Social Casework* (June 1983): 331–338.

Piva, Michael J. *The Condition of the Working Class in Toronto—1900-1921.* Ottawa, ON: University of Ottawa Press, 1979.

Piven, Frances Fox, and Richard A. Cloward. *Regulating the Poor: The Functions of Public Welfare.* Rev. ed. New York, NY: Vintage Books, 1993.

Popay, Jennie, and Yvonne Dhooge. "Unemployment, Cod's Head Soup and Radical Social Work." *Radical Social Work Today.* Ed. Mary Langan and Phil Lee. London: Unwin Hyman, 1989.

Posner, Wendy B. "Common Human Needs: A Story from the Prehistory of Government by Special Interests." *Social Service Review* (June 1995): 188–223.

Price, Karen (Ed.). *Community Support for Survivors of Torture: A Manual.* Toronto, ON: Canadian Centre for Victims of Torture, n.d.

———. "Doing the Right Thing: Suggestions for Non-Medical Caregivers: An Interview with Rosemary Meier." *Community Support for Survivors of Torture: A Manual.* Ed. Karen Price. Toronto, ON: Canadian Centre for Victims of Torture, n.d. 80–86.

Proctor, Bernadette D., and Joseph Dalaker. *Poverty in the United States: 2001.* US Census Bureau, Current Population Reports. Washington, DC: US Government Printing Office, 2002.

Reamer, F., and S.R. Gelman. "Is *Tarasoff* Relevant in AIDS-Related Cases?" *Controversial Issues in Social Work.* Ed. E. Gambrill and R. Pruger. Boston, MA: Allyn and Bacon, 1997. 342–55.

Reamer, Frederic G. *Ethical Standards in Social Work: A Critical Review of the NASW Code of Ethics.* Washington, DC: NASW Press, 1998.

Reamer, Frederic G. *Ethical Standards in Social Work: A Critical Review of the NASW Code of Ethics.* Washington: NASW Press, 1998.

———. *Ethics Education in Social Work.* Alexandria VA.: Council on Social Work Education, 2001.

———. *Social Work Malpractice and Liability: Strategies for Prevention.* New York, NY: Columbia University Press, 1994.

———. *Social Work Values and Ethics.* 2nd ed. New York, NY: Columbia University Press, 1999.

———. *Tangled Relationships: Managing Boundary Issues in the Human Services.* New York, NY: Columbia University Press, 2001.

Regehr, Cheryl. "Secondary Trauma in Social Workers." *Newsmagazine: the Journal of the Ontario Association of Social Workers* 28.3 (2001).

Reisch, Michael. "Defining Social Justice in a Socially Unjust World." *Families in Society: The Journal of Contemporary Human Services* 83.4 (2002): 343–54.

Reisch, Michael, and Janice Andrews. *The Road Not Taken: A History of Radical Social Work in the United States.* New York, NY: Bruner-Routledge, 2002.

Reitsma-Street, Marge, and Jennifer Keck. "The Abolition of a Welfare Snitch Line." *The Social Worker* 64.3 (Fall 1996): 35–66.

Reynolds, Bertha C. "Social Case Work: What is it? What is its Place in the World Today?" *Child and Family Welfare*, 11.6 (March 1936): 1–12.

Reynolds, Bertha C. *An Uncharted Journey, Fifty Years of Growth in Social Work.* New York, NY: The Citadel Press, 1963.

Richmond, Mary. *Friendly Visiting Among the Poor.* New York, NY: Macmillan, 1899.

Ritzer, George. *Contemporary Sociological Theory.* 2nd ed. New York, NY: Alfred A. Knopf, Inc, 1988.

Rivera, Felix G. and John L. Erlich. "A Time of Fear; A Time of Hope." *Community Organizing in a Diverse Society.* Ed. Felix G. Rivera and John L. Erlich. Toronto, ON: Allyn and Bacon, 1998. 1–24.

Robinson, Virginia. *A Changing Psychology in Social Case Work.* Chapel Hill, NC: University of North Carolina Press, 1930.

Rogers, Carl R. "The Interpersonal Relationship." *Interpersonal Helping: Emerging Approaches for Social Work Practice.* Ed. Joel Fisher. Springfield, IL: Charles C. Thomas Publisher, 1973. 381–91.

Rose, Stephen M. "Advocacy/Empowerment: An Approach to Clinical Practice for Social Work." *Journal of Sociology and Social Welfare* 17.2 (1990): 41–51.

———. "Reflections on Empowerment-Based Practice." *Social Work* 45.5 (October 2000): 403–12.

Rossiter, A., and Richard Walsh Bowers and Isaac Prilleltensky. "Learning From Broken Rules: Individualism, Bureaucracy and Ethics." *Ethics and Behaviour* 6.4 (1996): 307–20.

Rothman, Gerald C. *Philanthropists, Therapists and Activists.* Cambridge, MA: Schenkman Publishing, 1985.

Rothman, Jack. "Approaches to Community Intervention." *Strategies of Community Intervention.* 5th ed. Ed. J. Rothman, J.L. Erlichs, and J.E. Tropman, with F.M. Cox. Itasca, IL: F.E. Peacock, 1995. 26–63.

———. "Three Models of Community Practice." *Strategies of Community Organization.* 2nd ed. Ed. Fred Cox et al. Itasca, IL: F.E. Peacock, 1974. 22–39.

Rothman, Juliet Cassuto. *Contracting in Clinical Social Work.* Chicago, IL: Nelson-Hall, 1998.

Royal Commission on Aboriginal Peoples. *Final Report.* http://www.indigenous.bc.ca/rcap.html.

Rubin, Lillian B. *Families on the Fault Line: America's Working Class Speaks About the Family, the Economy, Race and Ethnicity.* New York, NY: Harper Collins, 1994.

Ryan, William. *Blaming the Victim.* New York: Pantheon Books, 1971.

Saleebey, Dennis (Ed.). *The Strengths Perspective in Social Work Practice.* 3rd ed. Boston, MA: Allyn and Bacon, 2002.

Satir, Virginia. *Peoplemaking.* Palo Alto, CA: Science and Behavior Books, 1972.

Satzewich, Vic. "Race, Racism and Racialization: Contested Concepts." *Racism and Social Inequality in Canada.* Ed. Vic Satzewich. Toronto, ON: Thompson Educational Publishing, 1998. 25–45.

Schwartz, William. "Private Troubles and Public Issues." *The Social Welfare Forum* (1969).

Selekman, M.D. *Solution-Focused Therapy with Children: Harnessing Family Strength for Systemic Change.* New York, NY: Guilford Press, 1997.

Selmi, Patrick. "Social Work and the Campaign to Save Sacco and Vanzetti." *Social Service Review* 75.1 (March 2001): 115–34.

Selmi, Patrick, and Richard Hunter. "Beyond the Rank and File Movement: Mary van Kleeck and Social Work Radicalism in the Great Depression, 1931–1942." *Journal of Sociology and Social Welfare* 27.2 (June 2001): 75–100.

Selvini-Palazzoli, M., L. Boscolo, G. Cecchin, and G. Prata. *Paradox and Counter Paradox.* New York: Jason Aronson, 1978.

Sepehri, Ardeshir, and Robert Chernomas. "Who Paid For The Canadian Welfare State Between 1955–1988?" *Review of Radical Political Economics* 24.1 (Spring 1992): 71–88.

Sharma, Sohan, and Surinder Kumar. "The Military Backbone of Globalisation." *Race and Class* 44.3 (January-March 2003): 22–39.

Shera, Wes, and Lillian M. Wells. *Empowerment Practice in Social Work.* Toronto, ON: Canadian Scholars Press: 1999.

Shor, Ira. "Education is Politics: Paulo Freire's Critical Pedagogy." *Paulo Freire: A Critical Encounter.* Ed. Peter McLaren and Peter Leonard. London: Routledge, 1993. 25–35.

———. *Empowering Education: Critical Teaching for Social Change.* Chicago, IL: University of Chicago Press, 1992.

Shulman, Lawrence. "Group Work Method." *Mutual Aid Groups and the Life Cycle.* Ed. Alex Gitterman and Lawrence Shulman. Itasca, IL: F.E. Peacock, 1986.

———. *The Skills of Helping Individuals, Families, and Groups.* 3rd ed. Itasca, IL: F.E. Peacock Publishers, 1992.

———. *The Skills of Helping Individuals, Families, Groups and Communities.* 4th ed. Itasca, IL: F.E. Peacock Publishers, 1999.

Simon, Barbara Levy. *The Empowerment Tradition in American Social Work: A History.* New York, NY: Columbia University Press, 1994.

Skodra, Eleni E. "Counselling Immigrant Women: A Feminist Critique of Traditional Therapeutic Approaches and Reevaluation of the Role of Therapist." *Counselling Psychology Quarterly* 2.2 (1989):185–204.

Solomon, Barbara Bryant. *Black Empowerment: Social Work in Oppressed Communities.* New York, NY: Columbia University Press, 1976.

Solomon, Robert, and Dawn A. Dudley. *A Legal Survival Guide for Social Workers.* Toronto, ON: Family Service Ontario, 1996.

Sorrentino, Constance. "International Unemployment Rates: How Comparable are They?" *Monthly Labour Review* (June 2000): 3–20. http//www.bls.gov/opub/mir/2000.

Specht, Harry, and Mark E. Courtney. *Unfaithful Angels: How Social Work Has Abandoned Its Mission.* New York, NY: The Free Press, 1994.

Staples, Lee H. "Powerful Ideas About Empowerment." *Administration in Social Work* 14.2 (1990): 29–42.

Staples, Steven. *Breaking Rank: A Citizen's Review of Canada's Military Spending.* Ottawa, ON: The Polaris Institute, 2002.

Statistics Canada. Target Groups Project, *Women in Canada 2000: A Gender-Based Statistical Report.* Ottawa, ON: Statistics Canada, 2002.

Steiner, Claude. *Scripts People Live: Transactional Analysis of Life Scripts.* New York, NY: Grove Press, 1974.

Swigonski, Mary E., Robin S. Mama, and Kelly Ward. "Introduction." *Journal of Gay and Lesbian Social Services* 13.1/2 (2001): 1–6.

Tafoya, Terry. "Finding Harmony: Balancing Traditional Values with Western Science in Therapy." *Canadian Journal of Native Education* 21 (1995): 7–27.

Taft, Jessie. *Family Casework and Counseling, A Functional Approach.* Philadelphia, PA: University of Pennsylvania Press, 1935.

Taylor, Sharon, Keith Brownlee, and Kim Mauro-Hopkins. "Confidentiality Versus the Duty to Protect." *The Social Worker* 64.4 (Winter 1996): 9–17.

Teeple, Gary. *Globalization and the Decline of Social Reform: Into the Twenty-First Century.* Toronto, ON: Garamond, 2000.

Thompson, Neil. *Anti-discriminatory Practice,* London: Macmillan, 1993.

———. "Social Movements, Social Justice and Social Work." *British Journal of Social Work* 32 (2002): 711–22.

Thyer, Bruce A., and Marilyn A. Biggerstaff. *Professional Social Work Credentialing and Legal Regulation: A Review of Critical Issues and An Annotated Bibliography.* Springfield, IL.: Charles C. Thomas, 1989.

Timms, Noel. "Taking Social Work Seriously: The Contribution of the Functional School." *British Journal of Social Work* 27 (1997): 723–37.

Tomm, Karl. "The Ethics of Dual Relationships." Lazarus and Zur 32–43.

Touzel, Bessie E. "A Social Workers Protest." *The Social Worker* 5.2 (November 1936).

Towle, Charlotte. *Common Human Needs.* 1945; London: George Allen and Unwin, 1973.

Townsend, Monica. *A Report Card on Women and Poverty.* Ottawa, ON: Canadian Centre for Policy Alternatives, April 2000.

Tracy, Elizabeth M., and James K. Whittaker. "The Social Network Map: Assessing Social Support in Clinical Practice." *Families in Society: The Journal of Contemporary Human Services* (October 1990): 461–70.

Trevithick, Pam. "Unconsciousness Raising with Working-Class Women." *In Our Experience: Workshops at the Women's Therapy Centre,* ed. Sue Krzowski and Pat Land. London: Women's Press, 1988.

Trolander, Judith Ann. "The Response of Settlements to the Great Depression." *Social Work* (September 1973): 92–102.

Tsetung, Mao. "On Practice." *Selected Readings From the Works of Mao Tsetung.* Peking: Foreign Languages Press, 1971. 65–84.

Turner, Francis J. (Ed.). *Social Work Practice: A Canadian Perspective.* Scarborough, ON: Prentice Hall, 1998.

Turner, Frank. "Legislative Protection Against Malpractice." *Canadian Review of Social Policy* 25 (May 1990): 63–64.

Van Voorhis, Rebecca, and Marion Wagner. "Coverage of Gay and Lesbian Subject Matter in Social Work Journals." *Journal of Social Work Education* 37.1 (Winter 2001): 147–59.

Vodde, Rich, and J. Paul Gallant. "Bridging the Gap Between Micro and Macro Practice: Large Scale Change and a Unified Model of Narrative-Deconstructive Practice." *Journal of Social Work Education* 38.3 (2002): 439–58.

Wagner, David. "Radical Movements in the Social Services: A Theoretical Framework." *Social Service Review* (June 1989): 264–84.

Wakefield, Jerome C. "Does Social Work Need the Eco-Systems Perspective? Part 1: Is the Perspective Clinically Useful?" *Social Service Review* (March 1996): 1–32.

———. "Does Social Work Need the Eco-Systems Perspective? Part 2: Does the Perspective Save Social Work From Incoherence?" *Social Service Review* (June 1996): 183–213.

Waldegrave, Charles. "Just Therapy." Social Justice and Family Therapy: A Discussion of the Work of The Family Centre, Lower Hutt, New Zealand. A special issue of *Dulwich Centre Newsletter* 1 (1990): 1–46.

Wallerstein, Nina. "Problem-Posing Education: Freire's Method for Transformation." *Freire for the Classroom.* Ed. Ira Shor. Portsmouth, MA: Boynton Cook/Heinemann, 1987. 33–44.

Warner, Tom. *Never Going Back: A History of Queer Activism in Canada.* Toronto, ON: University of Toronto Press, 2002.

Watson, David (Ed.). *A Code of Ethics for Social Work: The Second Step.* London: Routledge and Kegan Paul, 1985.

Weil, Marie O. "Community Building: Building Community Practice." *Social Work* 41.5 (September 1996):481–99.

Wenocur, Stanley, and Michael Reisch. *From Charity to Enterprise: The Development of American Social Work in a Market Economy.* Chicago, IL: University of Illinois Press, 1989.

West, Cornel. *Race Matters.* New York, NY: Vintage Books, 1994.

Wetzel, Janice Wood. "Human Rights in the 20th Century: Weren't Gays and Lesbians Human?" *Journal of Gay and Lesbian Social Services* 13.1/2 (2002): 15–45.

Wharf, Brian (Ed.). *Social Work and Social Change in Canada.* Toronto, ON: McClelland and Stewart, 1990.

White, Michael. "Deconstruction and Therapy." *Therapeutic Conversations.* Ed. Stephen Gilligan and Resse Price. New York, NY: Norton, 1993. 22–61.

———. *Re-Authoring Lives: Interviews and Essays.* Adelaide: Dulwich Centre Publications, 1995.

White, Michael, and David Epston. *Narrative Means to Therapeutic Ends.* New York, NY: Norton, 1990.

Whitehorn, Alan. *Canadian Socialism: Essays on the CCF-NDP.* Toronto, ON: Oxford University Press, 1992.

Whittington, Colin, and Ray Holland. "A Framework for Theory in Social Work." *Issues in Social Work Education* 5.1 (Summer 1985).

Wigdor, Hazel. "Social Work and Trade Unions," *The Social Worker* 12.2 (November 1943).

Wilding, Paul. *Professional Power and Social Welfare.* London: Routledge and Kegan Paul, 1982.

Wills, Gale. "Values of Community Practice: Legacy of the Radical Social Gospel." *Canadian Social Work Review* 9.1 (1992): 28–40.

Wise, Sue. "Becoming a Feminist Social Worker." *Feminist Praxis.* Ed. Liz Stanley. London: Routledge, 1990. 236–49.

Withorn, Ann. *Serving the People Social Service and Social Change.* New York, NY: Columbia University Press, 1984.

Witkin, Stanley L. "Human Rights and Social Work." *Social Work* 43.3 (May 1998): 197–201.

———. "If Empirical Practice is the Answer Then What is the Question?" *Social Work Research* 20.2 (June 1996): 69–74.

Wohl, Bernard J. "The Power of Group Work with Youth: Creating Activists of the Future." *Social Work with Groups* 22.4 (2000): 3–13.

Woodsworth, David. "An interview with Dr. David Woodsworth, Emeritus Professor of Social Work, McGill University." *Canadian Social Work* 2.2 (Fall 2000): 146–49.

World Conference on Human Rights, Vienna, 1993: *Vienna Declaration and Program Action*; Fourth World Conference on Women, Beijing (1995); *Beijing Declaration and Platform* and its followup, *Beijing Plus 5* (2000). http://www.who.int/hhr/readings/conference/en/

Wylie, Mary Sykes. "Diagnosing For Dollars?" *Networker* (May/June 1995): 23–33, 65–69.

Yalnizyan, Armine. *The Growing Gap: A Report on Growing Inequality Between the Rich and the Poor in Canada.* Toronto, ON: Centre for Social Justice, 1998.

Yelaga, Shankar A. *An Introduction to Social Work Practice in Canada.* Scarborough, ON: Prentice-Hall, 1985.

Zide, Marilyn R., and Susan W. Gray. "The Solutioning Process: Merging the Genogram and the Solution-Focused Model of Practice." *Journal of Family Social Work* 4.1 (2000): 3–19.

Zur, Ofer. "Guidelines for Non-Sexual Dual Relationships in Psychotherapy." http:drzur.com/dual-relationships.html.

INDEX